EDGARD VARÈSE

EDGARD VARÈSE

By *FERNAND OUELLETTE*

*Translated from the French
by Derek Coltman*

The Orion Press, New York

To Claude and Célinie Cortot, Varèse's grandparents,
to Louise Varèse, his wife,
to all those, friends and musicians,
who loved and who love him

FOREWORD

I am not naïve enough to claim that I am going to tell you Varèse's life. A man's life cannot be told. One can only walk around an abyss. Thus, there is no question of this being a biography in the sense that a dictionary gives the word. I am providing the *first document* concerning certain events in the life of a composer who was born in Paris and who died in New York. But Varèse cannot be reduced to those events. Who could capture the man as he was in himself? His works came from his fullness, from the wonder of his uniqueness; but Varèse cannot be reduced to his own works. I have taken a few signs as my starting-point, I have lived in his works so as to tame them, so as to come closer to this man's secret, closer to his greatness. But the mystery, inviolably, remains. Genius does pass among us; it confronts us, storms us, strikes us with its lightning, and yet is still an enigma to us. And what an enormity! The more his works work their violence upon us, the more the man escapes us. Not because there is no common measure between the creator and the man, but because we are made like that: dazzled, we become blind. The wider the genius spreads his wings, the more the man within becomes unreachable. All appearances become another wall. Thus I set out from silence and I return to silence.

As I have said, this book is intended as a first document which attempts to encompass the elements constituting the life of the composer Edgard Varèse. André Leroi-Gourhan has pointed out that "the mind is passably disarmed when it finds itself in the presence of facts for which it possesses no anterior references." [1] * And indeed, I have constantly felt the disproportion that exists between certain of the facts I recount and other, more important ones, of which I am ignorant. I did not choose the facts, or the documents, at my disposal; I simply recount what I know. I am conscious of having seemed to attribute importance to episodes which are relatively unimportant. But this impression arises only because there are *blanks* in the sequence of events, or, if the facts themselves are continuous, because they do not necessarily give rise to a sensation of progress and duration. I believe that with time those blanks will be filled in. It was therefore impossible for me, in this first work to be devoted to Varèse, to select my facts and to conceive a synthesis, a structure

(*) All notes and bibliographical references will be found at the end of the book.

capable of delighting the mind and making possible a freer style. It therefore seems inevitable to me, at this stage of our knowledge of the pertinent documents, that we should often come across groups of elements that are merely juxtaposed, not linked together in any organic way. I hope that this work, despite its profound lacunae, will be useful to the true biographer, to historians of music, and above all to Varèse's public.

Most of my conversations with Varèse were recorded. Those recordings were my primary source. Then I addressed myself to all those who could either provide me with clarifications or furnish first-hand evidence about certain events. I wish to offer my warmest thanks to those who replied. Lastly, thanks to the patience of Varèse himself and of Madame Varèse, I made a compilation of all the appropriate newspaper and magazine articles, without forgetting to consult any of those works in which Varèse's name might logically be expected to appear. Despite this labor, and the fairly considerable bibliography which I am publishing as an appendix, I am convinced that many facts, many words have escaped me. For it would have been financially impossible for me to visit all the great capitals in order to seek out, day after day, the documents I was lacking, or in order to complete a bibliographical reference. For the most part, I have been content to *quote* instead of offering *evidence of evidence.* Since I was not a witness to the majority of the facts I relate, I have allowed those who were present to speak in their own words, and particularly Varèse himself. I have so often been obliged to translate these texts, or have them translated, that translation itself seemed to me already a betrayal, and one which it was better not to compound by résumés. Since I am neither a musicologist nor a composer, I have permitted myself to approach the works themselves, not as a musician, but as a passionate music lover. I have left the task of analyzing them to the specialists.

My thanks to Louise Varèse who was kind enough to read and re-read my manuscript after Varèse's death. I also thank Mademoiselle Odile Vivier, my "angel in Paris," and Messieurs André Belleau, Marcel Houle, François Morel and Gilles Tremblay. And this work could never have been undertaken or brought to a conclusion without the help of the Conseil des Arts du Canada and of the Conseil des Arts and the Ministère des Affaires culturelles du Québec.

CONTENTS

LIST OF ILLUSTRATIONS

following page 114

1. Varèse, with his brothers and sister (1892–93).
2. Claude Cortot, Varèse's grandfather. (A charcoal sketch by the sculptor Julio Gonzalez, 1908.)
3. Varèse's birth certificate.
4. Varèse in 1910.
5. Varèse's admission papers to composition class, signed by Fauré.
6. Cover to the first publication of the score of *Hyperprism*, 1924.
7. The first sketch of *l'Astronome*, 1928.
8. Varèse and Villa-Lobos in Paris, March, 1930.
9. A letter from Claude Debussy, and a letter from Richard Strauss.
10. Varèse's gongs, in his studio.
11. A letter from Massenet (1906 or 1907).
12. Edgard and Louise Varèse, 1965.
13. Part of a letter from Romain Rolland.
14. Letter from Varèse to the author, February 3, 1964.
15. Varèse and the author, in front of a poster announcing the première of *Nocturnal* at Town Hall, New York, April 30, 1961.
16. Varèse in 1964.
17. Diagram of *le Poème électronique*.
18. Varèse's work table, at the time of his death (1965).

EDGARD VARÈSE

"Sometimes one sees so far that expression refuses to follow, as though it were afraid." *Varèse*

"All great works have some despair at their root." *André Suarès*

"Look, it is not Mozart struggling in your soul, but the gong, against the shapeless arm of death." *Yves Bonnefoy*

"The force of procreation, the first ecstasy in living and joy in the presence of growth turned the silence of contemplation into sound." *Maori Song*

1

Childhood

In about 1592, an Italian composer named Fabio Varese published his first works. Then, in about 1624, it appears that a certain Giovanni Baptista Varese also published some Masses and motets in Milan.

On January 24, 1772, Louis XV, le Bien-Aimé, conferred nobility on a *Varèse* family who were the lords of the province of Bastia in the north of Corsica. [1] Today, we have only to examine any map of Lombardy to discover a province, or a town, or a lake, named *Varese*. It is thus a name which seems to have fairly ancient origins.

Edgard,[2] Victor, Achille, Charles Varèse was born in Paris, in the 10th arrondissement, at four o'clock "in the evening," on December 22, 1883.[3] His father, Henri, Pie, Jules, Annibal, the son of Achille Varèse and Pauline Monnet, was born in Pignerol, a town in the Piedmont which was sometimes French, sometimes Italian, according to the caprices of history. His mother, Blanche-Marie, was also born in Paris. She was the daughter of Claude Cortot, from Burgundy, and Célinie Yasse, who was almost certainly born in 1838 in Lorraine. Edgard was his parents' first child. He was followed by two brothers, Maurice and Renato, and two sisters, Corinne and Yvonne.

Thus Varèse had roots in Piedmont, Burgundy, Lorraine, and Paris, all at the same time. As we know, Piedmont was the most progressive state in Italy; its hope, "the storehouse of its future" as one historian was to put it. With such a background, how should the young Varèse not have had a character of bronze? Moreover, he was born in that "happy twenty-six-year period which begins in 1876," a period which proved "capital through its real importance." The historian Maurice Baumont was even to write: "During this reassuring era of calm and regularity, a great change took place in the world. Civilization made progress in every domain." "The West was becoming more and more industralized." "The spirit of socialism . . . was impregnating the life of nations." "The colonizing impulse had seized the world's attention.[4] Bismarck's Europe was breaking up on all sides. The German hegemony was called into question. Economic internationalism was accompanied by intellectual internationalism. Jules Ferry had just formed a government. The name of General Boulanger, France's "General Revenge," was soon to be on everyone's lips. Paris was preparing for its forthcoming *Exposition Universelle*. Debussy was twenty. Nietzsche was writing *Thus Spoke Zarathustra*. Renoir had just painted *le Déjeuner des Canotiers*. Rimbaud's *Illuminations* were about to be published. Pasteur was working on the first anti-rabies vaccine. Also born in 1883 was Anton von Webern, the opposite musical pole, son, like Varèse, of an engineer. This analogy is not without significance. As Dostoevski, Wagner, Manet, Darwin, Emerson, Littré, Turgenev, Hugo, and Borodin were dying, so Spengler, Freud, Jung, Einstein, Apollinaire, Picasso, Stravinsky, Joyce, Jaspers, Kafka, Schoenberg, Bachelard, Max Linder, Klee, Toynbee, Dreyer, Heidegger, Jouve, Cendrars, Jouvet, Bernanos, Brancusi, Pevsner, Flaherty, Gropius, Léger, Chagall, Trakl, Teilhard de Chardin, Wiener, T.S. Eliot, and so many others were being born. The twentieth century was theirs.

Several weeks after his birth, the young Edgard Varèse was entrusted to the care of his aunt Marie and his uncle Joseph—brother of Varèse's maternal grandfather—who lived in Villars. This action is to be explained partly by the fact that Varèse's father was continually obliged to travel about, but above all by the very strong tensions which must have already arisen between the young Edgard's parents.

Elsewhere, Varèse's grandfather, Claude Cortot, kept a little bistro in Paris, on the rue de Lancry, near the Canal Saint-Martin, a little bistro which I believe still exists. Thus, it was for the most part his grandmother, Célinie, who used to go and visit the child at Villars. The grandfather was that huge, warm presence that the child returned to in Paris, almost certainly at 88, Faubourg du Temple, on the fringe of the 10th and 11th arrondissements. They were to go together to the market many, many times. And it was still accompanied by his grandfather Cortot that the young boy was to go to his first school in Paris. But Varèse, though he loved his grandfather deeply, loathed school. He thought of nothing but getting back to Villars, where he had a wonderful playmate in his cousin Marthe.

Villars, a little village of the former Comté du Mâconnais, is situated on the banks of the Saône, scarcely more than a few kilometers from Tournus, so famous for its magnificent Romanesque church, Saint-Philibert. Paris, Lorraine, Burgundy! What an inheritance of vitality those names imply! "Men of Burgundy be not so daft as to say goodbye without their draught!" Romain Rolland's hero, Colas Breugnon sings. What could be more Rabelaisian than a Burgundian? Moreover, it appears that "Burgundians always recognize one another, no matter what district they're from. The Burgundian is no myth." Let us not forget that Debussy's paternal ancestors were from Burgundy. It is certainly in that sane and healthy region that we should look for the roots of the prodigious passion for life which gave Varèse his vitality, as well as his humor and determination. No soil can be too rich and too healthy for a creator. And thus it was that Varèse spent the happiest days of his childhood in the calm air of Villars. Whether he was in Paris or Berlin, it was to Villars that he would always return until his grandfather's death in 1910. But let us listen to Varèse himself as he evokes the role his grandfather and that little village played in his life.

"There I grew up to boyhood, and I remember how I hated to return to my family to go to school in Paris. But later, when a student at the Paris Conservatoire and afterwards when I was living in Berlin before the first World War, I would always go back to Le Villars for vacations to stay with my grandfather. I often took friends with me, among others the Spanish sculptor Gonzalez, who made a drawing of him. Not having any fixative he used the juice of garlic as preservative. The portrait, a perfect likeness, still hangs in the room where I work, the only picture I have of my grandfather.

"At that time my grandfather was living alone in a little house which is a tiny part of a tenth century Prieure. There is a small Romanesque church connected with this, now dilapidated, old Prieure, which is not unknown to anyone who has read Anatole France's *Rôtisserie de la Reine Pédauque,* for it is outside this little church that his Abbé Jérôme Coignard dies.

"My grandfather, like all the other peasants in our village, had a little vineyard and made his own wine. He also did his own cooking and was an excellent cook. As a soldier he had visited several eastern countries and knew many Oriental recipes. One I remember that I have often made myself, Syrian I think, consists of cucumbers sliced very thin and prepared with sour cream and mint. This, as well as old familiar French dishes such as *Boeuf Bourguignon, Potée Bourguignonne, Coq-au-vin, Veau* (or *poulet) Marengo,* I learned from him. . . . I have inherited only one thing of value, the memory of my Burgundian grandfather.[5]

The most touching compliment Varèse was ever to make to his wife, Louise, was to confess to her that the two beings he loved the most were his grandfather Claude and herself. Indeed, one only had to talk to Varèse for a short while in order to realize that his grandfather was still the man he loved and admired the most. (He knew him for a much longer time than his grandmother, Célinie, who died some eighteen years before Claude Cortot). I still remember the fervor and emotion with which he spoke of him. Unlike Varèse's father, Claude Cortot was not an educator of the lion-tamer school. (Varèse was often to quote Jules Renard's remarks: "Everyone doesn't have the luck to be an orphan." And the childhood of Jules Vallès, the revolutionary writer, was similar.) Claude Cortot was more of a village Socrates, so strong was his instinct for maieutics when it came to the most elementary and vital truths. He was doubtless a good Republican, probably a radical, who took the young Varèse to sit with him on the café terrace during Sunday Mass.

It was at Villars that the first signs of Varèse's vocation as a composer appeared. Needless to say, the village had no orchestra, no choral society, no brass band; but there was the train whistle to be heard in the distance, the splashing of the Saône, the wind blowing over roofs and through the grass and trees. One night, the young Varèse was awakened by a long C sharp rending the silence.

It was the whistle of a train as it passed close by the village. It was not until much later, after his arrival in New York, during the period when he was living on West 14th Street, near the docks, that he was to rediscover that high, whistling C sharp of his childhood. Another marvel . . . The first time he heard an orchestra, in Turin, he had the impression "of a great stream flowing." The orchestra was reminding him of the Saône washing by at Tournus. Later on, we shall see what importance the river had in his "esthetic." The man who has once been marked by a river never forgets its motion. Moreover, the river is an unceasing call to travel, to escape, to set forth on magic quests. As he listened to the world, Varèse came to know that he would be a singer of sound; for it was as he listened that the world seemed to him magnificent. Thus Nature was his first teacher, as it has been for many great artists, as it was for Leonardo da Vinci himself.

On July 9, 1892, Varèse's grandmother Célinie died at the age of fifty-four. She was buried in the Pantin cemetery on Monday the 11th. Shortly afterwards, Varèse's father decided to settle with his family in Turin, where he had very considerable business affairs. It appears that Henri Varèse was one of those hard and ruthless businessmen so characteristic of the nineteenth century. After Villars and Paris, Edgard could only feel very much alone in that enormous, "sad" city, where everything was foreign to him: the customs, the language, and his father. It was in Turin, in effect, that the latent conflict between the boy and his father was slowly and tragically hatched. Everything was a source of opposition between them. Varèse took refuge in his memories, in contemplating the happy moments of his past. His roots were much more in Burgundy than in Piedmont, and Turin was in fact one long exile for him; an exile made even gloomier by the fact that it was being experienced by a child. We all know how sharp the torments of children and adolescents can be.

He learned Italian while playing with companions in the street. He was a hefty, quarrelsome boy, and played several sports. But since he had to get through five years of studies in only three, he was obliged to spend most of his time shut up in his room, where he spent many long hours, face to the wall, dreaming of the Saône, and pierced by the joyful cries of his friends rocketing up from the street. His father had done his engineering studies at the Polytechnicum Fédéral de Zurich, and his eldest son had to follow in his footsteps. But young Varèse, too familiar with the freedom of a great river and the open air, could only rebel and rise in defiant revolt against his industrially-minded father's authoritarian temperament and practical good sense. In fact, he was not to know joy again until the day his grandfather Cortot came to live with them in Turin.

During this period of his life, most of his vacations were spent with his family at Bergeggi, near Genoa, on the shores of the Mediterranean, where his father was in the habit of renting a house for the summer. It was there that Varèse discovered the sea. But sometimes, too, he would go to stay with his uncles in Pignerol. With them he went climbing for the first time and discovered the mountains.

However, it was in Turin, a twentieth century city, that he was to become conscious of *his* nature: the true sounds which characterize an industrial city. He was to love the city so much later on, especially New York, that he was to come to loathe the country, to feel himself an absolute stranger there. Varèse achieved a spontaneous harmony with what Henri van Lier calls the "median reality." In this sense, in the very heart of New York, he never felt alien. He was able to integrate himself with this new nature, created by the hands of man, with optimism and lucidity. There was a great distance between him and men like Georges Duhamel or Lanza del Vasto, between him and all that mulitiude of pessimists who have propagated the myth of the machine as a deadly thing, all those witch hunters of a new civilization! The man who achieves a consciousness of natural-artificial reality is truly a spirit apprehending his present. However, the majority of men do not succeed in this. They persist in hanging on to the Nature of the German Romantics or the Canadian trappers, then they are astonished at finding themselves left behind, dispossessed; they are astonished at finding themselves incapable of feeling the authentic works of their contemporaries. They have never managed to perceive that we have truly changed universes, and that the poetry of the countryside may have to give way, little by little, to the poetry of a city like New York. For it is already in the cities that the majority of men live; and it is those men who must be expressed. As Jean-Marie Domenach so rightly said. ". . . One can only resist the spread of uniformity by taking one's stand upon living particularities, capable of change, and not by regilding one's folklore." [6]

In the musical field, Turin had a conservatory and an opera house, which was used mainly by touring companies. It was during a visit of the Concerts Colonne that the young Varèse attended his first concert. The works performed were by César Franck, Paul Dukas, Richard Strauss, Wagner, and above all *Prélude à l'après-midi d'un faune* by Debussy. Thus, Varèse was fortunate in making contact with the majority of the important composers of the day almost simultaneously. He was always to retain a great admiration for the *Prélude à l'après-midi d'un faune*. It was the real shock for him. I do not believe he was to be struck again by Debussy in such a thunderbolt way until the revelation of *Jeux*. Shortly afterwards, he later admitted, he came under the spell of the mystery and sensation of distance produced by Sibelius's *Swan of Tuonela*. Nevertheless Varèse had, in any case, already been intrigued, and passionately so, by musical sound and instruments long before this meeting with musical works. While still in Villars, he had stretched the cords of a mandolin in a thousand different ways in order to delight in the new sounds and the new relations between those sounds he was able to produce. Leonardo da Vinci, you may recall, was similarly fascinated by musical instruments . . . In Turin there was, of course, a grand piano in his father's house. But as soon as the young Varèse's passion for music became too flagrant, his father locked the keyboard shut, covered the whole piano with a thick black shroud, and kept the key of the room himself. There could never be any question of musical studies for his businessman son, already sacrificed on the altar of industry, a future polytechnician, a future adult who must of course earn his living like any "proper man" and think of music as no more than a pastime for the well-to-do members of his class. Nevertheless, in secret, thanks to the money which he earned occasionally by working in his father's office, the adolescent began visiting the director of the conservatory, Giovanni Bolzoni. Almost immediately, the latter began to give him free lessons in harmony and counterpoint. Later, through his teacher, Varèse came into contact with the orchestra of the opera house, then became a member of the "percussionists." One day, when the orchestra's conductor suddenly fell ill, Varèse replaced him during a rehearsal for *Rigoletto*. He knew the score very well. But even before his first music lessons, in order to amuse his friends he had composed an "opera" entitled *Martin Paz* based on a book by Jules Verne.

At the age of fourteen, the young composer already had the intuition of his musical esthetics and of his vocation as a composer, as an "organizer" of sounds. After reading an account of the Zambezi, the great African river, in which the differing speeds of the many currents making up the general flow were discussed, Varèse imagined a transmutation of this fluvial polyphony into the sphere of sound. From then on, the whole of his musical thought and his vision of sound structures was to be impregnated by that intuition. But from that first insight to a work like *Intégrales*, for example, there was still a very long way to go. The horizontal polyphony of river currents . . . The vertical polyphony of volcanic eruptions . . . For this latter kind of polyphony seems to me to be as much present in his work as the horizontal kind. Doubtless this intuition was handed down to him, through his individual heredity, from the vast memory of humanity.

In 1900, Varèse went to Paris with his grandfather to visit the *Exposition Universelle*. Shortly after his return from the capital, it seems, his mother died. Once she was gone, the conflict with his father, constantly being stirred up anew, could only end in a stalemate. Henri Varèse had often been horribly brutal with his wife; so much so that on her deathbed, calling Edgard to her side, Blanche-Marie told him to protect his young brothers and sisters as well as he could, since he was the eldest, for his father was a "murderer." As a mother, she had been too much crushed, too much humiliated by her husband to display the normal warmth and tenderness that all children expect. It is possible that Varèse felt much more pity than deep affection for this mother who, it should be remembered, had entrusted him while still a young baby to one of his aunts, though doubtless under pressure from the father. However, Varèse always kept a photograph of his mother in his workshop, and a painting of her as a little girl in his drawing-room.

Henri Varèse remarried shortly afterwards. However, before long his anger was breaking out again, and he raised his hand in violence against his new wife. The latter, though, was a good-hearted woman who was kind to the children. Because of this, Varèse intervened firmly during the very first angry scene. This *father-son* crisis ended in drama in which all the bitterness, hatred, and anger Varèse felt, even while hating them, exploded into the open. Subsequently, any father-son type of relationship he became involved in was doomed to swift decay. As soon as any man established a relationship with Varèse involving authority over him (Rodin or Vincent d'Indy for example), that relationship was bound to fall apart very quickly. Behind the face of a d'Indy, there lurked the features of the father, hated since birth. Because of this, it took very little—a simple criticism, which Varèse disliked intensely—to make all his aggressiveness, his wilfulness, and his violence, burst through to the surface. He must certainly have struggled all his life to channel the violence which he had himself inherited; he must have struggled ceaselessly to exorcize the father-image that undoubtedly haunted him. In fact, I believe that he was to prove psychologically incapable of being a true father himself, when he became one in reality. How deep that hatred must have gone! This aggression manifests itself, it seems to me, even in Varèse's way of shattering or attacking a sound, or a chord, in his works. Needless to say, without that hatred, burning like a bed of coals under all his acts, he would not have composed the works we know today. His music would have been as powerful, but different. The tenderness he felt for his grandfather and his all-devouring passion for music no doubt saved him from the total hatred and revolt which would have made all creation impossible. For total hatred can engender nothing, it can only destroy.

After the break with his father, Varèse took up residence in Paris. There, he met a friend from Turin who had just begun his architectural studies in the French capital. It was with that friend, in a small hotel, that he was to live at first. Then, more than a year later, his father did everything within his power to see him again. He even went so far as to make a scene in Fauré's respectable conservatory. But Varèse, still inflexible, refused to see him even then. The bond had been broken forever. The wound could never be healed. It was still raw even at the age of seventy-five. Moreover, it was not until 1914 that he was to see one of his brothers again.[7] As for his grandfather, a few years after the departure of his grandson, Claude Cortot left Turin for Villars, where he lived until his death.

2

Formation

1903. Paris was in ferment. The City of Light was a meeting-place for thousands of men, all dreaming the twentieth century. Europe, with its four hundred million inhabitants and its extraordinary industrial power, dominated the world. Though there were a few "decadent" artists wonderstruck by Negro art, the white man was still absolutely convinced of his superiority over the yellow and the black races. Vallès was remarking that, since he could no longer attack other whites, the white man was using his bayonets to disembowel yellow men. The great colonial empires were being built. But despite everything, the old conceptions of the universe were exploding. On December 17th, the Wright brothers were to make their first flight, lasting twelve seconds. Max Planck had put forward his quantum theory and revolutionized modern physics. Rutherford was publishing his work on radioactivity. Einstein was at work on his first theory of relativity, Bertrand Russell on his *Principia Mathematica*. Durkheim, Lévy-Bruhl, Binet, Ribot, Husserl, and Bergson were making their marks. Picasso, Gris, Modigliani, Severini, Bartók and Klee were in Paris or on their way there. Julio Gonzalez had already been there three years. That year, Rouault exhibited at the Salon d'Automne, Matisse, Dufy and Marquet were at the Salon des Indépendants, and Gauguin was dying in the Marquesas Islands. In the musical sphere, the scandal of *Pelléas et Mélisande* had just died down. In literature, Proust, Gide,

Valéry, Claudel, Suarès, and Romain Rolland were coming to the fore. Péguy had founded his *Cahiers de la Quinzaine*. Apollinaire, Jacob and Cendrars were the new masters of the poem. Beside all this, Edward VII's visit to Paris, the cakewalk, or the first Tour de France on bicycles, were of little importance. In the heart of Paris, it was the hope raised by the advent of a new century that was being breathed deeply. Though Trotsky was able to write, and perhaps with reason, that "the development of art is the highest test of the vitality and the significance of any epoch," he was singularly mistaken when he also wrote that "art showed itself to be powerless, as it always is at the beginning of a great epoch."[1] Unless one is only going to admit the peaks of Classic art, it must be said that a new epoch was in fact being born with these men, and that its creators were admirably equal to the high task awaiting them.

As we have said, upon his arrival in Paris Varèse went to live with a friend from Turin in a little hotel on the rue Saint-André-des-Arts, in the 6th arrondissement. He was twenty. What music, what new works had Paris to offer him? There was, of course, Satie, at that time composing his *Trois pièces en forme de poire*, and Debussy, at work on his *Jardins sous la pluie*. But in fact, the Masters, the Venerables of that era were Saint-Saëns, Lalo, d'Indy, Charpentier, Widor, Dukas, Bruneau, Tournemire, Chausson and a few others. What new compositions were being revealed by the performances of the Concerts Colonne or those of the Société des Nouveaux Concerts run by Lamoureux? Both these associations, subsidized by the state, were bound to give first performances of a fixed minimum of works by French composers. Thus the Concerts Colonne in this year 1903 presented its audiences with *l'Amour des Ondines* by Bachelet, and *les Villes Maudites* by Max d'Ollone; as for the Concerts Lamoureux, their contributions were Witkowski's *Symphonie*, A. Coquard's *Eté*, *Ouverture* by Casadesus, d'Indy's *Symphonie in B flat*, G. Huë's *Trois poèmes maritimes*, and Saint-Quentin's *Harmonie du soir*.[2] These works represented the so-called new music. This was the true musical Paris. And it was in this atmosphere that the young Varèse was to pursue his studies. His only means of subsistence was to be his work as a copyist, and later a post in a library. He did so much music copying that his writing gradually shrank in size, eventually becoming the minuscule handwriting we know today.

In 1904, Varèse was accepted at the Schola Cantorum. This school had been founded in 1896 by Charles Bordes, and there Varèse studied composition and orchestral conducting with d'Indy, counterpoint and fugue with Albert Roussel, and medieval and Renaissance music with Bordes. In order to pay for his studies he accepted a post as librarian offered to him by d'Indy, thanks to the help of his second-cousin, the pianist Alfred Cortot. Little by little, however, d'Indy "conceived a tenacious enmity" for him. Twenty-four years later, in *Comoedia*, he was still attacking Varèse, even though he had not seen him then for twenty years. "The reason I left him," Varèse told me, "was because his idea of teaching was to form disciples. His vanity would not permit the least sign of originality, or even independent thinking, and I did not want to become a little d'Indy. One was enough."[3] D'Indy's teacher had written: "Only melody never grows old."[4] One can imagine what a gulf there was between the two men. But despite everything, the Schola opened up for Varèse all the riches of musical life before Johann Sebastian Bach. That in itself means a great deal. Léonin, Pérotin, Adam de la Halle, Guillaume de Machaut, Guillaume Dufay, Ockeghem—whose *Deo Gratias*, made up of four nine part canons, he was to copy—Josquin des Prés, Pierre de la Rue, Janequin, Palestrina, Giovanni Gabrieli, Thomas Luis de Victoria, Roland de Lassus, Heinrich Schütz—whom he admired more than Bach—Monteverdi, his "god," Marc-Antoine Charpentier and several others. We shall see later on with what religious respect Varèse regarded Leonardo da Vinci and Paracelsus. If one were to consider only the men he loved the most, then one might say, paradoxically, that Varèse was a man of the Middle Ages in the sense that Rouault was, or a Renaissance man like da Vinci. "Many of the old masters," Varèse wrote, "are my intimate friends—all are respected colleagues. None of them are dead saints—in fact none of them are dead . . . They are alive in the present."[5] And indeed, how could a great innovator like Monteverdi not have been a spiritual brother to Varèse? Especially when one thinks that the latter had to confront problems which, though doubtless different from those faced by the Italian, nevertheless led him inevitably to conceive a radical new art of sounds, an art nearer to that incorporated by the Middle Ages into the *Quadrivium* than to that of a man like d'Indy.

The critic and composer Paul Le Flem was a student with Varèse at the Schola. Here is how he describes Varèse the student (in a letter to me) : "We shared Debussyist sympathies, but Edgard was to go much further than myself subsequently . . . And above all, don't go thinking that at that distant time he was a poor contrapuntalist. He could have shown even the cleverest in that field a thing or two, and once more we find the truth of the old Latin adage verified: 'Ad augusta, per augusta.' He went to d'Indy's classes, but as an independent, and like some others, including myself, he knew enough to get out of them when he felt he would be better off elsewhere.

"Both Varèse and myself had a pretty tough time at the Schola, and we experienced moments of extreme financial depression which we managed to get through by plunging into the rising flood of new ideas and esthetics which was then breaking all around us. It was sometimes very tough going.

"We made our débuts as conductors together, in the orchestral class that d'Indy supervized every Tuesday. D'Indy used to advise us, and I can still see Edgard walking up to the conductor's desk, tall, his eyes flashing defiant lightning at the little girls playing the second violins— he made his début with the *Overture to Egmont*—and giving the signal to begin as he transfixed the players with those thunderbolt eyes."[6] This striking reminiscence of Le Flem's coincides with one of Varèse's own memories: "I was even the phenomenon of the class because of the ease and celerity with which I juggled with counterpuntal artifices. . . . I do not in the least regret having learned to master these jigsaw puzzles, and even now sometimes amuse myself with quite similar games."[7] In short, Varèse didn't think of himself as a composer because he could bring off a successful fugue, but since he was in full possession of his tools, of musical grammar, he was able to go in quest of his own music without having to bother about such matters of craftsmanship. Like all great innovators, he knew perfectly well what he was giving up or what he was rejecting.

While studying at the Schola, he met François Bernouard, who later became a publisher of Bloy, Barbey d'Aurevilly and Jules Renard. They were to introduce one another to many men who are now celebrities. At number 7, rue Ravignan, Varèse met Max Jacob, Picasso, newly settled in Paris, and Julio Gonzalez. He already knew Erik Satie. And later he also became friendly with Modigliani, Apollinaire, Rémy de Gourmont, Sâr Péladan, Salmon, Léon-Paul Fargue, Bertrand—the inventor of the dynaphone—and above all Léon Deubel. Needless to say, he became an habitué of the Closerie des Lilas, where he occasionally met Léautaud. "I've been a Montparnassian since my childhood," Varèse once said. "I was going to the Dôme in the days when all you found there at ten in the evening was a single customer fast asleep."[8]

On January 8, 1905, Varèse received the following card: "I am pleased to inform you that you have been accepted as a student of composition, in Widor's class, at the Conservatoire National de Musique et de Déclamation and are consequently requested to present yourself in the secretary's office on January 11th at 9 o'clock. Signed, Director of the Conservatoire, Gabriel Fauré." Varèse did, in effect, study with Widor. He even worked for the Prix de Rome, and we still have an unfinished fugue surviving from this period at the Conservatoire. But the Conservatoire had nothing new to offer him. As the German critic Stuckenschmidt has pointed out: "The generation of composers around the year 1900 was no longer caught up in the battle between 'pure music' and 'music drama.' The war it had to wage was situated on a quite different level, and its critical implications have proved more considerable: what was really at stake for this generation was the very validity of music's raw material."[9] This is what Varèse was already investigating while at the Paris Conservatoire. In Leonardo da Vinci's words: let us inquire toward what hope his thoughts were turning. From the very start, Varèse was passionate about men and their ideas. He weaned himself intellectually on Leonardo's *Notebooks.* Moreover, through Maurice Pelletier, a Latin scholar and the translator of Paracelsus, he initiated himself into "alchemical" thought. The son of an engineer, attracted by physics and mathematics, how could he not have been drawn to the great Leonardo? We know, for example, that Leonardo was a great observer of waves and water currents. As Odile Vivier has remarked, Leonardo wrote that "the waves of sounds and those of light (which) are governed by the same laws as those of water."[10] It will be remembered that Varèse was struck very early on in life by the diversity possible in water currents, by the polyphony of energies flowing in rivers. Music is "the art-science," he was to say.[11] Instead of talking about music, he preferred to talk about "organized sound"; instead of saying that he was a musician, he was to say that he

worked with rhythms, frequencies, and intensities. Moreover, as
Odile Vivier has written: "His cult of the Middle Ages and his passion
for the great inventors led him to read works of alchemy or Hermetic
astronomy and apply them in the musical field, then to the study of the
theories and discoveries of Renaissance scientists."[12] It is certainly
true that Varèse was amazed by Paracelsus' description of the "transmutation of elements," but we should not exaggerate this influence of
the "magus." Varèse did not actually believe in alchemy as such, any
more than in any of the other branches of occult knowledge. We must
not forget that he had studied physics quite extensively, and above all
that he was a contemporary of Einstein. Since he was striving to express
a new universe, naturally he turned toward those men who had had
similar problems, but he could only resolve his own problems con-
cretely *on his own*, in the course of a patient quest, in an unceasing
striving for lucidity, which is to say, for a lucidity of the kind that can
be conceived, and is necessary, in the universe of the "median reality"
spoken of by Henri van Lier. In order to find all Varèse's masters one
would have to go back in time to the School of Notre-Dame, and then
salute the true creators of musical tradition, such innovators as
Giovanni Gabrieli, for example.[13] One would have to talk of Monteverdi, of Beethoven, of Berlioz and Debussy. It was Berlioz, after all,
who wrote: "As you may well suspect, entirely new means will have to
be employed. Apart from the two orchestras there would be four
groups of brass instruments placed in the four corners of the performing area. The combinations would be quite new, and a thousand
propositions would emerge from this mass of harmony quite imprac-
ticable with ordinary means."[14] Berlioz, as we know, was to realize this
dream in his *Requiem*. It is men like that who were Varèse's masters,
his "colleagues." But since he had had a good scientific education, he
was particularly interested in the work of physicists. "When I was
about twenty," he has written, "I came across a definition of music that
seemed suddenly to throw light on my gropings toward a music I
sensed could exist. Hoéne Wronsky, physicist, chemist, musicologist and
philosopher of the first half of the nineteenth century, defined music as
'the corporealization of the intelligence that is in sounds.' It was a
new and exciting conception and to me the first that started me thinking of music as spatial—as moving bodies of sound in space, a conception I gradually made my own. Very early musical ideas came to me

which I realized would be difficult or impossible to express with the means available, and my thinking even then began turning around the idea of liberating music from the tempered system, from the limitations of musical instruments and from years of bad habits, erroneously called tradition. I studied Helmholtz, and was fascinated by his experiments with sirens described in his *Physiology of Sound*. Later I made some modest experiments of my own and found that I could obtain beautiful parabolic and hyperbolic curves of sound, which seemed to me equivalent to the parabolas and hyperbolas in the visual domain."[15] In 1905, among the other works to be found on his work-table, we would have noticed *The Musical Problems of Aristotle*. Later on, he was to interest himself particularly in Aristoxenes (*cf.* bibliography). It is thus apparent that Varèse was in fact one of those rare composers characterized by "an identical endeavor to return to the deepest sources, to call into question all the artistic principles then current."[16] The young composer was becoming conscious of *sound*, the physicist's raw material. And Western music was, in effect, wholly ignorant at that time of its raw material. Musical writing had become a game of graphics, but it was not music.

In 1905, however, it was still too soon for Varèse's intuitions and ideas to take concrete form in his works. His first manuscript efforts, unfortunately destroyed either by a fire in Berlin or by Varèse's own hand, have not come down to us. Nevertheless, we know that during that year Varèse had already composed: *Trois pièces* for orchestra, *la Chanson des jeunes hommes* and *le Prélude à la fin d'un jour*, inspired by a poem written by his friend Léon Deubel and entitled *la Fin d'un jour*. Elsewhere, in a letter from Léon Deubel to Emile Bernard, two works are mentioned: *le Fils des étoiles*,[17] an opera that Varèse was still to write, drawing his inspiration from the text of that title by Sâr Péladan, and the *Prélude à la fin d'un jour*. "I have never mentioned this young maestro to you before," Deubel writes. "He is at the Conservatoire, working in the composition class towards the Prix de Rome . . . I have a great love and admiration for him. I get great pleasure out of hearing him play Wagner and Beethoven in the evening. His works are already remarkable and you would certainly like them. At the moment he is just finishing a *Prélude à la fin d'un jour* for an orchestra of 120 musicians, which is colossal."[18] Unfortunately, the manuscript of this work was entrusted to Deubel's keeping and subsequently lost. Deubel was supposed to have conveyed it, through the intermediary of Emile Bernard, to the writer Elémir Bourges. Why? Subsequently, as is well-known, Deubel killed himself.

At that time, Varèse was being put up at the *Rénovation esthétique*. He was supposed to introduce Deubel to Péladan. Deubel and Varèse were very good friends, despite the dissimilarity in their characters. In his *Anecdotiques* of December 1, 1913, Apollinaire reports Varèse's remarks on the subject of his friend Deubel: "Léon Deubel was a misanthropist and very much a misogynist. As far as I know, he only loved one woman, Anna, a very plain little German girl. The only companion for whom he felt any truly lively affection was Louis Pergaud, in whose future he had a great faith. He also had an affection for Emile Bernard, who had always been very kind to him and got him into the *Rénovation esthétique,* where he had really spacious lodgings; he must have felt at least esteem for me, since he invited me to come and share his quarters with him. During the time I lived with him, Deubel read me everything he wrote. We spent some good evenings drinking white wine, which he liked very much and used to go out and fetch from the Coopérative on the rue Cardinale. I set several of his things to music: a sonnet called *Souvenir,* two pieces of rhythmic prose written especially for me, and which I don't think ever appeared in any of the magazines . . . I also wrote the *Prélude à la fin d'un jour,* a symphonic poem intended to serve as a prologue to *la Fin d'un jour,* one of the poems from *la Lumière natale.*"[19]

In 1906, Varèse composed his *Rhapsodie romane.* Only the piano version was ever performed, at the *Rénovation esthétique.* Having been marked himself by the architectural conception of Romanesque art, he wanted to achieve an identical austerity, an identical purity and strength. Since childhood he had been impregnated with the beauty of Saint-Philibert, the Romanesque church in Tournus under whose walls he had so often played. Thus he had an obscure need to go back to his childhood, and even further than that, to the sources of Western art, before endeavoring to achieve an expression of the century then being born. Péladan, who heard this work, said that Varèse "was writing a profane Gregorian chant."

Also in 1906, the composer founded the choral society of the people's University in the faubourg Saint-Antoine. This was a mixed choir of working men and women, and with it Varèse gave concerts at the *Château du peuple*. For him, a musician of the "belle époque" half starving to death, this was doubtless a way of rebelling against the bourgeoisie, a way of "committing himself." Apollinaire and others were to give several lectures at the University of the faubourg Saint-Antoine. Varèse said later, in a letter to Odile Vivier dated November 28, 1962: "Some of my choristers were old enough to be my fathers and mothers . . . and some constituted themselves my bodyguard after our late evening rehearsals, escorting me as far as the place de la Bastille, because the young toughs (apaches) of the neighborhood 'didn't know me yet,' as they put it. At that time, the neighborhood was one of the most disreputable in Paris." Indeed, it was scarcely four years before this that two gangs of apaches had done battle there for the beautiful "Helen of Troy of the sidewalk"—Casque d'Or. And at that particular time Varèse was living at 41, rue Monge, in the 5th arrondissement.

On September 19, 1907, thanks to the help of Clemenceau, then Premier, Varèse's certificate of exemption from military service was duly signed. He had been originally due for recruitment in 1905, but Varèse had more or less challenged the old "tiger," saying to him, you politicians never keep your word. But Clemenceau . . .

At the Conservatoire, Varèse met a girl named Suzanne Bing who was studying to be an actress. Two years later, on November 5, 1907, he was to marry her. They lived on the rue Descartes, in a large room without heating, a room of which one wall was made of sacks sewn together. It was in a similar hovel, at number 18 on the same street, that Verlaine had died ten years before. And it was in this room on the rue Descartes that Dullin, while still a student, came to hear Suzanne's lines in an Ibsen play. He was working at an audition he was about to do for Gémier. Louis Jouvet was another visitor.

It had taken Varèse only three years to become looked upon by several older masters of the time as a composer of the future. In order to prove to him the confidence they felt in him, Massenet and Widor obtained for Varèse, in 1907, the *Première Bourse artistique de la ville de Paris*. There can be no doubt whatever about the affection that Massenet felt for Varèse: "My dear Varèse," he wrote to him, "I want to prove to you what a great interest I take in you . . ."[20] Such words only serve to emphasize how powerful the magnetism emanating from Varèse's extremely forceful personality must have been. Some of the

Paris maestros considered him as a friend—a young man, scarcely more than twenty, who had arrived in Paris, poor and unknown, only four years before. But despite the warmth with which he was surrounded, Varèse found the musical life of Paris so distasteful that he resolved to exile himself to Berlin, a city to which he was drawn by the more favorable musical climate existing there. Later, when giving some of his reasons for leaving Paris, he was to say: "I left Paris impelled by a disgust for all the petty politics there, searching for a way of escaping from myself, for a way of escaping from middle-class sentiment, that sentiment which neutralizes the efforts and the sensibility of the most astute, the most intelligent of peoples, and of the French élite, the first in the world."[21] To Stravinsky, he was to confess: "The teachers were all ruled like music paper." One thing is certain: since his arrival in Paris there had been but little change in the musical world. For one Debussy writing *la Mer*, in 1905, how many other composers there were merely dozing! At the end of 1907, when Varèse left Paris, the Concerts Colonne and the Concerts Lamoureux gave first performances of the following works: *Symphony in C minor* by E. Cools, *Deux pièces en forme canonique* by Th. Dubois, *Chant de la destinée* by G. Dupont, *les Fugitifs* by André Fijan, *Selma*, a cantata by M. Le Boucher, *Contes de Noël* by Perilhou, *Ouverture dramatique* by Mazellier, *Etudes symphoniques* by Samazeuilh, *Fünn* by J. Poueigh, *le Livre de Job* by Rabaud, *Joré* by Bachelet, etc.[22] And these concerts were the only ones Varèse could afford to go to. The seats cost only ten sous.

3

Encounters

In Paris, in 1908, Fauvism was giving way to Cubism. Picasso had
already painted *les Demoiselles d'Avignon*. In the realm of cinema,
Max Linder had just made *les Débuts d'un patineur*. At the moment
when Bergson was publishing his *Evolution créatrice*, Gémier was
putting on Jarry's *Ubu-Roi* at the Théâtre Antoine. In the United
States, William James had just put his most important work before the
public: *Pragmatism*. In Berlin, Busoni was making himself felt with his
Sketch of a New Aesthetic of Music. Mahler was finishing *Das Lied von
der Erde*. Strauss had already, in the years since 1900, given his *Salomé*
and *Elektra*. Doubtless, official art was just as triumphant in the Berlin
of 1908 as it was in Paris or in Vienna; but the opposition to music was
less strong there all the same. Even Schoenberg himself, moreover, was
to turn away from Vienna, in 1911, and come to live in Berlin. "There
was a perpetual quest for new sensations," the critic Stuckenschmidt
notes. "The possibility of traveling more or less without hindrance
encouraged cultural exchanges and an intellectual rivalry more or less
unprecedented in the history of civilization."[1] But in the face of this
acceleration of history, of this cultural ferment, the gap between new
works and the public was in danger of becoming accentuated. The
creator was to be more and more a lone figure. "The greater the sensibility, the greater the martyrdom," da Vinci wrote.[2] There is, I believe,
no development slower and more painful than the progress of man's

sensibility. Its roots go down too deeply into his being, if not into the "collective unconscious." To change eras means, it goes without saying, to change sensibilities. And is there any art more deeply involved with the roots of sensibility than music? It is not astonishing, therefore, that the development of that art should so often prove slow and agonizing. Man's sensibility has a need for security which makes it cling to its memories, to the past, to what *has been* sublime. It is a matter, in short, of that contemplation of happy instants of which Delacroix speaks, and which he termed *happiness*. So that the sensibility hangs on to happiness as hard as it can, and for the majority of men, apparently, happiness is a long and penetrating gaze *behind*, into what has been.

Varèse settled, then, in Berlin (just as Scriabin was arriving in Brussels). In that foreign capital he found himself alone once more. Since he knew no German, he started off by working again as a copyist. He did remain constantly in touch, let us not forget, with his friends in Paris, and he traveled frequently between the two cities. Was he under the influence of the pro-Teutonic conversation of his friend Deubel? Was he attracted by those musician-prophets, by the German music of the time which was a vehicle for so many extra-musical ideas, as Paul Rosenfeld believes? [3] What is important is that during this year, 1908, he was to have two all-important meetings with two men whom he admired a great deal: Busoni and Debussy.

Varèse had just read Busoni's prophetic book. The latter's prestige as a composer was, at this time, immense. Nevertheless, despite Varèse's youth, this first meeting between the two men was an extremely warm one. "In 1907 (sic) I went to Berlin where I spent most of the next six years and had the good fortune of becoming an intimate friend (in spite of the great disparity of age and importance) of Ferruccio Busoni," Varèse wrote. "I had read his remarkable little book, *A New Aesthetic of Music* (another milestone in my musical development), and when I came across his dictum: 'Music was born free and to win freedom is its destiny,' I was amazed and very much excited to find that there was somebody else besides myself—and a musician at that—who believed this. It gave me the courage to go on with my ideas and my scores. Our views on music often differed radically, for his own music and his musical tastes were more orthodox than his theories. It was Busoni who coined the expression 'The New Classicism,' and classicism, new or old, was what I was bent on escaping. But it was also Busoni who said, 'The function of the creative artist consists in making laws, not in following laws already made.' In any case I owe him a debt of gratitude. He not only corroborated, clarified and encouraged my ideas, but being as magical a talker as he was a brilliant thinker, he had the gift of stimulating my mind to feats of prophetic imagination." [4] Busoni was for Varèse, in Socrates' magnificent expression, a *midwife*. Thus, his influence over him was much more intellectual than musical. "Busoni's pupils," one critic wrote, "have drawn strength from him, but without ever having to abdicate anything of their individuality. Busoni never modified their peculiar geniuses. He was an indefatigable searcher for new forms and new means of expression." [5] We are a far cry from men like d'Indy. In effect, Busoni reassured Varèse that what he was saying, what he was dreaming, what he was attempting, was not a way of escape, not a search for utopia. Varèse tells us that Busoni had said, as early as 1908: "I am more or less convinced that in the authentic new music machines will be necessary, and that they will play an important role. Perhaps even industry will have its role to play in the progress and transformation of esthetics." Kurt List also remarks, elsewhere, that: "With this postulate he set up a problem which hamstrung a whole generation of composers."[6] Busoni was the man who foresaw "the liquidation of the harmonic system based on the diatonic scale and the opposition of major and minor keys, as well as the advent of total chromaticism." [7] The young composer could have found no better friend than Busoni. Only yesterday, Varèse was still speaking of him with warmth and tenderness: "He was a great Renaissance lord with great depths of kindness," he used to tell me. "He hadn't the time for showing off." Varèse also told how he and Busoni first began to use the familiar *tu* when addressing one another. One day, when Varèse was showing him his score, *les Cycles du Nord,* or perhaps *Ödipus und die Sphinx*, Busoni had several observations to make. At several points he advised certain modifications, then asked if Varèse agreed. "No, Maestro!" the latter replied; and he gave his reasons. Whereupon Busoni came with: "From this moment on, I want to hear no more of 'maestro'—only Ferruccio and *tu*." When they were together, Busoni and Varèse spoke sometimes Italian, sometimes French. Varèse never got over his astonishment that the same man who talked to him about tthe Dynamophone, invented by Dr. Thaddeus Cahill in the

United States, composed those works so little in accordance with his own ideas.[8]

It was probably in that same year, which is to say in 1908, that Varèse met Debussy for the first time. (For it is not impossible, according to Louise Varèse's recollections, that her husband had already contacted Debussy while still a student at the Conservatoire, and that the latter had even tried to persuade Varèse not to leave that institution right away.) In any case, Debussy certainly received Varèse in a very friendly fashion at this time, at 80, avenue du Bois-de-Boulogne. He was interested, as a consequence of a letter Varèse had written him, in the latter's scores and ideas. At their first meeting, he gave Varèse a corrected score of *la Mer* inscribed: "To Edgard Varèse, in sympathy and with my best wishes for success. October 29, 1908." This score was later studied by several conductors during visits to New York. It contains corrections which were not to appear in the published version. Varèse wrote on the subject of Debussy: "I had the privilege of knowing Debussy when I was a student in Paris and from the many long talks I had with him I have kept the image of a man of great kindness, intelligence, fastidiousness and wide culture. He was also something of a sybarite and loved beautiful things and all the pleasures of the senses. I remember a carved sandalwood fire screen he kept in front of his wood fire, and how he delighted in the warm fragrance of the precious wood that filled the room. He was in his middle forties when I first knew him, I in my early twenties, but he treated me simply as a colleague without the least condescension. He was too intelligent to be self-important.

"Before I met Debussy I had heard on all sides that he was quite unapproachable, bearish and disagreeable. Later I told him that I had felt very ill at ease the first time I came to see him because of this reputation. His response was charming. He put his hand on my shoulder and said: 'And have I given you cause for complaint?' Being a rebel himself I think he liked my somewhat aggressive independence and my revolt against conformity. Although the tendencies in the scores I showed him were too foreign to his nature for him to really like them, he approved of them objectively. He would say: 'You have a right to compose what you want to, the way you want to if the music comes out and is your own. Your music comes out and is yours.' Everyone knows Debussy's aphorism: 'Rules do not make a work of art.'

"At that time I was very poor and Debussy tried to help me with introductions and recommendations. When I returned to Paris in 1929, the first time I saw Gaveau (head of the piano firm of that name) he told me that he had me to thank for the only Debussy autograph he possessed. This was Debussy's signature on a letter he had written Gaveau asking him to put one of his pianos at my disposal.

"Everyone agrees that Debussy was one of the greatest innovators of all time, but few people know that he was also one of the kindest men." [9]

Debussy was without doubt the composer closest to Varèse. Neither liked to explain his works, so that their conversation was bound to be as much concerned with painting and literature as with music.

Debussy's contempt for the Schola and the Conservatoire could only delight Varèse. "For Debussy," Strobel emphasizes, "the Schola was the citadel of the 'mandarins' who had made music into a pedantic science and barricaded up the windows which it is that art's aim to fling wide open." [10] "One should leave the Conservatoire as soon as possible," Debussy is supposed to have said, "in order to find one's own personality." [11] As Strobel points out, "Debussy's war cry was 'follow the ear rather than the rule.' " [12] These views were without doubt shared by Busoni. It is not astonishing, in consequence, that Varèse should have wanted the latter to meet Debussy. And in effect, in a letter dated February 10, 1909, Debussy did ask Varèse: "Would you ask your friend, M. Busoni, to come and see me, either tomorrow or on Saturday next, at eleven in the morning." Unfortunately the meeting did not take place.

Victor Segalen, after one of his conversations with Debussy, noted down the following remark of the composer on December 17, 1908: "I take great care to employ each timbre in its pure state." And Segalen comments: "Preoccupation of Debussy: insufficiency of percussion. (Note: Bring back set of gongs and cymbals from Far East)." [13] As early as March, 1907, Segalen had sent Debussy some notes on Maori music. And since we know to what extent percussion instruments were already fascinating Varèse as well, their conversations must have been memorables ones. They evidently enriched both composers. It is accepted today that Varèse introduced Debussy to some very important works. "What Debussy knew of the music of Schoenberg was therefore partly or entirely due to Varèse. The present writer asked Varèse what works of Schoenberg he remembered having submitted: it was the *Drei Klavierstücke,* op. 11, and the *Funf Orchesterstücke,* op. 16. No one among Debussy's friends and relatives had so deep and direct a knowledge of the musical scene in Germany. The alleged statement of December, 1913 (reported by Vallas), according to which Debussy knew nothing of Schoenberg at that time, is now definitely disqualified." [14] There is no doubt too, as Stravinsky has pointed out, that Debussy was an influence on Varèse. How, indeed, could the latter not have assimilated what was valid for him in the older man's work, just as Beethoven assimilated Mozart? He was perhaps "a debussyist" as Paul Le Flem [15] affirms, but that attitude was limited to the period during which he was attending Parisian institutions. Varèse, as an adult, could only be "a Varesian."

That same year, 1908, in the fall, [16] Varèse also met Ravel in Paris. He went with Ricardo Vinès, the Abbé Petit, and Jean Marnold, the editor of the *Mercure musical,* to attend the private première of *Gaspard de la nuit* at Ravel's house. The two composers also met again on cordial terms several times thereafter. René Chalupt has emphasized that Varèse "was at that time situated in the extreme forefront of the avant-garde."[17] We possess so little first-hand evidence of this period in Varèse's life that this simple remark seems to me important; though Varèse never, in fact, thought of himself as belonging to an "avant-garde." Indeed, he loathed the expression, and wanted only to be quite simply a voice of *his* time.

It was also in 1908, in Berlin, that Varèse became acquainted with the German poet Hugo von Hofmannsthal. Fascinated by *Ödipus und die Sphinx,* which had been published in 1906, Varèse went to see the poet at his home in Rodaun and suggested himself as the composer for a three-act opera to be based on that work. Not only did Hofmannsthal accept, but the two men continued to work in close collaboration together until the war, and became excellent friends. This was a signal mark of confidence on the part of the famous poet, since the composer was both unknown and not yet twenty-five years old. Hofmannsthal was also, of course, a friend and collaborator of Richard Strauss, who the previous year had set to music Hofmannsthal's "genial poem" *Elektra,* from which they had together fashioned "a wonderful libretto." [18] Varèse knew enough German by the end of 1908 to read it well enough, but he did not speak it really well. I have seen all the work he did, in red ink, on Hofmannsthal's book: so many passages, whole paragraphs, struck out, and a host of directions!

At the very beginning of 1909, Varèse, having finished his work entitled *Bourgogne,* began a symphonic poem called *Gargantua.* It was with these two manuscript scores that he introduced himself to Romain Rolland. The great writer has described this first meeting in a letter to Sofia Bertolini Guerrieri-Gonzaga dated January 24, 1909: "And look how curious it is!" he confides in her. "A second Jean-Christophe has just recently appeared on my doorstep, and an amazingly handsome one. Tall, with a fine head of black hair, pale eyes, an intelligent and forceful face, a sort of young Italian Beethoven painted by Giorgione. He's only twenty-five; but he has scarcely suffered any less than Dupin, though in a quite different way; for since the age of fifteen he has been wandering all over Europe (sic)—in Italy, in Germany, in France—working as a sort of orchestral Jack-of-all-trades; he's French with admixtures of German and Italian blood, and his name is Edgar Varèse; he will soon be going to conduct a concert in Prague. His passion is the orchestra. He has shown me a symphony entitled *Bourgogne* (the region where he spent his childhood) which seemed to me interesting, and above all remarkably written from the point of view of its instrumental color. He has a great admiration for Strauss; and even though he lives in Berlin he has never dared go to see him, because he's afraid of being badly received and losing his illusions about the man. Though he is certainly by no means timid, and yet he is, on this occasion, precisely because he admires Strauss so much. It occurred to me that if he did go to see him, perhaps it would be the scene between Christophe and Hassler. He has told me all the wretchedness he's been through and the indifference and cruelty of people, of colleagues, of other artists. He really did almost die, in harness. Now, he's more or less out of the wood. It gives me pleasure to feel at the moment that independent young artists come to me, and that they are right to come; for I can, truly, be of use to them—intellectually, and even in a practical way. Jean-Christophe is attracting his brothers struggling out in the world.

"But I've not told you the most amusing thing about my meeting with this Varèse: he is in the process of writing a *Gargantua* (a symphonic poem). And just at this very moment, Jean-Christophe is writing one too! Now say, after that, that my book is a 'novel'! My book isn't a novel. Jean-Christophe really exists. He is all around us, everywhere. I am merely writing about what is. I invent nothing . . ." [19]

This extraordinary coincidence must without any doubt have struck Varèse as much as it did Rolland. In effect, Rolland's *Dans la maison*, in which this *Gargantua* occurs, though finished in September of 1908, was not published until February 16 and 23, 1909, in the *Cahiers de la Quinzaine*. In a letter dated January 22, 1909, Rolland wrote to Varèse: "Your *Gargantua* seems to me the ideal for a living and popular subject (popular in the sense of 'a whole people'). But above all amuse yourself writing it! If you don't have a good time creating it, then it's not worth the trouble of creating it at all; unload yourself of all intellectual preoccupations; overflow!" His liking for this subject was equalled, however, by his efforts to dissuade Varèse from his project of writing an opera based on Hofmannsthal's play. Attacking this scheme in the same letter, he wrote: "I am extremely uneasy about the idea of *Ödipus und die Sphinx*. I know the work, and have even seen it acted in Germany; and despite some very fine lyrical moments (and even psychological ones—such as Jocasta's first meeting with Oedipus), I find it dreary and over-erudite. I personally don't like these barbaric cabinet dramas set in some decadent prehistory, and soliloquies for soliloquies I prefer our own Classical tragedy a thousand times. If you are attracted by the Greek myths, why don't you go and get them from the source! Have you read Sophocles and Euripides (not to mention the over-whelming Aeschylus)? Ajax, Oedipus, and Philoctetes are all divine things. I'm quite sure that if I'd been a composer I would have written a *Philoctetes* or a *Nausicaa* (taken from *The Odyssey*). And then there is the *Bacchae*, and so many other works by Euripides that are essentially lyrical and musical.

"Even here in France today we have a poet who has written an *Electra and Orestes* filled with a kind of harsh passion, a kind of larger than life feeling different from anything to be found in any of Hofmannsthal's works— (though it's true that his work needs revision) —I mean Suarès. But he isn't well known, because he despises cliques . . .

"I cannot believe that these works, such as *Ödipus und die Sphinx*, have the future on their side. That would mean that the Byzantinism (very refined) of the chosen few is going to prevail over the great popular movements now exerting their growing strength all over the world at this moment; and I hope that isn't so. . . . But, naturally, don't let what I say get in your way, follow your own inspiration." This passionate and sincere letter did not halt Varèse, even though it is extremely probable that Rolland was wholly in the right. Those words must have remained engraved in Varèse's unconscious throughout the years he spent working at this task. But once he had committed himself to a course of action. . . . This long letter of Rolland's makes it quite plain how great the novelist's interest was in the young composer. Rolland became a real friend, a confidant. And yet Varèse was not a man who confided easily. But to Rolland he told the story of all his disappointments, as though he had unconsciously found in him the absent, ideal father. And the writer, with affection, did his best to cheer him up: "My poor boy," he wrote in a letter dated November 25, 1909, "I pity you with all my heart. Don't let it get you down. It's no fun living every day, there are bound to be sad moments. I know a thing or two about that too, believe me. Go bravely back to work: only work can bring consolation—and vengeance. Don't say to yourself: I want to conquer. Say: I want to be. To be, when no one else would understand you to begin with. The rest comes as an extra, later on. But one has to be a stricter judge for oneself than even others are. Courage!" In this way, Rolland taught Varèse how to channel his eruptive energy, how to transmute it into a slow patience. For Varèse was, after all, his flesh and blood Jean-Christophe.

Gargantua was never finished, despite the request of M. Schiller, Yvette Guilbert's husband, who wanted a double-bass concerto version of it for Koussevitsky. *Bourgogne* was to be performed the following year.

The first meeting between Varèse and Richard Strauss undoubtedly took place during the spring of 1909. Varèse told me that they met in the street, by chance. He had never brought himself to go and knock on the Austrian composer's door, despite the letter of introduction from Rolland which he carried around on him. Nevertheless, Strauss already knew Varèse's name. Indeed, on February 21, 1909,

Romain Rolland had already written to him: "I talked a great deal about you this morning . . . with a young French composer who has been living for a year or two in Berlin, and who admires you so much that he doesn't dare to pay you a visit. His name is Edgar Varèse and he has talent; he seems to me to have a particular gift for orchestral writing. I think he might interest you. He has in him what you love, I believe, above all else (like myself) , and what is rare today: life." [20] Rolland's politeness notwithstanding, however, Varèse told me that he had not really been particularly struck by any of Strauss's work other than *Elektra*. But whatever the truth of this, according to the critic Paul Rosenfeld, a friend of Varèse's: "Varèse, no doubt, has learned considerably from Strauss in the way of dense instrumentation; just as he learned from Mahler, whose development of the orchestral role of the percussive instruments foreshadows his own prodigious one." [21] Though it is difficult, today, to know exactly what the young composer thought of Mahler, for example, in 1909, Varèse was to say to me, referring to *Das Lied von der Erde*: "The orchestration is good, but the material is so bad, so vulgar!" Varèse had met Mahler, by the way, in 1909.

That same year, Varèse struck up a friendship with the conductor Karl Muck. (Right up until his death he always kept the latter's photograph over his work-table with those of his wife, of Debussy, and the portrait of his grandfather, Claude Cortot). Muck had confided in him: "I sometimes play music I don't like, but which I know to be good. And precisely because I don't like it, it is my duty to work harder on the score." Honesty of that kind could not fail to fill Varèse with enthusiasm, for he hated the "star system" in art above all else.

Also in 1909, Varèse worked with Max Reinhardt, the great theatrical director who in 1903 had put on one of Strindberg's plays, as well as Gorki's *The Lower Depths*. Since 1905, he had been the director of the Berlin Deutsches Theater. After Ibsen's *Ghosts*, he had turned to Goethe and mounted *Faust* on a revolving stage. And since Varèse had started a mixed choral group, the Symphonischer Chor, Reinhardt engaged him several times to take part in his productions. It was in this way that the young composer collaborated in the mounting of *Faust* and *A Midsummer Night's Dream*. (Varèse must have met Reinhardt again in New York in 1940, since the great director died there in 1943) . Apart from these fairly infrequent engagements, Varèse specialized in the interpretation of medieval and Renaissance music.

While in Berlin, Varèse lived at 61, Nassauischestrasse. His wife and he only managed to subsist with great difficulty. In October, 1909, he was still without work, without a single pupil. His famous friends made several attempts to help him, usually without his knowledge. As early as April 10, 1909, Busoni had written to the President of the Paul Kusynski foundation: "On behalf of my young and dear friend, M. Varèse, from Paris, I am taking the liberty of drawing your attention to the intelligence and talent of this artist now at the beginning of his career. These, among other outstanding qualities, deserve to be taken into consideration and given support." On April 18th of the same year, Karl Muck declared to the same president: "M. Edgard Varèse is a very gifted musician with a remarkable training. I know one symphonic poem of his which displays a rich and original quality of invention, a lively imagination, and a complete mastery of musical technique. The references I asked for from my friends in Paris have been most favorable to M. Varèse: warmth, energy, unflagging determination, and upright and correct conduct in the face of the great difficulties confronting him in his daily life. It is more or less in these terms that all three verdicts, taken from different sources, are conceived. . . ." Even Strauss himself sent out several letters and cards. He wrote to Paul Kupfer, President of the Association of the Workers' Choral Societies of Germany, as follows: "Allow me to recommend M. Varèse to you warmly as director of your choir. If the fact that, being French, he does not yet know German is no obstacle, then you will have acquired an excellent musician and a conductor of the first rank—he is also a talented composer." Moreover, Strauss had also given him a card of recommendation couched in these terms: "I know Edgar Varèse as a musician of great worth and a very gifted composer. To anyone whom it may concern I recommend him very highly for the teaching of counterpoint and the study of singing and choral parts." [22] On October 29, 1909, Strauss held out a hope to Varèse: "M. W. Klatte, a teacher of counterpoint, has promised me that he will help you in looking for pupils. Please go to visit him tomorrow, Saturday, between four and five P.M. Do you speak English?" On November 17 of the same year, he wrote to Varèse: "I have spoken to my publisher, M. Furstner. I hope he'll be able to give you some work. He is expecting you tomorrow morning in his office."

Hofmannsthal also made efforts on Varèse's behalf. Among others, he approached Franz Schalk, the conductor of the Vienna Opera. Varèse sent him an excerpt from *Ödipus und die Sphinx*. The poet even succeeded in obtaining advances for him from a publisher on the strength of the unfinished opera. Nevertheless, all these concerted attempts did not succeed in obtaining Varèse any regular employment. The truth is that he did not, in any case, really speak German sufficiently well at that time. And I can imagine him presenting himself to all these people with a very proud and intransigent air.

4

First Works

For Varèse, 1910 was a year of mourning and of joy. Thanks to Busoni and Strauss, he obtained his first pupils. It was in this way that Ernst Schoen became not only his first pupil but later on his friend. A few months before his death, Schoen gave me his account of their first meeting: "I was Varèse's first and worst pupil. In 1910, at the age of sixteen, I had decided to become a composer of music. At that time I used to visit a lot at Busoni's house, since his eldest son, Benvenuto, was a schoolfriend of mine." Then, Schoen went on, his mother asked Busoni to find him a teacher. Busoni recommended young Varèse, who agreed to teach him 'for either ten marks a lesson or nothing.' Since the first alternative was out of the question he taught me on the basis of the second. He took me through the harmony course devised by Luis-Thuille (followed later by Schoenberg). . . ."[1]

Debussy and Varèse were still keeping in touch at this time, either in person when Varèse went to Paris, or by letter. Thus we find Debussy remarking in a letter dated July 12, 1910: "Berlin seems to be making you welcome as far as I can tell, for which I am happy, and congratulate you upon it sincerely. All the same, it takes a great deal of courage to acclimatize oneself in a foreign country. So many things, so many customs must be bothersome—not to say painful. One more or less drags one's country after one, and I confess that I have felt myself a foreigner even in France; which is some indication of how extraordinary you seem to me." Debussy was forgetting that Varèse had grown accustomed to living abroad, he was forgetting the years in Turin, and the Lorraine ancestry of his maternal grandmother. At that time, Varèse was studying the score of *Pelléas et Mélisande,* which is why we find Debussy asking in the same letter: "Send me the score of *Pelléas,* and although I have no confidence whatever in metronomic movement I will do what you ask. You were right to put yourself at the 'piano' first of all from the 'conductor' point of view, for yourself; one is so often betrayed by the so-called pianists! That I can assure you, for it just isn't possible to imagine how much my piano music has been distorted; to such an extent that I often hesitate before recognizing it!"

It is from another of Debussy's letters, this one written in October, 1910, that we learn of the birth of Varèse's daughter, named Claude in honor of her Burgundian great-grandfather. "Before anything else," Debussy writes, "allow me to send you all my good wishes on the arrival of your little daughter. You will find out that this is something much more beautiful than a symphony, and that the caress of a child of one's own is better than fame!" But by a cruel leveling of the scale, the birth of Claude Varèse occurred just at the same time as the death of Claude Cortot, the beloved grandfather who had been Varèse's real father; and also just as *Bourgogne,* which had been so titled in memory of those happy days in Villars and dedicated to old Claude Cortot, was about to be performed.

Stuckenschmidt tells us in his book *Modern Music* that "Edgard Varèse has, for example, been able to point out that as early as 1910 he had introduced combinations of sevenths and ninths into his compositions which established a sort of counterpoise between the twelve semitones." [2] In effect, *Bourgogne* did without doubt already reflect Varèse's own personality, even though his technique and musical mastery were to evolve profoundly later on. Varèse was to say: "I became a sort of diabolical Parsifal on a quest, not for the Holy Grail, but for the bomb that would explode the musical world and allow all sounds to come rushing into it through the resulting breach, sounds which at that time—and sometimes still today—were called noises." [3] In any case, Varèse himself did not consider this work sufficiently expressive of his personality, since he destroyed his manuscript score of it in about 1962. Nevertheless, there was a performance. It was

Richard Strauss who more or less forced Josef Stransky to put *Bourgogne* on the program of a concert given on December 15, 1910. Moreover, this was the first time that any work of Varèse's had been played. The performance took place in the Bluthner Hall in Berlin and was given by the Bluthner Orchester. Busoni was present. Varèse had been extremely anxious that Busoni should hear his work, but when he telephoned his house on the morning of the concert, Busoni's wife told him that her husband was in bed with a fever, and that his doctor had forbidden him to go out. This news upset Varèse a great deal. But then, to his great surprise, just a few moments before the concert began, he saw an unshaven Busoni, supported by two of his pupils, Zadora and Petri, suddenly making his appearance. Varèse reproached him affectionately for his imprudence. But Busoni riposted: "It's my duty!" One's mind immediately leaps to the inscription that Busoni had written, that same year, on the score of his *Berceuse élégiaque: "All 'illustre Futuro l'amico Varèse, affezionatamente."*

Bourgogne was played before an ordinary concert audience and not to an élite. The result was that the work provoked the first of the many scandals that Varèse's compositions were always destined to excite throughout the world. And although Schoenberg's *Pelléas et Mélisande* was played the same week, it was *Bourgogne* that caused the audience's anger to explode. Bruno Schrader, for example, announced in his review that it was an infernal din, mere caterwauling. This was the first such cliché in a long series of criticisms in the same style. But on January 3, 1911, the great German critic Alfred Kerr, having heard *Bourgogne,* wrote to Varèse as follows: "I still haven't thanked you for *Bourgogne.* I found it full of fascinating beauties. Would you like to say something about your way of envisaging your art; about your loves and hates in music? If so, I can put the pages of the magazine *Pan* at your disposal, since I have a certain influence there. I am told that you once said to Saint-Saëns: 'I have no desire to become an old fossil like you.' " Kerr was, of course, the *literary* critic of the largest Berlin daily at that time. So we see that from the moment of the very first public performance of one of Varèse's works, it was already the writers who were able to understand him far better than the musicians, if we make exception of the genuine creators such as Strauss, Debussy, and Busoni.

The writer necessarily had fewer prejudices than the little "neatly ruled" musician, than the little critic—without imagination and, above all, without creative power—who had been so completely molded and "academized" by the conservatories, etc.

In any case, despite the bad reception he had been given by the public and critics, Varèse was not crushed. A letter written to him by Debussy on February 12, 1911, confirms this: "You're right not to be alarmed by the hostility of the public. A day will come when you will be the best friends in the world. But waste no time in ridding yourself of your confidence that criticism in our own country is any more farsighted than it is in Germany. Criticism could be an art . . ., it is no more than a trade." Even Debussy probably did not imagine that in Varèse's case it would take almost fifty years before the public would slowly come around to him.

After the first performance of *Bourgogne,* while continuing to work at his opera *Ödipus und die Sphinx* Varèse also undertook a new work during 1911 entitled *Mehr Licht.* Though this title had a different meaning for him than that intended in Goethe's famous phrase, Varése intended to signify *more light,* as though it were a question of filtering the raw material of sound in order to render it more and more luminous. The work progressed no further than the sketch stage at this time, though later on, in 1912, having been wholly rethought, it became *les Cycles du Nord,* a work inspired by the wonder of the Aurora Borealis.

On October 9, 1912, in the Choralionsaal in Berlin, Varèse apparently attended the "final rehearsal" of Schoenberg's *Pierrot lunaire,* conducted by the composer himself "before an audience of musicians, critics, and friends." At least, according to a letter I received from the musicologist Herr Stuckenschmidt, dated December 22, 1966, this seems to be the most likely hypothesis. This would mean that the date of the first official performance was October 9th rather than October 16th, and that it was conducted by the composer himself rather than by Hermann Scherchen. Stravinsky was also present. At all events, it is certain that Varèse and Stravinsky did not meet. Performed as it was before a carefully selected audience, Schoenberg's work did not excite any uproar, according to Varèse's own recollection of the event. It was only later on, he told me, that the polemics started. There can be no doubt that Varèse was one of the very few musicians who grasped the import of the new work that day. Even Stravinsky was "in no way enthusiastic about the esthetics of this work." [4] However, the Russian composer's attitude remains ambiguous. According to Stuckenshmidt, Stravinsky wrote to W. G. Karatygin on December 13, 1912, to say that he found "the whole extraordinary physiognomy of its creator expressed with maximum intensity" in *Pierrot lunaire.*

The importance of the percussion instruments was becoming more and more widely felt at this time. Mahler and Strauss had introduced "instruments of an entirely new type, such as the hammer, chains, and the wind machine" into their scoring for symphony orchestras. As Stuckenshmidt says: "Since the nineteenth century, machines have been impregnating the life of modern man with their noise. The intensity of sound to be met with on the principal artery of a large city, in a machine depot, in a railroad station, or on an airfield, is greater than that contained in the entire world at the time of the stagecoach." [5] There is no doubt that Russolo's futurist manifesto *The Art of Noise,* which was published in Milan on March 11, 1913, was a conscious effort to come to terms with this new phenomenon of civilization. But the subsequent experiments of the noise-artists never succeeded in progressing any further than mere noise. They produced no work of art. There was no attempt to go beyond the simple imitation or unmodified utilization of familiar noises—such as that of the klaxon—on a stage. No understanding was achieved of the musical possibilities of a noise used as an integral element within a work. All the effort should have been applied to the transposition, the poetization of noises. So that the noise-art experiment had no consequences. It is a mistake to link Varèse's researches in any way with Russolo's. Although he was a friend of the man, he could not accept the noise-artist. Their conceptions were on two very different levels and could never have come together. We must not forget that Varèse had been interested in the siren since 1905; but what fascinated him was not just noise but *noise being transmuted into sound,* noise becoming *beautiful,* noise becoming timbre, timbre revealing its *spirit.* This is why, four years after the publication of *The Art of Noise,* Varèse was to express his savage opposition to the futurists. It became essential for him to state his own position, so that no ambiguity should subsist as to the direction and aim of his own attempts. His position was therefore expressed in Picabia's magazine *391*. This manifesto was written when Varèse was on the threshold of his great works: "That which is not a synthesis of intelligence and will is inorganic. Certain composers have nothing in view in their works but a succession of titillating aggregations of sound—material for the most part of terrifying intractability—and have no intellectual concern with anything but external sensorial effect; others shore up their thought with a lot of literary rubbish and seek to justify or comment upon a title by means of an arrangement of phrases. Oh, the Protestant mentality of those artists who ooze with boredom and work away as though at some unpleasant duty! The triumph of the sensibility is not a tragedy. *Let music sound!* Our alphabet is poverty-stricken and illogical. The music that ought to be living and vibrating at this moment needs new means of expression, and only science can infuse it with youthful sap.

"Italian futurists, why do you merely reproduce the vibrations of our daily life only in their superficial and distressing aspects?

"My dream is of instruments that will obey my thought—and which, by bringing about a flowering of hitherto unsuspected timbres, will lend themselves to the combinations it will please me to impose on them and bow themselves to the demands of my inner rhythm."[6] This seems clear enough. Varèse did not at any time wish to use noises or new instruments except within a creative and expressive process originating in his inner musical universe. In this respect he was much nearer to Debussy, who was also avid for new sonorities. Varèse wanted to express the sounds which he could hear inside himself, and which no ear before his had ever heard. There was no question, where he was concerned, of making himself into a loud-speaker for noises that any man could hear in his natural-artificial environment, that new nature produced by the hands of man: the twentieth century city; just as there was no question, in a Beethoven's case, of parroting Nature. Varèse knew that the timbres of the traditional orchestra were no longer adequate to express his universe. All the well-known instruments were inventions of other centuries, or of other civilizations, or of other sensibilities; they no longer had the true power of expression needed to give an account of the new civilization then being born. And it was not by means of the "musical gigantism" of a Mahler or a Strauss that the sound-energy, the audible personality of the new era were going to be released. Gigantism was not the solution. According to Varèse, such developments could only result in making the orchestra muddy. Because Varèse had become fascinated so early in life by acoustics, he knew what a sound was and could foresee its possibilities. But we shall return to *sound* a little further on.

In 1913, Varèse's wife, Suzanne Bing, decided to return to Paris in order to continue her career as an actress at the Vieux-Colombier. (She was to spend the summer of 1913 with its first company at Jacques Copeau's property of Limon.) Since it had thus become impossible for them to continue living together, they decided very amicably to end their marriage and seek a divorce. Their daughter, Claude, was to remain for a while in Berlin before being entrusted to the care of her maternal grandmother. Two months before Varèse's death, his daughter, who was living in Monte Carlo, and his granddaughter Marilyne, were to visit him in New York.

On May 29, 1913, it appears that Varèse was present at the first performance of *le Sacre du Printemps*. In any case, he was to say later, being a veteran of such scandals after the performance of *Bourgogne* in Berlin, in 1910, that Stravinsky's work seemed very natural to him, and that he simply thought of the Russian composer as having done his duty.[7]

In November, 1913, Varèse was back in Paris. Apollinaire mentions this visit in his *Anecdotiques*: "Though he is less well known in France than in Germany, where he is held to be one of the most original talents of our time, the musician Edgar Varèse will not take long to conquer Paris just as he conquered Berlin."[8] Marcel Adéma tells us that at that time Varèse and Apollinaire often met one another at the home of Louise Faure-Favier, "in that charming 'House of the Centaur' where she gathered her friends about her."[9] Paul Léautaud, having dined at her house, 45, quai de Bourbon, notes in his diary on December 27, 1913: "Mme Faure-Favier, a handsome woman, as they say . . . elegant house. A beautiful view, a view that says something to you, over the Seine, the quais along by the Hôtel de Ville, all those lights in the darkness."[10]

That year, Romain Rolland advised Varèse: "Draw on your passions; you are already the master of your musical language, with that virile youth and poetic talent I love. Don't be afraid to externalize yourself, you will never lose your French clarity." [11]

For some years now, it may be remembered, there had been some question of Varèse conducting a concert in Prague. Romain Rolland had alluded to the project in 1909, and Debussy had mentioned it several times in his letters to Varèse. There was even some question of Debussy himself going there at the time of his trip to Vienna and Budapest in 1910. It was Gabriel Astruc who became Varèse's impresario and who organized a European concert tour on his behalf for the year 1914. Because of the war, however, Varèse conducted only a single concert, the one in Prague, which took place on Sunday, January 4, 1914, in the Smetana Hall. This was the first step in his short career as a conductor. He had been invited by the Mojmir Urbanek Concert Society, and the program he had chosen consisted entirely of modern French works: G. Dupont's *Chant de la destinée,* Paul Dukas's *Ariane et Barbe-Bleue,* Albert Roussel's *les Dieux dans l'ombre des cavernes,* and a first performance in its concert version of Debussy's *le Martyre de Saint-Sébastien.* For the public and critics of Prague, Varèse, conducting the Czech Philharmonic Orchestra, was a revelation. We find the critic of the *Prager Tageblatt* writing on January 6: "But equaling the delight of the program itself was that of coming to know Edgard Varèse. His noble enthusiasm for the works of the masters is able to surmount all difficulties: after only three rehearsals with an orchestra that was strange to him he succeeded in revealing to us the very soul of the compositions which had been entrusted to him. The great love of Art which lives in this slender young man, the nobility of his manner, the precision and clarity with which he conducts, and which make it immediately clear that Varèse knows what he wants, all held the orchestra under his spell and immediately captivated the audience. The concert was a musical event, and it is to be hoped that we shall soon be able to hear this enthusiastic defender of modern music again, both as conductor and as composer." It therefore seems certain that a fine conducting career was about to open up for Varèse. When he was surprised by the war, in Paris, almost all his manuscripts were still in Berlin; among them his more or less complete opera, *Ödipus und die Sphinx.* However, Varèse was unable to return to Berlin until 1922, when he discovered the warehouse in which his manuscripts had been stored had been completely destroyed by fire.

François Lesure reports that in June, 1914, Varèse attended the performance of *Tristan* by Nickisch at the Théâtre des Champs-Elysées. "On the way out, he found Debussy who showed his enthusiasm in this way: 'In the name of God, our ears were cleaned tonight.' " [12]

In 1915, Varèse met Trotsky (having already known Lenin, in Paris, in about 1909). That same year, he took Picasso to visit Cocteau (at least, according to Varèse, who said that Cocteau was in bed at the time, whereas Cocteau, in R. Stéphane's broadcast program *Portrait Souvenir*, said: "Picasso, whom I was taken to visit by Varèse"). But in any case, it was certainly not in 1916 that Cocteau and Picasso first met—as has been claimed—since Varèse had already left France by that time.

Before his mobilization, Varèse was living at 49, rue de Seine. It was there, on March 27, 1915, that he received this *pneumatique* from Debussy, its words blurred by tears: "My dear Varèse, your affectionate sympathy touches me infinitely. The loss of my mother affects me more painfully than I can say, for I know that this is a time of tears for the whole world. No announcements have been sent out, and the funeral will take place, in the strictest 'privacy' tomorrow, Monday, at ten in the morning at Notre-Dame d'Auteuil."

On April 18th, the newspaper *l'Intransigeant* announced Varèse's mobilization in these terms: "Gunner Guillaume Apollinaire has arrived at the front. The musician Edgard Varèse has been posted to the School of War. André Billy has been mobilized again." In fact, Varèse was posted in the first place to 25th Staff Headquarters as a bicycle messenger. After some six months, he asked to be transferred to the first machine-gun battery, but his medical examination showed him to be unfit for military service and he was invalided out. Double pneumonia. It is quite obvious that Varèse, who was above all international in spirit, both by origin and upbringing, in the same way as Romain Rolland, could not but feel a great esteem for German culture. We must not forget that he had been living in Berlin since 1908, and that he had lived in Turin from 1892 till 1903; consequently, he could not be as French in his attitudes as someone like Péguy. He must therefore have felt a deep revulsion against this war which was setting the two peoples he esteemed the most at each other's throats.

As may be imagined, though invalided out of the army, there was no possibility of Varèse's continuing his career as a conductor in Europe. He therefore decided to go for a while to New York. For one thing, his friend Karl Muck was at that time conductor of the Boston Symphony Orchestra. Also, at that time no one thought that the war was going to last as long as it did. So Varèse left the majority of his manuscripts in a hamper in his Paris apartment, and early in December, 1915, André Lhote, the painter, came to take him from 12, avenue du Maine, to Bordeaux. Varèse embarked on the *Rochambeau* on December 18, 1915. The crossing lasted twelve days. At the time, he intended to be gone only a few weeks; but he was not to return to Paris, and then only briefly, until 1922. The pressure of circumstances was to make him settle definitively in the United States.

5

The New World

On December 29, 1915, at the age of thirty-two, Varèse stepped off the boat in New York. He had only ninety dollars in his pocket and knew only two words of English. The reason he had chosen New York, rather than Buenos Aires, was not only that his friend Karl Muck was already in the United States, but also because the musical life was much more intense there than in South America. Muck was able to introduce him into musical circles in New York and into the German colony there. At the very beginning, Varèse went back to being a copyist, doing orchestrations, or giving lessons. During the first few months of his stay in America, Varese lived at 110 West 88th Street.

Scarcely had he arrived in New York when he received a card, on February 6, 1916, from his friend Erik Satie, who lived at Arcueil: "Dear Old Fellow—Did you get my note of Thursday last? I have sent my *Gymnopédies* to you by Rouart. I asked you to keep my music for *A Midsummer Night's Dream* in cold storage. Will you do that? The stuff isn't ready anyway. In exchange, I am sending you a curious piece by A. Verley—one of my good pupils. Read this work with your usual lucidity, *mon Gros Père* . . . The other day, Debussy talked to me about you . . ." It is apparent how intimate the friendship and spirit of comradeship was between the two men. On August 22, 1918, Satie wrote to him: ". . . Our poor Debussy is dead. He has been very ill, dear fellow that he was, for a long while."

Chennevière-Rudhyard (a Frenchman named Daniel Chennevière, but known in America under the name of Dane Rudhyar), painter writer, "mystic," and composer, wrote in his book, *Art as Release of Power:* "Western classical music has given practically all of its attention to the framework of music, what it calls musical form. It has forgotten to study the laws of Sonal energy . . . in terms of energy which is life. . . . Therefore the Oriental musicians often say that our music is a music of holes. Our notes are edges of intervals, of empty abysses. The melodies jump from edge to edge. . . . It is a music of mummies, of preserved and stuffed animals which look alive enough perhaps, yet are dead and motionless. *The inner space is empty.* The tone entities are dead, because they are empty of sonal energy, of sonal blood. They are but bones and skin. We call them 'pure' tones. They are so pure they will never do any harm!"[1] It is important at this stage to understand the sickness of Western music if we are to grasp the scope and depth of the revolution Varèse achieved. For Varèse had already been obsessed for a very long time by this question of *sound,* by this energy emanating from living matter. And it was thus by attacking the sonic anemia of our orchestra, and the limitations of its instruments, that he was to accomplish the first step of his radical metamorphosis. André Schaeffner, a musicologist, has given us a very pertinent account of the roots of this orchestral sickness: ". . . The instruments have lost in rawness of timbre and in variety of types what they have gained in extension of register, ease of playing, and capacity for nuances. The ideal our music pursues may be compared to that of painting when it mastered chiaroscuro and confined itself to that effect. We need only compare the equipment of our orchestras with that used outside Europe. It is in the case of percussion instruments of all kinds that our poverty or our insensitivity is most clearly revealed: where we produce only noise, the musicians of other cultures direct their efforts toward the projection of true sounds, with very definite timbres, usually tuned, abounding in harmonics, and, when necessary, of supreme intensity. We have restricted the field of percussion already by taking great pains to eliminate it even from the attack of the very least of our instruments; this definite improvement is also impoverishment . . . Lastly, because they lack vigor or diversity, it has been necessary to increase the size of our orchestras so that they may once more achieve those maximum degrees of intensity which primitive musicans attain at such a small cost. Jazz, the only exception—though only within the limits of certain sectors—has taken entire families of instruments and torn out of them sounds wholly unheard before, especially in the upper registers; though even there, the invention at work is not ours."[2] It is sad that this musicologist, writing these words in 1958, should have known nothing of Varèse's thought and works. But how can one blame him? He would have understood why Varèse became so interested in the siren as early as 1905, and why he felt so passionately about percussion instruments that he produced that great masterpiece *Ionisation*. It was not by chance that Varèse addressed himself to the question of *sound* and *instruments*. Like all great innovators, he was perfectly well aware of the novelty and the consequences of his art, of his revolution. To decide in favor of percussion, until such times as new instruments arrived, was to take up a position on the side of the life, the beauty, and the richness of *sound*. When Varèse struck a gong in his workshop and marveled like a child at its sound, he was returning, for his own pleasure, to that liking "for timbre for timbre's sake" characteristic of childhood games. It was this freshness of attitude, this childlike lack of prejudice, which enabled him to accomplish one of the profoundest revolutions in Western music. He taught us to strike all the gongs of earth, all its drums, its very mountains, in order that our dead ears may come to life again, in order that they may believe once more, with the Hopi Indians, that sound is the very essence of man, that it engenders light, and that it is a manifestation of the spirit.

Three months after his arrival in New York, in March, 1916, Varèse gave his first interview to the *New York Telegraph* and the *Morning Telegraph*. At that time he made his position very clear and explained both the intent of his musical researches and the meaning of his esthetic. "Our musical alphabet must be enriched," he said. "We also need new instruments very badly. The futurists (Marinetti and his noise-artists) have made a serious mistake in this respect. Instruments, after all, must only be temporary means of expression. Musicians should take up this question in deep earnest with the help of machinery specialists. I have always felt the need of new mediums of expression in my own work. I refuse to submit myself only to sounds that have already been heard. What I am looking for are new technical mediums which can lend themselves to every expression of thought and can keep up with thought." [3]

What freedom in those words, and what an absence of sectarianism. Varèse was never to deviate from this line of conduct. Moreover, at the very beginning of a lecture which he gave at Princeton University on September 4, 1959, he was to emphasize this again: "It must be quite widely known by this time, since I have been boring people on the subject for almost a half a century that my aim has always been the liberation of sound—to throw open the whole world of sound to music. I began to break the rules when still very young, feeling even then that they were barring me from this wonderful world, this ever expanding universe." [4] One can say without fear of contradiction that if electronics had existed in 1916, Varèse would without doubt have been the only composer at that time able to make use of them. He was the only one to conceive of such a universe of sound. It is not without reason that he is unanimously considered to be the precursor of what is called concrete or electronic music. Varèse's whole tragedy, as a composer, was that his poetry and his thought were thirty years ahead of the technological discoveries he needed. He was forced to express his thought—which was alone perhaps in belonging truly to the twentieth century, together with that of Webern—through the medium of a nineteenth century orchestra. As the Canadian composer Serge Garant wrote: "There is at least this, which is at the root of their creative procedures: they are the only two composers of this generation whose spirit is entirely, and without any admixture of nostalgia, *modern*. Stravinsky, Berg, Schoenberg, Bartók; all of them yielding to the great temptation presented by a musical past with tried recipes . . . The spirit animating them is either eighteenth or nineteenth century," [5] Stravinsky himself was to say: "Few composers have dedicated themselves so exclusively to 'purity of sound' as an ideal, and few, if any, have been as sensitive to the totality of sound characteristics." [6] Thus the New World became in a way the symbol of the new universe of sound that Varèse was seeking to make manifest. Odile Vivier has very well expressed one aspect of Varèse's problems which came into prominence at the time of his arrival in New York: "Varèse rejects the tempered scale, which is an arbitrary system . . . Even within the limitations of our present instruments, we are forced to admit the production of certain sounds which our notation is powerless to express. He purposely does away with the 'note' in order to replace it with a 'sound,' which is to say by a number of frequencies, the only conception which is in conformity with acoustical truth . . . a D was not thought in this case as a D but as a number of frequencies in relation with other frequencies." [7] Varèse might well have said, with Satie: "I came very young into a very old world."

Varèse had scarcely settled himself in New York before he was knocked over by an automobile on the sidewalk. He was to spend eleven weeks in a hospital bed.

It was the following year, on April 1, 1917, that he made his first entrance onto the New York musical scene, and as part of a gigantic musical spectacle. On March 19th, it will probably be remembered, the American ship *Vigilentia* had been torpedoed and sunk in the Atlantic by a German submarine taking part in the American blockade. Next day, President Wilson announced that a state of war had existed between Germany and the United States from the very moment when that torpedo had struck; and it was on the eve of that declaration of war between the United States and Germany, Palm Sunday, April 1st, that Varèse conducted the famous Berlioz *Requiem,* in memory of the dead of all nations, in the Hippodrome. It may be imagined in what an electric atmosphere Varèse directed the work that day. The cost of the concert had been met by New York's greatest celebrities. The Hippodrome was a vast theater, seating from five to six thousand people, situated on Sixth Avenue between 43rd Street and 44th Street. "It had a huge stage," wrote Irving Kolodin, "with mechanical means of depressing sections of it and a tank beneath, into which lines of show girls could march and disappear . . . Not all relished the pungent aroma which lingered in the Hippodrome from the annual invasion of elephants and horses of a Dillingham 'Spectacular' or the circus . . ." [8] That evening, Varèse was conducting an orchestra of a hundred and fifty musicians and a choir three hundred strong: the Scranton Oratorio Society of Pennsylvania, one of the most famous choral societies of the time. Since most of its members were Pennsylvania miners, rehearsals had been going on for six months at the bottom of a mine, into which a piano had been lowered. In fact, when Varèse conducted the work on that April Sunday in 1917 he had exactly the same number of executants as Habenek had when he directed the first performance on December 5, 1837, in the church of Saint-Louis des Invalides. Varèse must certainly have loved several parts of this work. How could he have failed to react with enthusiasm to that extraordinary idea Berlioz had conceived of placing four fanfares at the cardinal points of the church? How could he not have been particularly impressed by the end of the *Hostia et preces* in which the flutes and trombones play against each other? One might say that this stroke of invention on Berlioz' part was an annunciatory sign of Varèse's own works. Berlioz too was passionately interested in *sound*.

Varèse was very well received by the critics. Paul Rosenfeld in *The Seven Arts Chronicle* of June, 1917 reported: ". . . For Berlioz did manifest himself that night at the Hippodrome in a veritable blaze of power. He manifested himself in a manner that revolutionized all our conceptions. It is not as the romanticist, the loud Victor Hugo of music that he appeared, nor was it as the literary musician, or the bizarre technical innovator. It was as perhaps the most classic artist who ever composed music." On April 2nd, the *Evening Mail* observed: "Mr. Edgar Varèse who made his American debut as a conductor seemed to possess the inspiration of genius."

On March 17, 1918, Varèse conducted the Cincinnati Symphony Orchestra at Music Hall, Cincinnati. The program he gave combined works by Wagner, Bizet, Verdi, Borodin, Satie (the three *Gymnopédies*), Charpentier, Debussy (*Prélude à l'après-midi d'un faune*) and Dukas (*l'Apprenti sorcier*). The concert was a great success. Next day, the critic of the *Cincinnati Commercial Tribune* certainly summed up the general impression when he wrote: "An immense audience was present to greet this program with interested attention and, at the end, received it with the most enthusiastic applause . . . Mr. Varèse, who is evidently a well-routined conductor, was warmly applauded and repeatedly called to the box, the audience lingering at the conclusion of the concert to express its appreciation."

A true creator, Varèse was always passionately interested in poetry and painting. He was to say, in fact: "During the greater part of my existence my friends have tended to be painters, poets, architests, and scientists, rather than musicians . . ." [9] One cannot be a friend of Apollinaire and Cendrars, or of Max Jacob, without having a taste for poems and being tempted to write them. As a challenge to Picabia, Varèse did in fact write one, which he then had published in the celebrated magazine *391*. It was entitled *Oblation* and was "dadaistically" dedicated to Picabia. Michel Sanouillet says that the poem "was composed in 1916 (sic) (1917 is more likely), after an evening spent drinking with Picabia on the great iron bridge that links Manhattan to Brooklyn. According to Varèse, Picabia was a 'whisky sentimentalist' who indulged himself when in his cups in mock romantic excesses, a tendency which his friend intended to make fun of here."[10]

> The sky is waiting
> A woman's laugh has caused me so much pain
> My heart is heavy
> The stars are lighting up and the river is carrying past
>   the world's unhappiness.
> Speculative ideas
> The sun has refused the moon a wedding ring
> I shall never be a congressman or an ambassador
> Metarcarpal palms
> The Orange of Malta
> I shall order the Saturnalia of Brooklyn Bridge to start
> Opposite the skyscrapers bristling with amazement
> My love is dead. [11]

We must not forget Dada . . . Which does not necessarily mean that the poem did not, in fact, have its roots in an unhappy experience with a woman. In Paris, Max Jacob was publishing his *Cornet à dés*. Julio Gonzalez was working at the Renault factories and learning how to weld. Fernand Léger was entering his machine or "tubist" period. In a few months the October Revolution was to explode in St. Petersburg.

After April, 1917, Varèse was to stay for awhile with Albert Gleizes on 88th Street. He frequently had to fight down moods of acute discouragement. The war seemed interminable, his exile was weighing upon him, and he had not yet found a way of earning a living. It was at this moment that his whole life was changed by an all-important meeting.

Sometime late in 1917, Varèse and Louise Norton met one another in a bar. No word exchanged between them. At their second meeting, they were extremely rude to one another about nothing whatever. At their third meeting they fell abruptly and deeply in love. Louise Varèse, nee McCutcheon, was born in Pittsburgh on November 22, 1890. At the age of sixteen she left that city in order to go to school at Smith College in Massachusetts. By the time she went back to live with her parents again they had moved to New York. She then married Allen Norton, a poet and journalist. One son, Michael, was born of this first marriage.

In 1916, Allen and Louise founded *Rogue*, a little magazine of Dadaist-Picabian inspiration which foundered in December of the same year. Marcel Duchamp became a friend of theirs upon his arrival in New York during June of 1915.

As soon as their respective divorces became official, Edgard Varèse and Louise Norton were married, and during the long and difficult years that followed, Louise was to be not only a wife to Varèse but a collaborator and a support as well. She believed in Varèse, in his ideas, in his art, always. She said to me one day: "Varèse didn't have to be famous as far as I was concerned. His presence and the certainty I felt about his genius were all I needed." Later, of course, Louise Varèse became one of the best translators from the French in the United States. Among other works, she translated Rimbaud's *Illuminations*, Saint-John Perse's *Eloges*, and works by Bernanos, Julien Gracq, Henri Michaux and Simenon. In a copy of *Eloges*, Saint-John Perse was to write: "To you, dear Louise, incomparable Ally, my affection and gratitude." Always questing, a fervent admirer of Beckett (the antidote to Teilhard de Chardin, she was to say to me after reading the latter's work), receptive to all new knowledge, full of enthusiasm, she was truly for Varèse the magnificent companion who enabled him to go on at the moment when he himself came to doubt the value of his works and question the direction of his efforts. After Varèse's death, Saint-John Perse wrote to her: ". . . who (Varèse) drew sustenance from you as much as you drew sustenance from him . . . Death is no separation, but an even more essential integration, between two beings as united as you have been. You are still walking hand in hand. His presence is forever that of the companion, the admirable companion, that he was for you. Believe in the survival of the soul, and think of the pain that the slightest pain for you always caused him . . ." [12]

In 1918, Varèse made the acquaintance of the famous harpist Carlos Salzedo. They became the best of friends and collaborators. Salzedo had come to the United States in 1908 at the invitation of Toscanini, who had himself just arrived to settle in America. But let us listen to Salzedo telling about his first meetings with Varèse in his own words. "I met Varèse in 1918. Before we actually met, there was a peculiar feeling of enmity between us . . ." As a matter of fact, since the country was at war, Salzedo had been obliged to conduct the French and American national anthems. Varèse, an "internationalist born," had looked upon this "concession" on Salzedo's part with a disapproving eye. But, Salzedo goes on, "Fredo Sidès, a mutual friend of ours, deplored that state of enmity and urged me to take the first step in view of dissipating it. I decided to telephone Varèse and we made an appointment for the following morning. The contact was cordial but cold. We soon found a ground of understanding through Debussy and Ravel, whom we both knew in Paris. Stokowski, with whom I was in close contact, and who, later on, was to play an important role in Varèse's career, was the topic of our conversation. We became so involved in our unexpected friendship that we forgot to lunch (a strange happening for two Frenchmen). I arrived at Varèse's at ten and left at four! Varèse struck me as an indomitable and generous nature with an amazing vision: a tonal engineer, a prophetic musician, a courageous and loyal individual. I felt that a vital friendship was about to replace that peculiar enmity. Varèse told me of his idea to introduce contemporary music in this country, which at that time was strongly dominated by a provincial Germanic sentimentalism." [13]

As Salzedo's words have just indicated. Varèse had for some time been thinking of founding an orchestra which would play nothing but contemporary works. To do battle for the acceptance of his colleagues' works was indirectly to prepare the ground for the more difficult struggle on behalf of his own music. The public's ear had to be accustomed to the profound mutation then in preparation. Stuckenschmidt has observed: "Corresponding to this tendency toward the organization of a new musical order, we find the organization of musical associations (and) magazines intended to spread a knowledge of the new music. After years of individual sniping, the decision had been made to unite." [14] Already, in 1918, a circle of musicians had been constituted to which Erik Satie had given the name of the "nouveaux *jeunes."* A concert had taken place on January 15, 1918, in Paris. But the group was not really constituted until two years later under the name of *"les Six."* This, however, was not essentially a society for the promotion of concerts. In Berlin, on February 16, 1919, the statutes of an association for the organization of *private* concerts were published. The idea was Schoenberg's. But it was a closed society. Every member, for instance, had to be present at every rehearsal. At the same time, Varèse founded the New Symphony Orchestra, an association based upon the principal of the co-operative society in which every musician was to receive his share of the profits. The programs were to include only the works of modern composers and occasionally a work by an old master that had been neglected by the other two New York orchestras. The greatest innovation of Varèse's part was that this orchestra's concerts were intended for the widest possible public. For Varèse, quite evidently, there was no question of defending a particular theory or school. He was to be entirely free in his choice of compositions. The risk was great. The public was not yet ready. Having summoned a meeting of journalists, Varèse said to them: "There is urgent need for an organization that shall take what *has been* for granted and lay stress upon what *is* . . . Until we possess and support such an organization, we are, so far as music is concerned, nothing but careless bystanders, heedlessly watching the painful growth of art without doing a thing to help it along. Musical history is being made now. American composers should be allowed to speak their messages into the ears of those for whom they are intended—the people of today."

The first concert took place on April 11, 1919, at Carnegie Hall. For this opening program, Varèse had chosen: Debussy's *Gigue,* Casella's *Nuit de mai,* Bartók's *Deux Images pour orchestre,* Dupont's *Chant de la destinée,* and an excerpt from Bach's Cantata no. 31, *Der Himmel Lacht die Erde Jubiliert.* If we except the critic of the *Christian Science Monitor,* who found the experiment worthwhile, it must be admitted that the concert was very badly received. Needless to say, Varèse's conceptions constituted a threat to a deeply rooted conformism which provided many people with their livelihood. Another experiment followed. But after this too had failed, the orchestra's administrative council, and above all the musicians playing in the orchestra who found their efforts insufficiently profitable, tried to make Varèse conduct more popular works. Varèse handed in his resignation. Salzedo, who witnessed this failure of the New Symphony Orchestra at first hand, told me that "Varèse refused to prostitute his plans. . . . The post was offered to Rachmaninoff, who declined it. He explained his refusal as follows, 'Varèse was absolutely right in his plans. . . . Frankly, I do not understand Varèse's own music, but I admire him too much as a man to take his succession.' The Board of Directors then approached Arthur Bodansky, who grabbed the job without any scruple.[15] For these Americans feverishly building a new world, rushing around on the floor of the Stock Exchange and submitting themselves to the requirements of Taylorism, music was becoming a royal road to escape, a cloud cuckoo land. They had not yet achieved sufficient control over their new environment, their daily lives, their new terrors. And so, at concerts, it was not discovery nor the shock of wonder that they sought, but only mere repose.

6

Amériques

In 1920, Varèse began work on his first great work, one that he was
to recognize as being truly an expression of his universe: *Amériques.*
It became for him the symbol of a break with "Europeanism," and
it also became, more particularly, the first manifestation of the truly
new world of sound he was to reveal. Perhaps in no other work of his
was Varèse to be so rich, so dionysiac, so immense. One might even
say that within this continent of sound in which all questions and all
discoveries are possible, we can already perceive the outline of *Déserts,*
that profoundly interior and at the same time cosmic landscape which
he was not to depict for us until 1952, after emerging from a long
darkness.

Varèse has himself explained the meaning of the titles he gives his
compositions. "A title is generally given after the score is written in
order to catalogue the work, or it may occur to me while I am composing, but it always derives from some association of ideas in relation to
the score, and has, needless to say, an imaginative appeal to me
personally. . . ." [1]

The great Cuban writer Alejo Carpentier has brought out very
clearly the significance for the composer of this first work conceived
in his imagination after arriving in New York. "North America im-
presses him with a sensation of vastness and extent," he says. "In
passing, one can cast an absent-minded glance from the window of a

railroad train at the largest waterfalls on earth. In the depths of canyons, there are cities creating their own storms . . . For him, New York is neither jazz nor 'musical comedy,' nor even Harlem dives. He stands apart from those ephemeral characteristics of this new world, but feels himself profoundly moved by the tragic meaning which he perceives in the implacable rhythm of its labor, in the teeming activity of the docks, in the crowds at noon, in the bustle of Wall Street. . . . *Amériques* begins to ripen. Encouraged by the possibilities for its realization, Varèse conceives the work on a vast scale. He will not attempt to create a score that will convey the external or picturesque side of American life, but rather throw himself courageously into the discovery of new horizons." [2] Indeed, Varèse himself had written: "I did not think of the title *Amériques* as purely geographic but as symbolic of discoveries—new worlds on earth, in the sky, or in the minds of men." [3]

Amériques is dedicated to his "unknown friends in the spring of 1921." This refers, in fact to two anonymous patrons who sent Varèse regular sums of money to live on while he was composing *Amériques*. In its first version, the work was written for a hundred and forty-two instruments, including two sirens. It lasted about thirty-five minutes. In its final version, it is conceived for two piccolos, three different kinds of flute, three oboes, one cor anglais, one heckelphone, five clarinets of various kinds, three bassoons, two double bassoons, eight horns, six trumpets, five trombones of various kinds, two tubas, and two harps; for a string group of normal dimensions, and lastly for a percussion group of twenty-one instruments, including a whip, a siren, and a string drum or "lion's roar"—all of which are divided up among ten executants. In his program notes for the first performance in 1926, Zanotti-Bianco wrote: "The forward movement of the score could be represented as a series of varied and continual displacements of levels and volumes of sound around a number of solid pivots which support the composition's framework without themselves being apparent . . . The recall of the theme is achieved by means of passages with different characteristics which function as elastic bodies between the principal masses. At several points, the work presents us with sudden shifts, breathtaking leaps which give it a barbaric flavor. This characteristic is even more condensed in the first few pages, which form a swift synthesis of the whole work, summing up all its essential elements." [4]

Continuing Zanotti's commentary, Paul Le Flem added after hearing
the second version: "There are two densities at work above all in
Amériques: the orchestra proper and its stimulant, the percussion.
The role of the percussion is not to provide rhythmic punctuation or
to accentuate certain cadences, but to penetrate into the masses of
instrumental sound, to lend them special and varied vibrations. The
percussion element will thus be sometimes deep, sometimes flexible
and light, the rhythm explosive and nervous." [5]

We shall see later on, when we come to the work's first performance
in 1926, how the public and the critics reacted. But it was obviously
only too easy, since Varèse was using sirens for the first time, to take
the work as a description of some great city, such as New York, and
discuss it in those terms. This is why, the day after the first performance, Varèse countered such comments in this way: "This composition is the interpretation of a mood, a piece of pure music absolutely
unrelated to the noises of modern life which some critics have read
into the composition. If anything, the theme is a meditative one, the
impression of a foreigner as he interrogates the tremendous possibilities of this new civilization of yours. The use of strong musical effects
is simply my rather vivid reaction to life as I see it, but it is the por-
trayal of a mood in music and not a sound picture. . . . Now, as to
the use of unusual sounds throughout the piece. I do that to avoid
monotony. I employ these instruments with a definite fixed pitch to
serve as a contrast in pure sound. It is surprising how pure sound,
without over-tones, re-interprets the quality of the musical notes with
which it is surrounded. Actually, the use of pure sound in music does
to harmonies what a crystal prism does to pure light. It scatters it into
a thousand varied and unexpected vibrations. It is often said that I am
bringing geometric elements into the field of music. Sudden stops,
sharply broken intensities, exceedingly rapid crescendi and diminu-
endi give an effect of pulsation from a thousand sources of vitality.

"To be modern is to be natural, an interpreter of the spirit of your
own time. I can assure you that I am not straining after the unusual." [6]

It is perhaps a good thing to have given Varèse's own categorical
statement of his position here so fully, as we approach the period of
his great compositions. Too many people, from weakness of imagination, refuse to conceive of new works as anything but forms of imita-

tion or description. Out of a desire for security, they look for analogies instead of having the courage to confront the new work itself in all its singularity. Varèse, as we have seen, speaks of states of soul, of geometry and the spirit of the age, and does music not, after all, as one sociologist put it, "evolve between the nebula of emotion and the geometry of reason"? [7] However, before venturing further into the Varesian universe, it may perhaps be useful to try to fix certain concepts as they have been realized in his works, or as Varèse himself has explained them.

First of all, harmony. The American composer Henry Cowell has remarked that Varèse does not break any of the rules of ordinary harmony, but that those rules do not even enter into consideration, since they are not pertinent to the different art at which Varèse is aiming. "One key to a comprehension of Varèse's music," Cowell continues, "is the fact that he is more interested in finding a note that will sound a certain way in a certain instrument and will 'sound' in the orchestral fabric than he is in just what position the note occupies in the harmony, except of course, in so far as its harmonic position will pertain to its 'coming out' in the scoring.

"One must consider that besides the harmony of notes, which with Varèse is somewhat secondary, there is at any given time also a harmony of tone-qualities, each of which is calculated to sound out through the orchestra. For example, Varèse will use a certain chord. Superimposed upon this chord and more important than the chord itself to Varèse, is the harmony resultant from the tone-qualities of the instruments owing to their particular sound in the register in which he scores each; so that, while the chord might be found in many a modern composer's work, it assumes a character found only in Varèse when we see it in his particular scoring." [8] Shortly after Varèse's death, André Jolivet wrote: "At all events, if we take Hindemith as our reference (in his *Treatise on Harmony*), then Schoenberg's works are still faithful to the traditional harmonic functions of sub-dominant, dominant, and tonic. Varèse, on the other hand, arrived at a point on this syntactical level where he truly succeeded in dominating tonality (so as to exclude it) to an extent that produces effects of detemperization." [9] Gilles Tremblay, a Canadian composer, has this to say: "One of Varèse's principal contributions is to have broadened the scope of harmony . . . by restoring it to its primitive role as resonance and timbre." [10] Lastly, François Morel, another Canadian composer, adds: "Varèse looks upon chords as objects, as bodies of sound similar to superimpositions of frequencies and not as vertical coagulations above the harmonic functions proper." [11]

As for timbre: "Whereas the Romantic orchestra, with Berlioz and Wagner, was aiming at a fusion of timbres," Odile Vivier writes, "for Varèse, on the contrary, timbre has to create the differentiation between waves, levels, and volumes; one could compare it to the line and the play of light which give certain drawings the precision and the perspective of space." [12]

Rhythms and intensities are another concept. Stravinsky has said, in conversation with Robert Craft: "Varèse was also one of the first composers to employ dynamics as an integral formal element . . . and he was also among the first to plot the intensities of a composition, the highs and lows in pitch, speed, density, rhythmic movement." [13]

As Gilles Tremblay insists: "The essential role of rhythm and *dynamics* (intensity) will be to model the sound, to surround it in all its dimensions and to sculpt it . . . Thus we may say that durations give sound its dimension in time, whereas dynamics shape its volume. Here, the rhythm of the music is created by the combination of the two and is centered on the formation of the sound, since in Varèse's work it is the sound which is master of everything else." [14]

Speaking of rhythm as he conceived it, Varèse observed: "Rhythm is the element in music which not only gives life to a work but holds it together. It is the element of stability. Cadence or the regular succession of beats and accents has really little to do with the rhythm of a composition. In my own works, for instance, rhythm derives from the simultaneous interplay of unrelated elements that intervene at calculated, but not regular, time lapses. This corresponds more nearly to the definition of rhythm in physics and philosophy as 'a succescession of alternate and opposite or correlative states.' " [15]

As far as melody is concerned, Henry Cowell writes that "one finds that dynamic nuances on the same note, or repeated tones, often take the place of melody. He very frequently does away with melody entirely by having only repeated tones for certain passages. Removing from the listener's ear that which it is accustomed to follow most closely, sometimes almost to the exclusion of everything else, naturally induces a keener awareness of other musical elements such as rhythm and dynamics. Varèse, however, is always careful to supply the ear with subtleties of dynamic change which take the place of melody in certain passages." [16] Analyzing Varèse's use of melody, François Morel described it thus: "The phrase, generally composed of disjunct or linked notes, moves constantly from one register to the other and allows itself to be attracted by the magnetic force of these "pivot-notes," (kinds of dominants) either changing its timbre and color, or not, by means of differing instrumentations . . ." [17] Gilles Tremblay writes: "When the body of sound thins down till it is monody, the musical fabric, as though relieved of a burden, springs to life and becomes melodic. This is perhaps a transmutation of the vertical into the horizontal, to use one of the terms of alchemy. . . " [18]

Speaking of orchestration, Varèse has said: "To me, orchestration is an essential part of the structure of a work. Timbres and their combination—or better, quality of tones and tone-compounds of different pitch, instead of being incidental, become part of the form, coloring and making discernible the different planes and various sound-masses, and so creating the sensation of non-blending. Variations in the intensity of certain tones of the compounds modify the structure of the masses and planes. Contrasting dynamics are based on the play of simultaneously opposing loudnesses—loudness as defined by Harvey Fletcher as 'the magnitude of sensation.' " [19] Henry Cowell observed on this subject: "I have frequently noticed that when Varèse examines a new score, he is more interested in the orchestration than in the musical content. . . ." [20]

In his lecture at Princeton University in 1959, Varèse explained his conception of form. "Each of my works discovers its own form," he said. "I have never tried to fit my conceptions into any known container. . . . Conceiving musical form as a resultant, the result of a process, I saw a close analogy in the phenomenon of crystallization. . . . There is an idea, the basis of an internal structure, expanded or split into different shapes or groups of sound, constantly changing in shape, direction, and speed, attracted and repulsed by

various forces. The form of the work is the consequence of this in-
teraction. Possible musical forms are as limitless as the exterior forms
of crystals . . . Form and content are one." [21] This conception reminds
me of the remark made by the Roumanian poet Tudor Arghezi
during a radio interview: "I try to make more and more delicate
crystals." It becomes easy to understand, when one considers Varèse's
concept of form, how each work is the most profound vital experience
it is possible for there to be. The composer has given up all security.
He is advancing along a road without milestones. By him, through
him, the crystallization of a new being is taking place. He is the
agent of a crystallization struggling to assume a form in the border-
land between matter and spirit. Creation, as Varèse conceived it, was
an absolute risk. According to whether or not the work is brought off
successfully, so the spirit becomes more powerful or is weakened.
And if the new musical being is beautiful, that is because it is essentially, in its singularity, a new quality that was needed by the
spirit which animates the forward march of humanity. Varesian form
is the wager of a man who cannot live intensely unless confronting
the abyss. Such a creator is all tensions, and those tensions are the
dialectical forces that bring about the crystallization. Though talent
in another may reassure us, "genius exasperates us." [22] As Varèse
has made clear, it is not art's function to reassure. True art calls
our being into question. Varèse's challenge in art was so radical that
he produced only a few works. Calling being into question is not
a game. And Varèse was not playing. He was too attentive to the quality of his work to be concerned with quantity. Quantity is often the
supreme form of escape for the man who merely possesses talent.
But genius such as Varèse's has so profound a respect for quality,
for true value, that its progress is painful. Nothing comes easily to
it. It is obliged to tear everything out of its own being and out of
the universe. Creation, for such a genius, is like a slow violence. On
the horizon, there are marvelous suns of sound spinning in the
infinite. It is towards them that Varèse made his way, and he reached
them only on the other side of despair.

From this little "anthology" of Varesian concepts, a very precise
vision emerges in my mind. For Varèse, the living man, the work was
a living organism. (I prefer that word to "structure".) An organism
in which life truly continues to express itself; in which cosmic energy,

still alive, continues its development. If you like, the work grows like a tree, a new tree, a new species, to borrow our terms from phylogenesis. Thus, in the evolution of music, every new work should be a new being. It is not a matter of producing ten fir trees, but rather ten new species of conifers altogether. So that "music would be the example and the privileged domain of a sociology of the dynamics of signs," [23] with the poem conceived equally as a living organism.

This brings me to the question of the "open" work as conceived by a Pousseur, to the problem of so-called "aleatory" music. "The poetics of the 'open work' tend," Pousseur says, "to encourage 'acts of conscious freedom' in the interpreter, to make him the active center of an inexhaustible network of relationships among which he works out his own form, without being determined by any necessity derived from the structure of the work itself." [24] I understand why Varèse was opposed to this conception, and Gunther Schuller could bear out what I say. I wonder myself whether the solution of so-called aleatory music does not raise a false problem, since it relies upon the lucidity of the interpreter, upon the possibility of multiple works emerging from a different arrangement of structures. For what is important is not so much the action of the interpreter as the reaction of the listener to a work perceived within a given space of time; and that listener will not, in any case, have the opportunity to exhaust the entire multiplicity of possible forms. So that we find ourselves faced once more, and definitively so, by the same problems involved in any work which is entering into contact with a listener within a given time. And Varèse, who was only thinking of that listener, could only conceive of a finished work. He did not believe that a choice of structures made by an interpreter would augment the probability of the work's quality, which is the only important thing on the creative level. He had more confidence in his own choice as a creator. Throughout his life, for the most part, his interpreters had done him much more disservice by their incompetence and insensitivity than they had succeeded in manifesting him in his profound and powerful uniqueness. It is therefore not astonishing that he should have seen a greater possibility of freedom in the organization of sounds on tape, thus eliminating the need for any interpreter, than in the future of a work subjected to the choice of its interpreters. Though, needless to say, the work as conceived by Varèse was "open" in any case, since not only could it be "envisaged" and understood according to a "multiplicity of perspectives," [25] but it must also be as different and as unique as a crystal can be. I wonder, therefore, whether the solution provided by so-called aleatory or unfinished music is not, in a way, merely an irresponsible method of avoiding the tension, and the patience, that any truly new form demands on the part of its creator, or at least, form as Varèse conceived of it. Even in the event of a direct participation on the part of the listener, to what degree would that participation produce a work superior to that conceived by a genius? The whole problem is there: to what degree can a listener help a genius to produce a work superior to one that has been elaborated by the totality of his being? The predominant problem is that of the relationship between listener and work.

It is therefore much less a matter "of a new dialectic between the work and its interpreter" [26]—since that is an *a priori* question of no interest to the listener who is the true recipient—than it is, above all, of a dialectic between the work and the listener, the public. What is important above all else is the injection of new life that the work may give that listener. So that we are still confronted, once and for all, with a work which the listener, who receives it in a given space of time, must necessarily consider as a *whole*. It is that *whole* alone which is important. There is either contact or there is not. Either a shock, or not. If a so-called "aleatory" work should strike a listener "by chance," it is not because it is aleatory, but rather because the *whole* constituted by the sounds that listener has perceived, in that precise space of time, possessed qualities which made it a *work* rather than a mere aggregate of structures. And Varèse quite simply believed he could achieve this result more directly, more surely, by means of a patiently worked out and unified work than by means of an incomplete or aleatory work. He preferred to rely upon the long and patient process whereby his inner ear selected a sequence of particular structures, which were then crystallized into a living organism, than upon the more or less considered choice of a more or less sensitive and intelligent interpreter. Despite everything, I personally believe that the field of probabilities of any given structure possesses new possibilities of expression to the degree in which the work, the organism, has been previously mastered and controlled, as form, by the creator. The delimiting by the composer of the structures to be incorporated in a work is an aperture, and consequently one more means accorded itself by music of accomplishing its mission of liberating the spirit of sounds.

7

The International
Composers' Guild

After the failure of the New Symphony Orchestra, Varèse still did not abandon the idea of organizing a society devoted to the interests of the living composers of his time. The International Society for Contemporary Music had still not been formed, though the magazine *Melos* had recently been founded (in February, 1920) by Hermann Scherchen and his friends, and there was also Carlos Salzedo's magazine *Eolus* in New York.

It was on May 31, 1921, that Varèse, with the aid of Salzedo, founded the International Composers' Guild. Varèse asked William R. Shepherd, Maurice J. Speiser, M. Jagendorf, Charles Recht and Alfred Kreyreymg to attend the foundation meeting, which took place at the Liberty Club, 120 East 40th Street. The first members to accept places on the administrative council were Adam Gimbel, Benjamin F. Glazer (treasurer), Charles Recht, Mrs. William R. Shepherd, Maurice J. Speiser, and Joseph Stella, the painter. The technical advisors were Edgard Varèse, director, Alfredo Casella, Acario Cotapos, Carl Engel, A. Walter Kramer, Julius Mattfield, Carlos Salzedo, Karol Szymanowsky, and Emerson Whithorne. Mrs. Harry Payne Whitney and Mrs. Christian Holmes were the principal patrons. Mrs. Whitney had been persuaded to support the guild by her secretary, Mrs. Juliana Force, to whom *Intégrales* was to be dedicated. For seven years, these two patrons were to enable Louise and Edgard

Varèse not only to live comfortably but to keep the I.C.G. going.
In July, 1921, the I.C.G. published its manifesto:

"The composer is the only one of the creators of today who is
denied direct contact with the public. When his work is done he is
thrust aside, and the interpreter enters, not to try to understand the
composition but impertinently to judge it. Not finding in it any
trace of the conventions to which he is accustomed, he banishes it
from his programs, denouncing it as incoherent and unintelligible.

"In every other field, the creator comes into some form of direct
contact with his public. The poet and novelist enjoy the medium of
the printed page; the painter and sculptor, the open doors of a gal-
lery; the dramatist, the free scope of a stage. The composer must
depend upon an intermediary, the interpreter.

"It is true that in response to public demand, our official organizations occasionally place on their programs a new work surrounded
by established names. But such a work is carefully chosen from the
most timid and anaemic of contemporary production, leaving absolutely unheard the composers who represent the true spirit of our time.

"Dying is the privilege of the weary. The present day composers
refuse to die. They have realized the necessity of banding together
and fighting for the right of each individual to secure a fair and free
presentation of his work. It is out of such a collective will that the
International Composers' Guild was born.

"The aim of the International Composers' Guild is to centralize the
works of the day, to group them in programs intelligently and organically constructed, and, with the disinterested help of singers and instrumentalists to present these works in such a way as to reveal their
fundamental spirit.

"The International Composers' Guild refuses to admit any limita-
tion, either of volition or of action.

"The International Composers' Guild disapproves of all 'isms';
denies the existence of schools; recognizes only the individual."

Clearly this manifesto was in no way an esthetic credo; nor does
its tone suggest a surrealist pamphlet. It was essentially a manifesto
of the freedom to be himself, and to be played, that was the right of
any composer. It is even easier to understand after reading this manifesto how Varèse came to acquire his allergy to a *certain* kind of

so-called aleatory music. There is Boulez and . . . And Varèse liked Boulez.

At the I.C.G., Varèse and Salzedo, aided by Louise Varèse, divided up the work and responsibilities between them. Varèse, for example, since he knew the composers so well and had very reliable taste, chose the works to be played; whereas Salzedo, who had been living in New York since 1908 and thus knew the American musical world very well, engaged the players. In most cases, Salzedo rehearsed the orchestra himself right up until the last rehearsal.

In all, fifty-six composers from fourteen nations were given performances during the I.C.G.'s six years of existence. The first concert took place on February 19, 1922, at the Greenwich Village Theater. Three hundred persons were present. At the end of the sixth year, there was an audience of fifteen hundred filling the Aeolian Hall. Among the many works revealed to the American public by the I.C.G. were the following: Schoenberg's *Pierrot lunaire,* Stravinsky's *les Noces,* Webern's *Movements for String Quartet,* Berg's *Chamber Concerto for violin, piano, and 13 winds,* Hindemith's *Concerto for violin and chamber orchestra,* and Honegger's *Easter in New York.* The principal guest conductors were Eugene Goossens, Otto Klemperer, Fritz Reiner, and Leopold Stokowski.

In the fall of 1922, Varèse went to Berlin, where, together with Busoni, he founded a German I.C.G., the Internationale Komponisten Gilde. (That same year, through the intermediary of Arthur Lourié, a composers' association in Moscow became affiliated to the Gilde; then, in the following year, came the affiliation of Casella's society for new music). He was also anxious to introduce his wife, Louise, to the man he admired the most, and Karl Muck was there in Hamburg to welcome him. In July of that year, 1922, the mark had lost 99% of its value. Varèse was to tell me that in those days "people's suits were held together by memory, just from the habit of being worn." It was in these painful and uncertain conditions that Varèse managed to bring together several Berlin composers "such as Tiessen, Hermann Springer, Werner Woffheim, Jarnach and Erdmann." [1] Tiessen, in particular, had been one of the founders of the magazine *Melos.* Busoni, although already rather ill, agreed out of friendship for Varèse to become president of this new society. Tiessen became vice-president, C.-J. David its administrator, Dr. jur. Fritz Kalischer the treasurer, and Ernst Schoen the secretary. The committee consisted of Alfredo Casella, Bernard van Dieren, Eduard Erdmann, Alois Hába, Paul Hindemith, Philipp Jarnach, Ernst Krenek, Arthur Lourié, Felix Petyrek, Heinz Tiessen, and Edgard Varèse.

The first concert under the auspices of the Berlin I.C.G. took place on Wednesday, November 1, in the Gesellschaft der Freunde Hall. Works by Busoni, van Dieren, Hindemith, Arthur Lourié, and Varèse had been programmed. The Varèse work was *Offrandes*, already performed in New York the previous April but now receiving its first performance in Germany.

Varèse took advantage of his stay in Berlin to have the immense score of *Amériques* copied. However, the German I.C.G. crumbled away again almost immediately, to be replaced before long by the International Society for Contemporary Music, a very well-known organization today.

Shortly after Varèse's return to New York, a group of members split off from the main body of the I.C.G. and founded the magazine *Modern Music,* as well as the League of Composers. One should be careful not to confuse the two organizations, as one American critic recently did. Varèse and Salzedo had nothing to do with the League of Composers, which was merely an imitation of the I.C.G.[2] It was six years later, in November, 1927, that Varèse decided to break off the I.C.G.'s activities. In an open letter, written on November 7th and sent to the magazine *Eolus,* Varèse explained his action as follows: "The International Composers' Guild will give no more concerts in New York for the present. Many of our friends who have expressed surprise at our decision will readily understand it if they stop to remember the reason for our existence.

"When, in 1921, with a group of friends, I founded the International Composers' Guild there was an imperative need for such an organization, the American musical public having been kept in practically total ignorance of the music of its own time.

"The reception our concerts enjoyed, the keen interest shown by the growing public which followed and supported them, proved the vitality of our enterprise and was our efforts' desired recompense.

"The war had forced composers to limit their work to a very restricted number of instruments. The return to chamber orchestra form was dictated, except in a few cases, by necessity rather than, as many would have it, by a desire to return to the past to copy its forms.

"It is a satisfaction now to see that the great orchestral organizations are following in our footsteps and are beginning in their turn to present the contemporary works of all schools and tendencies to a public now enlightened or at least compliant. This evolution in the policy of the symphony orchestras and the return to normal living allow the composer today to realize his conceptions untrammeled, and assure him a perfect execution by the large orchestras and their distingushed conductors.

"This happy condition frees the International Composers' Guild of the responsibility which it undertook in the name of all the young composers of today. For the moment it sees no need for continuing its concerts. The I.C.G. was started for composers by composers. Its purpose accomplished, that of awakening an interest in living composers at a time when they were neglected, it leaves to other organizations the purely managerial task of continuing to entertain the public which now takes pleasure in hearing (thanks to its own ears) the works of its young contemporaries.

"The I.C.G. can only live in the exhilarating atmosphere of struggle. It therefore retires at the approach of the official laurel wreath, holding itself in readiness at any time to respond to a new call to battle." [3]

Varèse was a man made for combat and not for complacency: for him, victory was not white and dazzling but dark as death. There is more death in the triumph than in the struggle, he seemed to feel. He feared repose as nature abhors the vacuum. By making possible so many contacts with others and their works, the I.C.G. had, of course, stimulated him. And though there were few of those works that inspired him in his role as a creator, nevertheless the I.C.G. period was also his own most fertile one. At bottom, Varèse, like so many composers, only composed when he had some concrete expectation of the work's being performed. He felt the need of establishing a swift contact between the public and himself. Despite appearances, a feeling of insecurity was certainly anchored deep in his unconscious. The existence of the I.C.G. meant that his works were played. Moreover, Varèse had proved that one cannot blame the public if it is ignorant of new works, since if those works are presented to it, it listens to them and reacts. No, one's criticism must rather be directed at the impresarios and star-performers, who procure a fragile and futile glory for themselves by drugging the public with the works that everyone already knows. It is they who stand in the way of the creators and who prevent the public from discovering the works of their true contemporaries. This profound conviction of Varèse's was to be corroborated, much later, by the observations of several sociologists: "The incomprehension and lack of success of musical works," one of them writes, "even if their value is recognized later on, are generally less due to the public than to members of the profession, to the critics, and to colleagues, all of whom base their judgments upon a theoretical and practical education which presents as immutable rules those very traditions which the works in question have moved beyond. The tendentious notion of a regressive public is therefore not in accord with the actual state of musicological and sociological knowledge." [4]

It is important that we should remember these facts, and Varèse's action in dissolving the I.C.G., later on, when we find him hammering against the wall of indifference, or walking alone, or, above all, when we find him being accused of reaping the fruits of "others" labors. At the time of the I.C.G., Varèse's works were played and known to the public. This is why he was always to reply to those who talked about the "divorce" between the creative artist and his audience today: "There can't be a divorce, because there was never any marriage. The public doesn't know the works because they are not presented to them."

On January 12, 1921, Varèse signed the manifesto *Dada soulève tout*,[5] a pamphlet which was later distributed on the occasion of a lecture given in Paris by the futurist Marinetti. This manifesto was for Varèse another opportunity to make public expression of his opposition to Marinetti and futurism. He had already expressed this opposition once, during March, 1916, in an interview. We should be very careful to note here, however, that this does not mean Varèse ever seriously belonged to the Picabian-dadaist movement. He was so deeply independent by temperament that he was incapable of belonging to any movement. In number III of the magazine *391*, during March, 1917, we do of course find a report that Varèse is claiming to have finished "the orchestration for his *Cold Faucet Dance.*" But let us not forget that Varèse had been friendly with Satie ever since 1904. Moreover one must also keep in mind the charm and ebullience of the Picabia group he belonged to at that time, as well as the feeling of loneliness by which he was always haunted. It was natural that his contact with Picabia, Duchamp, or Gleizes should have been stimulating for him. Like them, Varèse had been fundamentally a rebel since his childhood, and in a certain way could only despise organized society. In that respect there was certainly a dadaist spirit in his aggression and his negative acts. But we must not forget the soil from which his rebellion had first sprung, the conflict with his father. Varèse's collaboration on the *Pilhaou-Thibaou* manifesto on July 10, 1921 (number XV of the magazine *391*), was simply a mani- festation of solidarity with his friend Picabia. I am convinced that he had no grudge whatever against Tzara. The most one can say is that he was instinctively opposed to any person who attempted to play the leader or pope. This is why, when Aragon writes that Varèse was "the only musician of the dada period," [6] he seems to me to be restricting the scope of Varèse's esthetics very considerably. Varèse was, certainly, one of the rare creators in the musical field whose activity coincided, in time, with the dadaist or surrealist move- ment. But the tone of his own manifesto for the I.C.G. has nothing particularly dadaist about it. Varèse was himself to write to Thomas H. Greer, on August 14, 1965: "I was not interested in tearing down, but in finding new means. Unlike the dadaists, I was not an icon- oclast." [7] Of course, it was after the breakup of Picabia's group that Varèse was to renounce all his previous works and begin to compose what he considered *his* works. But doesn't it always take a long time for a musician, and above all an innovator, to find his own language? It was therefore quite natural that Varèse should have approved of any valid work, whether it was dadaist or tachist or not. His contact with the Picabian group alone certainly cannot explain the break with all his previous works, and above all not the appearance of the truly *Varesian* works. We must not forget the *Bourgogne* scandal of 1910, which had literally forced him out of the "beaten paths," or Chalupt's remark that Varèse was considered in 1908 as being a musi- cian "in the very forefront of the avant-garde." And all this several years before the meeting with Picabia. Varèse himself had a person-

ality strong enough to influence men like Picabia and Duchamp quite
as much as they were able to stimulate him in return. There could
be no question of anything but a meeting of creators on an equal
footing. The process of metamorphosis had begun in Varèse's unconscious as early as his twentieth year, when he was becoming
familiar with physics. Certainly the element of "originality" in a
work (as he was to tell Georges Charbonnier in a broadcast interview in 1955) was enormously important to him, even though the
quality of a work could not, of course, be reduced to that element
alone. In his eyes, the valid work of art could certainly not be reassuring; on the contrary, at the time of its first appearance it
could not help but be a disturbing element, calling the whole
social structure into question and prodding our dozing consciences.
Though Varèse, like Baudelaire, believed that "the beautiful is always bizarre," that "the unexpected, and astonishment are an essential part of beauty and characteristic of it," he never believed
that anything uncompleted, or even the most dazzling accidents produced by chance, could provide a substitute for the patient search
for finished expression and form. He was often to say: "I do not
write experimental music. I offer a 'finished product'; it is for the
audience, when they hear it performed, to make the experiment of
confronting a new work." No one was to be further removed from
automatist methods of working, from perfunctory experiments, from
the futurist spirit and all its avatars. One has to grasp the fact right
away that Varèse was a man of patience, given to slow and painful
labor, as Boulez clearly sensed. For it takes a great deal of time to
reflect one's own time in depth. It is no paradox to say that, in a way,
Varèse was closer to Pasteur than to Russolo or Antheil. To use
Michel Seuphor's beautiful expression, Varèse was Einstein's "comple-
ment."[8] But how he loved imagination too! The words of
Paracelsus quoted as an epigraph to the score of his *Arcana* are
proof enough of that. Baudelaire was right when he wrote that "the
more imagination one possesses, the greater one's technique must
be in order to keep up with the imagination on its adventures, and
overcome all the difficulties that it seeks out so avidly." Varèse was
wonderfully that man of imagination and technique. So that he was
"bizarre," in the Baudelairian sense, to the degree in which that
bizarreness constituted and defined his individuality. And he was

"Romantic," in the Varesian sense, insofar as his work expressed his own personality. For to Varèse himself, any creator who expresses himself is, by definition, *Romantic*. Only the work, if it survives the test of time, can become what we have agreed to term *Classic*. In view of this, it seems to me that nothing could be more inexact than to say that Varèse "created a music that was no longer the language of man speaking to man."[9] If that had been so, then men would not have been overwhelmed when they heard his works. Varèse expressed himself and expressed us. Yes, for we can truly recognize ourselves in his universe. That world is indeed ours. And its tragic force is a spiritual explosion. So that Beethoven and Varèse, across the centuries, are linked by their humanity and their indivuality. Both were truly faithful to their natures. Both were men who "believed."

8

Varèse's Universe

In 1921, Varèse dreamed that he was in a telephone booth talking to his wife, who was at that time in Paris. His body became so light, so immaterial, so evanescent that suddenly, limb by limb, he disintegrated and flew away toward Paris, where he was reconstituted, as though all his being had become spirit. This singular experience, in a dream, of another duration and another space haunted him for a long while. It was not until ten years later, with the *Astronome,* that he was to attempt to express something of it in a work.

In Paris, Louise had made the acquaintance of the Chilean poet Vicente Huidobro, who in the years since 1917 had published several collections of his work in French illustrated by Juan Gris, Picasso and Delaunay. Louise Varèse brought several of his books back with her to New York. It was in one of these that Varèse came upon the poem entitled *Chanson de là-haut,* which was to provide his text for the first section of *Offrandes.* (This work was at first entitled *Dédications,* and its two parts constituted two more or less different works.) For the second section of the work, Varèse chose a poem called *la Croix du Sud* by José Juan Tablada, a Mexican who had been living in New York since 1914. The two sections of *Offrandes* were completed in 1921. The first is dedicated to his wife, Louise, and the second to his friend, Carlos Salzedo. The work was composed for a single soprano voice, strings, piccolo, flute, oboe, clarinet, bassoon, horn, trumpet, trombone, harp, and eight percussion instruments. (The texts of the two poems are given in note 1.)

Attempting to situate *Offrandes*, Richard Stokes remarked: " (Varèse's work) represents not so much another step in musical evolution as what physicists term another phase. . . . A similar revolution in texture, abrupt and decisive, characterizes *Offrandes*. . . . The alteration is one in the music's very tissue—a sudden break with tradition which run back to the harmonic ratios discovered by Pythagoras." [2] Alejo Carpentier, on the other hand, tried to convey the atmosphere produced by the sounds used in *Offrandes:* "The percussion section plays an important part," he emphasized. "The musical discourse is tender, tremulous, full of glittering sparks of sound. Mysterious panting sounds, pianissimo, alternate with sudden, brutal, searing expressions that surround the words with an atmosphere sometimes stormy and sometimes murmurous." [3] Stravinsky, referring to this work, has said that "the most extraordinary noise in all Varèse is the harp attack ('heart attack,' I almost said and that is what it almost gives one) at measure 17 in *la Croix du Sud.* . ."[4]

But this profoundly lyrical work did not apparently give the impression of being so to anyone who slipped unseen into the hall where it was being rehearsed. Tryon, the critic of the *Christian Science Monitor*, has described his impressions when in that situation: "Rehearsal rooms when they sound like the racket of a street under elevated trains. . . . At 11:10, it was a clatter that could be partially analyzed, being made up of scrapings, tootings and poundings in primitive pulse and measure. At 11:20, it was a balance of string, wood, brass and percussion sonorities, set off against a woman's voice. At 11:30, it was a beautiful song in the modern chamber music form. . . ." [5]

The first performance of *Offrandes* was given under the title of *Dédications*. It took place on Sunday, April 23, 1922, at the Greenwich Village Theater at 8:30 P.M. Carlos Salzedo has told me: "*Offrandes* is an extraordinary work. The performance met with the composer's approval. It was so warmly received that we had to repeat a part of the work." [6] This distant recollection on the part of the conductor who led the first performance is confirmed by the only criticism I have been able to unearth of it. Apparently the only critic present was the one representing the magazine *Musical America*. For we must remember that this was the first time a work by Varèse had been played in America, and only the second performance of any work of his since he first began composing. Thus we read in *Musical America*: "They are vital pieces, experimental in a certain sense, the music of an artist who knows and admires Arnold Schoenberg. . . . There was great enthusiasm, and recalls for composer, singer and conductor."[7]

In July of that year, Varèse told the critic of the *Christian Science Monitor*: "What we want is an instrument that will give us a continuous sound at any pitch. The composer and the electrician will have to labor together to get it. At any rate, we cannot keep on working in the old school colors. Speed and synthesis are characteristics of our own epoch. We need twentieth century instruments to help us realize them in music."[8] If, in Pierre-Jean Jouve's words, "genius needs time to become what it is,"[9] no other composer will ever have been forced to wait so long before gaining access to his true acoustical raw material, not describable in words and approaching the fullness of which he dreamed. If, as the musicologist Gisèle Brelet affirms, "every composer who wishes to create a truly original work must create fresh acoustical material, which is to say, impress sonority with a new form,"[10] then it is easy to understand that Varèse, while waiting for new instruments to be invented, should have turned so passionately to the percussion and brass of *Hyperprism*, and that it should have been with these instruments that the Varesian spirit affirmed itself most strongly in all its originality.

Varèse almost certainly began composing *Hyperprism* in September, 1922, and finished it in February, 1923. The work is conceived for flute, clarinet, three horns, two trumpets, two trombones and sixteen percussion instruments.

Recalling "Varèse's constant preoccupation with form," Pierre Boulez has said: "In this state of mind, *Hyperprism* appears, with its refusal of all thematicism and the plastique of its fluctuating tempi, as the most imperious of projections."[11] One could perhaps classify Varèse among creators of the "formal type,"[12] but we must never forget that Varèse the man, with his torments and his joys, cannot in any way be dissociated from the composer. It is his very personal vision of the universe which summons up the new forms. Alejo Carpentier has given a very good account of the importance of *Hyperprism* in Varèse's development: ". . . This work, the performance of which takes only a few minutes, is one of the composer's most complete successes. He has never given us a more tightly knit, a more clear-cut conception than this is as a whole. Faced with certain passages, full of blanks, reduced to essentials, one thinks of certain Picasso drawings in which two incisive strokes suffice to send us leaping across the whole universe. The instruments set out, intertwine, escape from one another, form into groups, change levels, all with utter sure-footedness. The percussion section becomes a subtle, elastic, personal organism, whose noises, following the progress of the other sounds, trace out arabesques. The orchestra gives out sounds of power. Everything is in its place. Three notes less, and an equilibrium would have been shattered. . . . It would be futile to seek for any influence from the past in *Hyperprism*. In this work Varèse is like no one but Varèse."[13] Nor should we forget that those lines were written in 1929, which is to say before *Ionisation, Ecuatorial, Déserts,* etc. More recently, the American conductor Robert Craft, in an analysis of this work, wrote: "*Hyperprism* begins with percussion alone. Two other passages for percussion solo can be counted. Otherwise, with the exception of one rhythmic unison with the brass, the percussion group is always distinguished from the winds by differences of rhythmic pattern. The one-pitch rhythmic figure with appoggiaturas, already mentioned in connection with *Intégrales* and *Octandre,* is the source here of music in—for so short a piece—a variety of tempi and moods."[14]

The first performance of this work took place on March 4, 1923, at the Klaw Theater, New York, with the composer conducting. This was the first great scandal in New York's musical life. One critic was to remark that Varèse was the cause of peaceable music lovers coming to blows and using one another's faces for drums.[15] But let us listen to W. J. Henderson of the *New York Herald,* who took the trouble to describe the uproar in detail: "After the Varèse number a large part of the audience broke into laughter, which was followed by hisses and cat calls. The supporters of the musicians then began to applaud and amid the uproar Salzedo jumped to his feet and, after calling to the audience to be quiet, cried: 'This is serious.' Apparently for the purpose of restoring order, the musicians played the Varèse number over again while about half of the audience left the building." [16]

Paul Rosenfeld, in an article entitled "We want Varèse," tells an anecdote which conveys very well the unconscious relation of the composer to his environment. During the first performance of *Hyperprism*, he recounts, Varèse noticed that the repetition of a certain piercing C sharp drew nervous laughter from the audience. Then that evening, while working back at his home on 8th Street, he was struck by the familiar sound of a siren coming off the river. Only then did he realize that this sound, which he had heard many times during the six months spent composing his work, was that same piercing C sharp.[17]

Hyperprism was performed again on November 7 and 8, 1924, in Philadelphia, and on December 16th in Carnegie Hall, with Leopold Stokowski conducting. The work was apparently no better received. Never mind, Rosenfeld concluded: "Varèse undoubtedly has done as much with the oral sensations of contemporary nature as Picasso with the purely visual ones."[18] In the *New York Tribune,* Lawrence Gilman wrote that it seemed that Varèse was on the way to giving birth to new planets in the heavens. He never lowered himself, Gilman continued, to compromises similar to those of his more traditional colleagues. While listening to the *Five Pieces for Orchestra* by Schoenberg, one recalled Wagner; Casella's *Alta Notte* reminded one of Schoenberg; but while listening to *Hyperprism,* one thought only of Varèse. Few composers have had access to such total freedom. Gilman wrote that Varèse indeed accepted no master in music. He found his musical expression incomparably unique.[19] Then there was the reaction of the composer Charles Martin Loeffler, which seems to me most typical. "It isn't music, but . . ." How often I've heard these words! Thus we find Loeffler confessing in an interview, after having heard *Hyperprism:* "It would be the negation of all the centuries of musical progress, if I were to call this music. Nevertheless, I seemed to be dreaming of rites in Egyptian temples, of mystic and terrible ceremonies which history does not record. This piece roused in me a sort of subconscious racial memory, something elemental that happened before the beginning of recorded time. It affected me as only music of the past has affected me."

Curwen, the London publisher, who was present at that memorable first performance on March 4, 1923, decided to publish Varèse's scores. He invited him to London. And so the first of Varèse's compositions to be published was *Hyperprism,* in 1924.

On June 11, 1924, Varèse arrived at le Havre and went directly to Paris. Then he went on for a few days to London, where he stayed until July 27th, the day of his friend Busoni's death. *Hyperprism* was to be broadcast by the B.B.C. in a performance conducted by Eugene Goossens. The event was given enormous publicity, and took place that July. Instructions had been given that the broadcast must not be interrupted except in an emergency. Just how poor the sound quality of such a broadcast must have been in 1924 is easily imagined, and the reaction was very violent. There were remarks about "four minutes of noise-making,"[20] "Bolshevism in music,"[21] "lions' roar,"[22] etc. Several newspapers, among them the *Daily Mail* and the *Evening News,* gave Varèse the opportunity to explain himself.

"There has always been misunderstanding between the composer and his generation. The commonplace explanation of this phenomenon is that the artist is in advance of his time: but this is absurd.

"The fact is the creative artist is representative in a special way of his own period, and the friction between himself and his contemporaries results from the fact that the masses are by disposition and experience fifty years out of date.

"Nothing has changed fundamentally, or is likely to change in art. Mehods of expression, however, have changed and must change. . . .

"Why we should be so conservative in music it would be difficult to explain. Stringed instruments are still the kings of orchestras, despite the fact that the violin reached its zenith in the early part of the eighteenth century. Why should we expect this instrument, typical of its period, to be able to carry the main burden of the expression of today? The rest of the conventional orchestra of today precludes the exploitation of the possibilities of different tone colors and range. . . .

"It must not be forgotten that the division of the octave into twelve half-tones is purely arbitrary. There is no good reason why we should continue to tolerate the restriction.

"Just as the painter can obtain different intensity and graduation of color, the musician can obtain different vibrations of sound, not varying, ultimately, from vibration to vibration.

"In order to exploit the art of sound (i.e. music) we shall require an entirely new medium of expression. We certainly should forget forthwith the pianoforte and all the arbitrary mechanical restrictions which it has imposed. . . .

"Music is antiquated in the extreme in its medium of expression compared with the other arts. We are waiting for a new notation—a new Guido d'Arezzo—when music will move forward at a bound." [23]

At that time, it was already several years since Varèse had begun saying that traditional musical instruments are obsolete. Yet forty years later, we find two musicologists seriously asking themselves: "Is it not abnormal, however, that we should still continue today to use equipment perfected a century and a half ago, and adapted to a music whose principles have today been profoundly shaken and whose whole framework is in the process of dissolution." [24] (They do not acknowledge Varèse's efforts in this field at all.)

During the whole summer of 1924, if we except the week spent in London, Varèse lived in Paris, in the studio that Fernand Léger and another painter used to hire to give classes in during the winter. Before returning to New York, Varèse stopped off at 86, rue Notre-Dame des Champs in answer to an invitation from Ravel.

During 1923, Varèse composed *Octandre*. This work is written for flute, clarinet, oboe, bassoon, horn, trumpet, trombone and string bass. Charpentier remarks that in *Octandre*: ". . . everything is clockwork, movement, muscle, gaiety. There is a perpetual bound and rebound of cries and songs. . . I remember having heard this fresh and rumbustious work being acclaimed by hundreds of students and artists, in Mexico, when it was played in the amphitheater of the National Preparatory School, beneath Diego Rivera's frescoes there." [25] (This is a reference to the performance on December 18, 1925, conducted by Carlos Chavez.) Odile Vivier notes: "The work is constructed like a triptych, in which the oboe opens the first panel, the piccolo at the bottom of its register the second, and the bassoon the third." [26] As Robert Craft has emphasized, it is the only work by Varèse that is divided into movements, even though the second and third movements do not in fact have any break be-

tween them. Thus Varèse begins with a *fairly slow* movement, progresses to a *very lively and agitated* one, then finishes, after a *somber*
rest passage, with an *animated and jubilant* section.

Octandre was first performed on January 13, 1924, at the Vander-
bilt Theater in New York. On the whole, the work was better received than *Hyperprism*. W. P. Tryon, in his review, said that
Octandre was for him the musical event of the year. The composition of the work is so personal and so powerful, he also said, that
it has enough in it to provide the foundation of a whole musical
school.[27] After the work had been played once, the conductor, Robert
Schmitz, asked the audience if they would like to hear it again.
Commenting on this gesture, the critic of the *New York Evening Post*
wrote: "What grim species of humor prompted the audience to
redemand it? . . . If Varèse's composition was the worst offender, there
were others which ran it a close race for hideousness and insanity—
songs by Carl Ruggles, Anton von Webern, Alban Berg."[28] This
account seems to contradict that given by Tryon. Is sympathy or is
aversion more likely to lead to objectivity? The veracity of any
evidence must rest ultimately upon the quality of the witness.

Octandre was played the following year in Mexico, in one of a
series of *Conciertos de Musica Nueva*. In the program notes for that
particular concert, Chavez stated: "Here is the gold of pure music.
His technique is the essence of his nature. Varèse creates music, he
does not make harmonized melody or melodious harmonies. He has
an all-embracing, sonorous concept which comprises all possible
material means, a phenomenon common to all musicians of genius."[29].

In revealing his own universe of sound, with the creation of *Offrandes, Hyperprism,* and *Octandre*, Varèse was not only appearing for
the first time in all the originality of his genius, he was also causing
music as a whole to take an immense leap forward. Another beacon
had been lighted to continue the great chain of authentic musical
tradition. The cause of music could never be the same again after
1924. A mutation had taken place. *Hyperprism,* for example, that
black diamond, will always inflict a lasting wound on those who know
how to hear, on those who are able to encompass its tragic dimension,
on those who allow themselves to be lacerated by the cries that pierce
its silences.

9

Intégrales

Varèse began composing *Intégrales* during the year 1924 and completed it early in 1925. It is a very important date not only in Varèse's
work but in the whole history of music. It was in reference to this
work that the expression "spatial music" was to be formulated for the
first time. And it is by keeping this great composition in mind that we
are best able to grasp the import of these comments made by a former
pupil of Varèse, the English composer Marc Wilkinson: "Lacking the
facilities he needed, Varèse has had to make do with conventional
means of performance, choosing the instruments that would come
nearest to the timbres and effects he had in mind. There exists therefore a strained duality in his music, for while composing with techniques based on fluctuating values, he must contrive to work within the
fixed values of temperament and within the limits of timbre, dynamics, and duration imposed by our mechanical instruments. Varèse
favors woodwind and brass because they produce clear sounds, relatively clear of such clouding factors as *vibrato* and approximate pitch;
their attacks and releases can be made neat and varied, even in
ensemble, and their timbres contrast but will also blend. His fondness
for percussion instruments is precisely due to their lack of pitch, which
allows almost unbounded rhythmic development outside the tempered
scale." [1] In his notes on *Hyperprism, Octandre* and *Intégrales*, Gilbert
Amy was to remark: "Starting from these three 'terms' one is able to

discern the entire Varesian project, in its multiple and radical determination: melodic, harmonic, rhythmic, acoustical. From the very start, these works appear as emanating from a single block whose rites of articulation may be taken, in a way, as the different facets of an identical intuition, of its 'crystallization' as Varèse himself likes to put it. . . Varèse definitively banishes the Classical (academic) notion of the orchestra, as he does that of tonality, and even of temperament. He recreates for himself a totality of means in conformity with his needs for 'spatial' and 'rhythmic' efficacity . . . The body of the acoustical design itself is formed by the mass of the brass and woodwinds, their registers being completed at one end by the use of extremely high-pitched instruments (piccolos, clarinet, piccolo trumpet) and at the other by extremely low-pitched ones (trombone and contrabass)." [2]

Intégrales, dedicated to Juliana Force, is composed for two piccolos, two clarinets, an oboe, a horn, trumpet, piccolo trumpet, three trombones, and seventeen percussion instruments played by four executants.[3] Varèse was to write: "*Intégrales* was conceived for a spatial projection. I constructed the work to employ certain acoustical means which did not yet exist, but which I knew could be realized and would be used sooner or later. . . Whereas in our musical system we divide up quantities whose values are fixed, in the realization I wanted, the values would have been continually changing in relation to a constant. In other words, it would have been like a series of variations, the changes resulting from slight alterations of a function's form or from the transposition of one function to another. In order to make myself better understood—for the eye is quicker and more disciplined than the ear—let us transfer this conception into the visual sphere and consider the changing projection of a geometrical figure onto a plane surface, with both geometrical figure and plane surface moving in space, but each at its own changing and varying speeds of lateral movement and rotation. The form of the projection at any given instant is determined by the relative orientation of the figure and the surface at that instant. But by allowing both figure and surface to have their own movements, one is able to represent with that projection an apparently unpredictable image of a high degree of complexity; moreover, these qualities can be increased subsequently by permitting the form of the geometrical figure to vary as well as its speeds . . ." [4] It was while listening to the scherzo of Beethoven's *Seventh Symphony,* one day in the Salle Pleyel in Paris, that Varèse first had the sensation of a "projection in space." "Probably because the hall happened to be over-resonant . . . I became conscious of an entirely new effect produced by this familiar music," Varèse said. "I seemed to feel the music detaching itself and projecting itself in space. I became conscious of a third dimension in the music. I call this phenomenon 'sound projection,' or the feeling given us by certain blocks of sound. Probably I should call them beams of sound, since the feeling is akin to that aroused by beams of light sent forth by a powerful searchlight. For the ear—just as for the eye—it gives a sense of prolongation, a journey into space." [5] Talking about the "movement of masses," Varèse was to say in 1936: "Taking the place of the old fixed linear counterpoint, you will find in my works the movement of masses, varying in radiance, and of different densities and volumes. When these masses come into collision, the phenomena of penetration or repulsion will result. Certain transmutations taking place on one plane, by projecting themselves on other planes which move at different speeds and are placed at different angles, should create the impression of prismatic aural (auditory) deformations. Here you have again as a point of departure the same devises that are found in classical counterpoint, only now adapted to new necessities, but still acting as a basic discipline for the imagination." [6] It was at this point that Varèse was to find his expression "sonic beams." Varèse-Gambara!

The first performance of *Intégrales* took place on March 1, 1925, in the Aeolian Hall in New York, and was conducted by Leopold Stokowski. The work, though well received by certain critics who had always admired Varèse, was on the whole ridiculed, especially by the critics of the great dailies. However, the majority of the audience was enthusiastic, to the point of clamoring that Stokowski should repeat the work then and there. That evening, most of the critics racked their imaginations in order to convey the sensations they had felt, sensations which were, to say the least, curious and strange. Thus Olin Downes of the *New York Times* (though he was to repent of his words later) judged that "the *Intégrales* of Edgar Varèse was the final offering of the illuminati. . . . For those of us who live in outer darkness, the music is merely very noisy and extremely dull. The composer lacks the courtesy of Satie, who, with far more wit, bowed himself out of the room as soon as he realized he was becoming a bore. . . . If you make bad noises, make them just as loudly and as badly as you possibly can. Some people will be impressed." [7] D. Taylor, in *The World*, reduced the work to a struggle between two groups of instrumentalists from which the percussionists emerged victorious, thereby earning great applause from the audience.[8] The critic of the *New York Evening Post* said it was like being in a shunting yard, like listening to the bellowings and shrieks from a zoo, like the din of passing trams, like the hammering of a drunken woodpecker, or like a thunderbolt striking a tinplate factory.[9] Today, all these judgments are bound to strike us as a little unlikely, and at the very least rather unworthy of "serious" critics. But since criticism is only a *trade*, as Debussy said . . . Even then, however, there were other men, though very few of them, for whom criticism was still an art, and even, one might add, a gift. Paul Rosenfeld was one of these. Indeed, he has even been nicknamed "the Elie Faure of the New World." After hearing *Intégrales*, he wrote in his column in the magazine *Dial*: "Varèse stems from the fat European soil quite as directly as Schoenberg does. It is the serious approach, the scientific curiosity of what of the nineteenth century remained on the Continent, that strengthened and sent him onward. But his experience has been the New World in dream and in contact. He has felt it directly, imaginatively, and through music bridged a way to greater apprehension. Varèse never has imitated the sounds of the city. . . . He has come into relationship with the elements of American life, and found corresponding rhythms within himself set free. Because of this spark of creativeness, it has been given him to hear the symphony of New York. . . . Varèse's polyphony is very different from the fundamentally linear polyphony of Stravinsky. The music is built more vertically, moves more in solid masses of sound. Even the climaxes do not break the cubism of the form." [10] Lawrence Gilman, in the *New York Herald Tribune*, wrote: "Whatever you might decide to think about Mr. Varèse's *Intégrales*, you will probably admit that there is nothing like it under the canopy. It is as remote from Schoenberg and Stravinsky as it is from Debussy, Strauss and Wagner and the Romantics."[11] Carpentier, as always, grasped the meaning of *Intégrales* very well: "These close-knit pages are given life by an underlying pathos. The music explodes from time to time, leaps out into the streets, howls, then comes back to itself, closes in upon itself again. . . The percussion section, at the highest pitch of tension, sometimes flutters with pain and grief. One feels oneself being disturbed by the harshness of the sounds that mask, beneath, a strange well of tenderness." [12]

In this year of marvels, as though drawn to earth by Varèse's "sonic beams" and brasses "full of sun," Pierre Boulez was born. At that same time the great Erik Satie died. Stravinsky arrived in the United States on his first tour. Maurice Ravel's *l'Enfant et les sortilèges* was performed. Alban Berg's *Wozzeck* had its triumphant opening under the baton of Kleiber. In Paris, the first Surrealist exhibition took place. In London, Curwen had published the score of *Amériques* and was selling it at twenty-five dollars a copy. *Octandre* was played in Los Angeles.

On November 25, 1925, Varèse bought his house, 188 Sullivan Street, New York, where he was to live until his death, if we except the years spent in Paris between 1928 and 1933, and the years spent visiting California.

In 1925, there began a period during which Varèse gave himself up entirely to the composition of *Arcana*,[13] which he was to complete in February, 1927. There was a period of meditation and creation before confronting the public once more, in the spring of 1926, with the first performance of *Amériques*. This was a year during which much was written about him and about his works. He was *temporarily* famous. For instance, we find the great Russian writer Mayakovsky paying him a visit during his stay in New York. But this fame never really took root. It was largely occasioned by the scandals and the curiosity that his works aroused. In fact, there were few people who truly understood the importance of his efforts, who felt the tragic gravity impregnating Varèse's thought. Yet it is there, as the lamentation in the theme of *Intégrales* tells us; in order to find anything resembling it one has to change worlds, to visit that of the Tibetan monks of Sikkim, which was revealed to us much later on by one of Serge Bourguignon's recordings. There is no music closer to *Intégrales* than that profound and slow *Lamentation for the Dead*. When I played this record to Varèse, in 1960, he was moved to tears and kept repeating: "How beautiful it is!" (though this did not stop him also pointing out the performers' lack of precision). Varèse's themes have a validity as archetypes. They are in a sense *signs*, emerging from the "collective unconscious." Their resemblance to the Tibetan laments is proof of this. It is apparent that Varèse found a way back, beyond the area of musical form, to the very essence of song in its most spontaneous manifestation: the sacred chant of man faced with the mystery of God and the beyond, with the mystery of Nature. How could the New World that was being born not bring with it also a new Nature, new mysteries, and new hopes? And this being so, how can one not be struck by the authenticity of Varèse's music, by its sincerity, and its purity?

10

Arcana

The first performances of *Amériques* took place on April 9 and 10, 1926, in Philadelphia, and on April 13th in New York, under the baton of Stokowski. A minimum of fourteen rehearsals was required. It will be remembered that this work was completed in 1921, and that it was scored for a hundred and forty-two instruments. In New York, the rest of the program on that Tuesday evening, April 13th, after *Amériques,* which opened the concert, consisted of *The Swan of Tuonela* by Sibelius (which Varèse had admired a great deal in his adolescence), Mozart's *C Major Symphony* (the "Jupiter"), and a Bach passacaglia transcribed for orchestra by Stokowski.

In Philadelphia, the *Philadelphia Evening Public Ledger* ran a headline: *Amériques hissed at first playing.* But the applause must in fact have been considerable, since Stokowski was called back for three bows. The critic of the above-mentioned newspaper wrote: "It would be difficult to accept this work as serious music were it not for the form which Mr. Varèse has employed in its construction." [1]

In New York, in the venerable Carnegie Hall, there was a near riot. W. J. Henderson, still quite flabbergasted, described the events as follows: "The outbreak, moderate at first, swelled gradually to an indescribable turmoil. Some men wildly waved their arms and one was seen to raise both hands high above his head with both thumbs turned down, the death sign of the Roman amphitheater. . . . The demonstration lasted more than five minutes, which, as political meeting experts well know, is a long time." [2]

W. P. Tryon, fired with enthusiasm by the work, wrote: "It is simply a great structure. . . . Now this work, dispassionately regarded, may be said to mark a date in the history of art. In all reason, it may be accounted the first absolutely original score for grand orchestra that has been made in America since the twentieth century began. . . . Here we are far past Strauss, Debussy, Schoenberg or Stravinsky. We are, that is to say, at the forefront of time in instrumental expression. . . . The most memorable night of modern music in New York, no doubt, since Pierre Monteux's bringing out the *Sacre du Printemps* of Stravinsky with the Boston Symphony." [3] Lawrence Gilman, however, was not entirely convinced: "He might, we think, have made it more completely out of the stuff of his own imagination. It is not so original, so daringly self-sprung, so independent, as his *Hyperprism*. . . . Not all of it is equally taut and stringent . . . But in the end the sense of power and release, the violent, irrepressible exultation of the thing, makes its effect. . . ." [4] After having exclaimed, in 1926, that "Edgard Varèse is a genius who has the orchestra in his skin," three years later, Paul Rosenfeld would say: "*Amériques* itself is something of a transitional expression, exhibiting the peculiarities of such pieces. Its inner coherency is weaker than that of its successors. . . ." [5]

I wonder whether Gilman and Rosenfeld really understood *Amériques*. It is precisely the absence of apparent logic and coherence that constitutes this work's power and originality. It is in this a complete break with the *Sacre du Printemps,* which reassures us with its logic. *Amériques* has the sun in it; it diffuses itself through space by a series of explosions in every direction. Who can deny that the sun in fusion possesses its own logic? It is a logic drawn both from its magma and the long, bright illuminations of the lightning. As the light breaks against the darkness in successive waves, with an even deepening undertow, so a thousand worlds are made manifest. We are demiurges rubbing day against night, as fascinated as though we were giving birth to a new "world for men." This is the logic of the miracle, the logic of celebration, the logic of life at white heat.

But, in any case, all these critical judgments refer only to the first version of *Amériques*, and in order to hear the reactions to the final version it was necessary to wait until its performance in Paris, in 1929. After that, the work was never played again. It has only just been recorded. Varèse had not foreseen the ruthless demands of the trade unions of the artistic world, particularly in the United States. Later on, several composers, using precisely this impossibility of obtaining the necessary rehearsals as a pretext, because of the prohibitive costs involved, were to direct their attention to the most formless kind of aleatory music. Thus they were able to put works that required very little rehearsal before the public.

"When talking about music, what must never be forgotten is that the listener, in order to hear music, must before anything else be subjected to a physical phenomenon. . . Each time a work is performed, it can only be so by means of a machine which produces sounds—the instruments composing our orchestras, which are subject to all the same physical laws as all other machines." And then Varèse quotes O. Knutsen: "From the very earliest antiquity, in India, in China, in Egypt, the origin of acoustics was always the scientific study of music. Acoustics has always been the handmaiden and the mistress of music." [6] Did Berlioz himself not say that it was in a way necessary that the body itself should become vibration? And then there is Balzac's *Gambara*, a work written in the same year as Berlioz's famous *Requiem* . . . Sound had long since become the dimension which interested listeners least, and apart from *Amériques*, its equal in this respect, no work has ever required so profound a knowledge of sound as *Arcana*. No other work has ever perhaps caused the body to participate so profoundly in the phenomenon of vibration talked about by both Berlioz and Varèse. The latter noted, in 1928: "It is perhaps in *Arcana* that you will truly find my thought." [7]

As I wrote earlier, Varèse completed the composition of *Arcana* in February, 1927. He was later to modify only a few details of the score for the definitive version of 1960. This final version requires one hundred and twenty players and considerably more instruments: seventy strings, about forty percussion instruments, eight horns in F, five trumpets in C, four trombones, two tubas, three piccolos, two flutes, three oboes, one English horn, one heckelphone, five clarinets, three bassoons, two contrabassoons. During the time that Varèse was composing *Arcana,* his wife Louise showed him *The Hermetic Philosophy* by Paracelsus, translated by Arthur Waite, which she had just bought. This work reminded Varèse of what he had read in 1905. Not only did he then decide to give his work the title *Arcana,* but he also selected an extract from Paracelsus to serve as an epigraph to the score. It reads: "One star exists higher than all the rest: this is the star of the Apocalypse. The second is that of the Ascendant. The third is that of the Elements, which are four in number. There are thus six stars established, and besides these yet another star, Imagination, which begets yet another Star, and a new heaven." Varèse was to say of this epigraph: "This extract is equivalent to a dedication; it makes of my symphonic poem a kind of tribute to the author of those words; but they did not inspire it, and the work is not a commentary upon them." [8] Varèse said to me one day: "You can add Paracelsus to the list of my friends!" Odile Vivier has established the living relationship that was able to exist between Paracelsus and Varèse: "The precepts of Paracelsus," she writes, "contain in a deliberately obscure form the scientific truths that our modern world is beginning to discover. Many of these precepts concern phenomena whose technique Varèse was able to apply in his musical works. For example, Paracelsus, following the alchemists, describes the transmutation of elements. Varèse constructs his works in accordance with this principle: he attempts neither development nor transformation, but rather the transmutation of an initial cell or agglomeration, which he subjects to different tensions, different dynamics, and different gravitational functions in accordance with the attraction and density of further elements. . . . Varèse considers, in effect that 'the new concepts of astronomy enable us more than ever to look upon rhythm as an element of stability, and not as the means of ordering certain cadences or certain metrical displacements.' Moreover, we should never forget the comparison with the phenomenon of crystallization, which was very important to Varèse himself." [9]

Arcana is composed in one continuous movement; it is an unbroken fresco which moves through fourteen different tempi. Rosenfeld wrote: "A basic idea, the banging eleven-note phrase which commences the work *fortissimo,* is subjected to a series of expansions and contractions." [10] Gilman, in his program notes for the first performance, wrote: "This form might be regarded as an immense and liberal expansion of the passacaglia form—the development of a basic idea through melodic, rhythmic and instrumental transmutation." Alejo Carpentier described *Arcana* in his usual vivid style as follows: "With *Arcana,* Varèse, the alchemist of sounds, sets out on a quest for the Philosopher's Stone. He gives his principle of the transmutation of acoustical material full play . . . Each group of instruments is a retort which receives the initial material in a new phase and fulfils its task of transforming it yet again. The theme turns, leaps, falls back, splits; it becomes liquid, incandescent, steam; it returns to its first form and sets forth once more in an impressive *coda.* From knell to whistle, from mechanical vibration to piercing bells, from bronze to crystal, the diabolical transmutation takes place without cease, in this work which is probably the most powerfully controlled of all Varèse's conceptions." [11]

The first performances of *Arcana* were given on April 8 and 9, 1927, in the Academy of Music, Philadelphia, and on April 12th, at Carnegie Hall, in New York. All three concerts were conducted by Leopold Stokowski and played, according to the conductor, by "musicians who detested the work." In New York, there was yet another uproar. W. J. Henderson of *The Sun,* an accurate reporter, as we have already seen, wrote: "There was an outbreak of hissing last evening, of genuine hissing, which could be heard above the resolute applause. Hissing is an honor rarely bestowed upon a composer in this town." [12] Ah well . . . But the critic of the *New York Telegram,* Pitts Sanborn, must certainly have been seated in a different part of the hall, since he emphasized the fact that the boos were drowned by the applause. [13] Doubtless each of these accounts is in fact a confirmation of what the critic, whether more or less consciously, wanted to see and hear. The imaginative critic of the *New York Times* was once more unable to restrain his pen. (Though he was, of course, to regret his remarks later.) "His composition *Arcana,*" he proclaimed, "achieved much of the tonal frightfulness that Mr. George Antheil wished to accomplish but could not. . . . But there is a temperament back of this music, if nothing else. . . . The day may—might—come when he might realize himself in terms of genuine, sustained music. But that, also, is speculative." [14] Richard Stokes, on the other hand, wrote just as boldly: "It (this music) is the product of a mind adult, robust, and expert, and of a heart audacious and imaginative. . . . He has transmitted into tones the Age of Steel." [15] Paul Rosenfeld compared Varèse to Leonardo da Vinci: ". . . Enormous over Carnegie Hall there fell the shadow of Leonardo da Vinci. *Arcana* is music born of Leonardo's synoptical and comprehensive type of vision. . . . A passion for discovery in Varèse appears to be referred to the technique of art, and the exciting scientific perspectives of the day related to his new emotional and auditory experiences. . . . Not frequently has the prime importance, which a new synthetic intelligence of the capacity of the Vincian's would have for us, been so apparent. . . . The composition seems to proceed from the feeling of unity in present things; and to move toward a form for the entire man of the times."[16] Gilman was not afraid to say that "we are far, here, from the blatant emptiness and the flatulent longueurs of Mr. Antheil's *Ballet Mécanique*. . . . There is portent and mystery in this music. . . . It is good to hear it and thus to be perturbed." [17] Stokowski was to say to Rosenfeld after the concert: "There are no holes in the score. Those you heard during the performance were the consequence of insufficient sonority given me by my orchestra. The men detested the piece." [18] (It should be emphasized that Antheil's *Ballet Mécanique* had been included in the same program.)

It is possible to speak of transmutation in reference to *Arcana*; but it is less a matter of alchemy than of volcanoes erupting blazingly into the night. Etna, here, has the same symbolical dimension as Prometheus. It is even his double. We are being confronted with an endeavor, Promethean in scope, to possess the cosmos *by* and *in* sound. It is Prometheus rebelling against the false gods who have mummified sound, and not only sound but life, social institutions, ideas. Prometheus wreaks havoc upon those who prefer the frozen forms of life, and take refuge in bygone centuries. Prometheus is almost mad with fury, so angrily does he lash out in his attempt to pulverize our minds with what he can hear within his being and in the cosmos; mad with fury that the immense and powerful birth of this new civilization is not more evident to men. Some listeners are incapable of tolerating such a multitude of eruptions penetrating, annihilating, purifying them. Terror freezes us when we are confronted with the words of Etna. Prometheus is not a magician, he is a liberator. It is often necessary to awaken men despite themselves, to plunge them into the abyss so that they may feel the necessity for their liberation. One could perhaps make an analogy with Nietzsche, with Zarathustra; but there is so much more energy and violence, so much more purifying power, in *Arcana*. Zarathustra may be dead, but Prometheus is immortal.[19]

11

Return to Paris

During the summer of 1927, Louise and Edgard Varèse spent their vacation in Antibes. (Varèse used to love watching the fishermen carrying a statue of the Virgin in procession to a chapel dedicated to her and named Sainte-Marie du Port). Then, having undergone a minor prostate operation, Varèse returned to New York on October 26th. It was at this point, at the age of forty-three, that he received his certificate of American citizenship.

In 1927, *Amériques, Hyperprism, Octandre* and *Intégrales* were all added to the catalogue of J. Curwen and Sons of London. Varèse was at this time president of the music committee of the American Society of Cultural Relations with the U.S.S.R.

At this period, no other city better symbolized his passionate quest for a new universe of sound than New York. Yet even after the revelation of *Arcana,* he still had no more than a small group of friends around him who truly loved and understood his works. For most people, he was either a charlatan or a sorcerer. After seven years of intense creative work and activities on behalf of the I.C.G., he doubtless felt a need for warmth, for an atmosphere in which he could expand. He wanted to see his work catch the light and shine, especially in his native country. In France, his friend Julio Gonzalez, experiencing the same solitude, was producing his first works in forged and sheet metal. Antheil, as we have seen, had composed his *Ballet*

Mécanique, and Mossolov his *Iron Foundry;* but these works are almost caricatures of Varèse's own profound procedures. They are all agitation on the surface, but they leave no wound. They call attention to the social pressures affecting the creation of works, but they do not attain to the true epiphany of the authentic creator, who can alone draw sustenance from those pressures and transcend them. Varèse himself was to state with great precision: "I refuse to take into consideration the ephemeral qualities in any work, its showy tricks intended for the diversion of idle snobs and esthetes which win for it its epithet of *modern.* There are no modern or ancient works, but only those which exist in the present. Ideas change, and with them their medium of expression. In the works of today and in those which have preceded them the same elements and principles are common to all. The composer should not be held responsible if habit and mental laziness prevent some people from following the process of perpetual transformation of these elements and principles and make them wish to stop this pitiless movement and to substitute for these elements and principles, stereotype formulas."[1] Varèse suffered the fate of all true creators. We must take care not to delude ourselves: the stir caused by the performances of his works during the twenties in no way diminished his feeling of loneliness. Americans adore any kind of spectacle, and it has been observed that the vocabulary of many of the critics of that period was derived from the world of show business, from the circus ring or the sports stadium. Varèse's compositions created scandals, but they did not reach through to people's sensibilities. The gap between his thought, his imagination, and the sensibility of an audience fascinated by Gershwin was considerable. There was still no inventor creating an instrument that would correspond to Varèse's needs. Jorg Mager, who had introduced the spherophon in London, in 1923, seems to have escaped Varèse's attention. Léon Teremine had not yet arrived in New York; Bertrand and Martenot were working in Paris; Trautwein had not yet demonstrated his trautonium. However, at least the old 78 r.p.m. phonograph record had come into general use. And in Paris, the first successful television experiments had even been made. Varèse therefore decided to change environments, to go and find out for himself what results Bertrand and Martenot were obtaining in Paris.

On November 7, 1927, he announced the dissolution of the I.C.G.

In April, 1928, together with Henry Cowell and Carlos Chavez, he
founded the Pan American Association of Composers, which was to
have as its aim the performance of works by composers from the
three Americas. Most American composers became members. Nicolas
Slonimsky was to be the Pan American Association's principal conductor, and he gave a great many concerts in that capacity, in Europe
as well as in America.

Tryon, having met Varèse before his departure for Paris, wrote
on October 4, 1928: "Stravinsky had to wait as long for general acceptance of his music in America as Varèse will have waited then,
though his experience, possibly, is not one for us to measure by.
Stravinsky needed about thirteen years; Schoenberg, a more original
composer, is taking a still greater time. Varèse, unsurpassed at
invention, bolder than Stravinsky in use of color and subtler than
Schoenberg in manipulation of harmonies, may require the most extended period of all." [2] He could scarcely have been more accurate.
Varèse was to wait for thirty years.

On October 10, 1928, Varèse left New York with the painter Stella.
Louise Varèse was to join him a little later. Before his departure,
Stokowski gave him two thousand dollars though Varèse had a small
fortune of his own at that time, enough to enable him to live with
his wife in Paris, without any income, for five years. He was welcomed
off the boat, at le Havre, by a friend of his early days, François
Bernouard, who had come to take him back to Paris with a car and
chauffeur. To begin with, Varèse took a room at the Hôtel Jacob, on
the rue Jacob. Then, having arrived for a few months, he was to
stay, as we have said, five years.

Shortly after his arrival in Paris, the weekly *Figaro* printed an
article on Varèse and the painter Stella, with interviews. The composer
said at that time: "Truth exists only insofar as art gives it a meaning.
The joy of the artist is in the hunt. . . . For my part, I cannot resist
that burning desire to go beyond the limits. Truth and beauty
must always be caught by surprise, just beyond our expectation. We
can never hold them. . . . Do you think it is in order to '*épater les
bourgeois*' that I am at this moment having the laboratory of an electric company do research into certain instruments which we hope
will have a voice more in conformity with our age? Everything is in
the meaning of things; they do not exist until an intelligence has

given them one." [3] For Varèse, coming to Paris meant, in effect, that he was still pursuing his truth. No work has expressed this thought better than *Arcana.*

In 1928, the only Varèse composition Paris had heard was *Octandre.* It had been conducted by Vladimir Golschmann on June 2, 1927, under the auspices of the Pro Musica. Upon arrival in Paris, it was Varèse's intention to open a school of composition; but, as he himself said, he did not expect any great success in the venture. It was a little later, in about 1930, that Paul Le Flem, his classmate at the Schola Cantorum, was to send him a young musician named André Jolivet. Having asked the young man to write a piano version of *Octandre,* Varèse accepted him as a pupil. At this period, Varèse's principal companions were Artaud, Pascin, Calder, Villa-Lobos, Zadkine, Miró, Desnos, Giono, Russolo, Asturias, Huidobro, Ozenfants, Carpentier, and a few others. He also made the acquaintance of Dr. Cournand, the future Nobel prize winner, who was to become a good friend later in New York. Before leaving Paris for good, Varèse was to give Jolivet "a certain number of fetish-objects which both recognized as possessing a sort of magic power: a wood and brass puppet named 'Beaujolais,' a 'bird' and a 'cow,' two sculptures by Calder, a Balinese straw doll nicknamed 'the Princess,' and two raffia figures, 'the Goat' and 'Pegasus.' These were the titles of the six movements of *Mana,* the general title which to the Polynesians signifies the immaterial power immanent in particular beings and objects." [4] André Jolivet was to dedicate this work to Louise Varèse.

Varèse confronted Paris with *Intégrales,* on Tuesday, April 23, 1929, during one of the Concerts M.–F. Gaillard given in the Salle Gaveau concert hall. Gaillard was the conductor. On the whole the criticisms were much more lucid than those expressed in New York. Paul Le Flem observed that: "The welcome accorded this work—an entirely new one to us—the other evening did not at any point take on the character of a revolt. . . . Before all else, the performance revealed a musician in love with research, prodigiously expert in the art of grouping sonorities, of regulating their volume and duration, and of creating unprecedented balances between his timbres. . . . There is in this sober, powerful style a sort of purging of means which disdains facile skills. It is direct art, and art impregnated with a profound lyricism, not the kind of lyricism directed towards meditation or afflatus, but that which is born of action or superimposed upon it. For this music is active and vigorous. . . . it inspires a strong and virile emotion whose greatness cannot be denied." [5] Pierre Wolff, who did not know Varèse personally, remarked: "What strikes one above all in this score is this power, this pulsating vigor, sign of a prodigious vitality. . . . A great and truly new work." [6] Lastly, the critic of *le Monde musical* asserted: "It was a revelation. It is indisputable that Varèse has a profound knowledge of instrumentation, and each instrument yields up its most beautiful resources. . . . He knows what he wants, where he is going, and he gets there. No sensibility, no lyricism; this is toughened metal, screaming as it is contorted by the forces of fire and rhythm. It is a precursor of the music of the future? We must hear more of Varèse's works before formulating a more definite opinion." [7]

However, the reception given to *Amériques* by the audience in the Salle Gaveau on May 30, 1929, was not so calm. An uproar broke out. Gaston Poulet was conducting. Tryon, then on a visit to Paris, was to say after being present at one of Poulet's rehearsals: "I have never before heard a conductor with such a talent for discipline. . . ."[8]

Varése himself told me that for this performance of *Amériques* he was forced to use the ondes Martenot as a substitute for the sirens, which could not be found in Paris. (Curiously enough, in 1961, in New York, he was obliged to replace his ondes Martenot with oscillators). Joseph Baruzi, in *le Ménestrel*, described the uproar *Amériques* provoked as follows: "At every entry of the percussion, every time the moanings of the siren (sic) spread their swelling menace as it were over the ground—in orchestra seats and balconies alike, shocked voices were startled into cries of rage. . . ." [9] Elsewhere, the respected critic Adolphe Piriou declared: "I have read this enormous orchestral score very carefully, and attempted very sincerely—especially since M. Edgar Varèse is a colleague for whom I feel much sympathy—to enlighten myself. . . . Then I put myself in the place of the listener, by which I mean the unprejudiced listener. . . . It is materially impossible that M. Varèse should be followed and understood by such a listener. . . . All these laboratory experiments kill music rather than revivify it. There is nothing more difficult than to invent a new and musical melody, with a beginning, a middle, and an end. . . . . [10] Taking the opposite point of view, Carol-Bérard, the editor of the *Revue internationale de musique et de danse,* wrote on June 15th: ". . . it was a revelation. One felt that no orchestra has ever attained such a power of sonority. . . ." And the poet Robert Desnos was brimming over with enthusiasm: "I have good ears," he wrote. "I can hear, and I heard Varèse's music. I am therefore qualified to speak of the emotion that was felt at the magnificently executed performance of his *Amériques.* . . . And during that performance, it was truly the pursuit of never-endingly renewed discoveries that we experienced, in an arduous, virile ascent, rising by successive stages in which the most charming first fruits were resolved into human, continuous, tenacious, persistent strivings toward a new summit. We held our breath as we followed this male endeavor. Yet what new breezes came blowing against our faces! Human music in the most absolute sense of the word, acting at the same time on our muscles and on our faculty for deams. And as the endeavor became ever more heroic, as the muscles strained toward an ever greater effort, so the horizon and the tragic grandeur of this work took on ever vaster proportions. To such a point that, at the finale, as half of the audience was howling its indignation in the face of a manifestation powerful enough to stand their wretched little lives on their heads, those very voices seemed to harmonize with the orchestra and to take part, as though it were the most natural thing in the world, with that immense and immensely moving clamor raised by the hundred and fifty instruments playing there. Unassailable music, proof against all degradations, closed against all intrusion, and generating the most profound emotion it has been our lot to feel for these many, many years." [11] But Desnos was not the only artist present. Tristan Tzara had to be given four stitches for the wounds he received that night. And as for Joan Miró: "They were howling," he wrote to me. "I have the greatest admiration for his work, and for his integrity as a man. It goes without saying that I couldn't talk about the one without the other." [12]

It was in 1929, while Varèse was playing a game of billiards with his friend Ortiz de Sarate, the painter, in the Café Billiard that the filmmaker Thomas Bouchard first saw the composer; though it was not until 1933, in New York, that he was to become one of the latter's close friends and ask him to write the music for his films on Miró, Léger, and Kurt Seligmann. At this time, in 1929, Varèse used to go regularly to the "Sundays" given by Villa-Lobos. It was there that he met Jean Giono, with whom he became fast friends, the photographer Brassaï, and several others.

It was in 1929 that Varèse began working on *Espace*, which I shall return to later, and sketched out his scenario entitled *l'Astronome*. It was to this work (which was never completed, as I shall explain) that Alejo Carpentier was referring when he wrote: "He is there working on a new piece, a miracle—*The one all alone*—based on a text by Robert Desnos and myself. . . ." [13] Jean Giono was also to collaborate with Varèse: "I have already begun working—in my head—for you," he wrote to Varèse on December 17, 1930. "I have the feeling more and more that with you, and only with you, I know how to walk; you are the only one who has enriched me in Paris, and even then, how long was I with you?" This letter, from such a source, gives one some idea of just how magnetic Varèse's personality was. We also find the famous Russolo inscribing a copy of his *Manifesto*: "To my dear and great friend Edgar Varèse, my soul still filled with the passionate enthusiasm aroused in me by his magnificent *Amériques*. May 29, 1929." The photographer Brassaï has left us a description of the Varèse he met in 1930: "We often met at the Dôme, at the Petit Napolitain, sometimes late at night in the Jockey-Bar. A handsome man, a Maupassant with the mustache shaved off, Varèse had curly hair, gray-blue eyes of a very rare shade, the cold eyes of a conqueror." [14] A journalist on the paper *la Liberté* has also left us a portrait: "His head, topped with a great thicket of hair, is placed on his shoulders like a great cobblestone on top of a rock. Beneath the bushy eyebrows, of the same texture as his hair, the gaze is by turns innocent, mischievous, and often abstracted." [15] Moreover, a photograph taken of him with the ailing Antonin Artaud, in 1932, gives us an idea of the force expressed in Varèse's face at the age of fifty.[17]

During this long stay in Paris, Louise Varèse had rented a little house on the banks of the Yvette, at Garnes, in the valley of the Chevreuse. Varèse would go there weekends to play belote with his friends Alejo Carpentier and Russolo. But the rest of the time he preferred to stay in Paris.

After staying for a while at the Hôtel Paris-New York, he then went to live at 31, rue de Bourgogne; then, in June of 1931, he moved to 3, villa des Camélias, a house which had once belonged to Pascin; then, from 1932 until he left Paris, he lived at 7, rue Bellini.

12

Ionisation

On March 14, 1930, Varèse himself conducted performances of *Octandre* and *Offrandes* in the Salle Chopin, which is part of the Pleyel building. At the same concert, Villa-Lobos and Mihalovici also conducted their own works. The musicologist Adolphe Boschot, a Mozartian, remarked in reference to *Offrandes*: "Perhaps you don't understand? But there are some members of the audience who are applauding, and who think they have understood." [1]

Varèse had for some time been nursing a great project: he wanted to found a music laboratory and a service for the composition of new music. Thanks to Ernst Schoen, who sent me a copy of the document before his death, I have the text of this project as formulated by Varèse at that time.

"Only students already in possession of their technical means will be accepted in the composition class.

"In this department, studies will concentrate upon all the forms required by the new conceptions existing today, as well as the new techniques and new acoustical factors which impose themselves as the logical means of realizing those conceptions.

"Also under Varèse's direction, with the assistance of a physicist, there will be a working laboratory in which sound will be studied scientifically, and in which the laws permitting the development of innumerable new means of expression will be corroborated, outside all empirical rules. All new discoveries and all inventions of instruments and their uses will be demonstrated and studied.

"The laboratory will possess as complete a collection of phonographic records as possible, including examples of the music of all races, all cultures, all periods, and all tendencies."

Even though this project did not come to anything, it is extremely indicative of Varèse's preoccupations. One sees that it was above all else the scientific study of sound, as the foundation for new means of expression, that seemed to fascinate him. And the history of musical instruments teaches us that their appearance has always preceded, by a greater or lesser period of time, and permitted the study of, a great many acoustical phenomena. So that it has taken more than two thousand years, it seems, to arrive at "a scientific explanation of what the very earliest bell founders already knew in China or elsewhere."

Moreover, the historian André Schaeffner has emphasized that primitive man was much more obsessed with particular *timbres* than with *sound* as the physicist knows it. As we know, Varèse was ceaselessly searching for instruments and was also interested in *sound* scientifically. Despite everything, the attitudes of Varèse and primitive man were not so much opposed as they may first appear. Like the primitive man, Varèse sought out the particular timbre which would rejoice his ear and people his dreams. Nevertheless, the instruments he needed were of such complexity—which is to say that their invention was bound to rely more and more upon a technology of such complexity—that it had become a practical necessity for the musician and the technician to work as a team. We must not forget that the instruments of the future would be expected to serve the imagination, the sensibility, and the quest for new sounds of a twentieth century genius, of a contemporary of Braun, not those of a shaman. This is why Varèse's researches are essentially a return to music's origins, and thus, in the profoundest sense, a rebirth. This return to music's origins was something that Varèse accomplished not only in time but also in space. For though he wished to embrace the music and the instruments of past and dead civilizations, this does not mean that he forgot the worlds of sound that have survived and are still alive today among the Japanese, the peoples of India, the Chinese, the Mongols, the Javanese, the Vietnamese, the aborigines of Australia, the headhunters of Borneo, the Aymaras of Peru or Bolivia, and in the multiple cultures of Africa, Europe, etc. We may imagine to what degree of perfection these new instruments were to be brought by the fact that even after the *Poème électronique,* for which Varèse had the most advanced techniques at his disposal, he was still not satisfied. He had still not succeeded in realizing the sounds he could hear inside himself. Even in 1965, the available techniques were still not sufficiently developed.

In 1930, Varèse took part in a roundtable discussion on the future mechanisation of music which also included the writers Ribemont-Dessaignes, Huidobro, Ungaretti, Carpentier, Desnos, and the composer Arthur Lourié. In the course of this discussion, which was taken down in shorthand and published, we find Varèse making some truly extraordinary statements, especially when one considers that this was at the very height of the neo-classical revival. "Now, all the new paths have been opened up to us by actual possibilities: developments in the use of electricity, waves, etc. But it goes without saying that these means should not lead to speculation as to how to reproduce already existing sounds, but, on the contrary, to ways of making possible the realization of new sounds in accordance with new conceptions. . . . The present tempered scale system seems to me worn out. It no longer suffices to provide musical expression of our emotions or conceptions. . . . Nor is it any longer in accord with our need to forge new modes of expression. With the tempered scale system we are restricted to arbitrary rules, whereas we now possess new means which offer us unlimited fields of speculation on the laws of acoustics and logic. Though the two systems can cohabit, of course, the difference being that any new, non-tempered system will be able, because of elasticity, to adapt itself to the exigencies of the former. In fact, one day when I happened to be in an acoustical laboratory of the sort that only exists in America, I noticed that when integral instruments were operated in conjunction with tempered scale instruments, the 'dirtiness' of the sound as a whole which resulted, and which could be improved, came from the interference produced between differing frequencies which, theoretically, according to the systems in use today, ought to have been the same. . . .

"We are still in the first, stammering stages of a new phase of music. . . . The instruments that the electrical engineers must perfect, with the collaboration of musicians, will make possible the use of all sounds—not only arbitrary ones—and also, in consequence, the performance of any tempered scale music. They will be able to reproduce all existing sounds and collaborate in the creation of new timbres; all this depends solely upon the development of known principles. Once adapted to the acoustics of actual halls, they will be capable of putting out unlimited acoustical energy. Until (today) variety in the realm of timbre has been more or less non-existent. Nor can acoustical intensities be very much varied. With the mechanical system, no hope is impermissible, whether from the point of view of timbre or from that of intensity. Taking the sounding elements as one mass, there are possiblilities of subdivisions in relation to that mass: it can be divided into other masses, other volumes, other levels, all by means of loudspeakers arranged in different places, thus giving a sense of movement through space, whereas what we have today is no more than a kind of ideogram. In the bass frequencies, although much improvement is still needed, we have reached the maximum that the human organism can register. Various acousticians have different opinions as to the highest frequencies encompassed by the average human ear. A physicist like Bouasse gave the approximate limit as 38,000 cycles per second, others give it as more. Certain other physicists, basing their opinion upon statistics arrived at in laboratory tests, claim that the average ear, from the age of 40 onwards, cannot hear anything below 10 or above 12,000 vibrations per second. I personally think that we could very safely take an average of 18,000 c.p.s. as a basis to start from, and add at least two octaves to the limits of our present-day instruments with an absolute certainty of their being perceived, and being still within the realm of music. Moreover, it is by no means certain that an ear poorly developed at first may not succeed in improving its auditive faculties." [2]

Even Pierre Schaeffer, when he wrote his book *A la recherche d'une musique concrète*, in 1952, spoke of Varèse only as a magician with percussion. He can have known nothing of the time and energy that that magician had expended on the study of "machines for the production of sound." As early as 1930, for example, Varèse had conceived a path of loudspeakers located in various spots that would really permit the music to move through space. However, it was not

until the realization of his *Poème électronique,* thirty years later, that
this dream was to take actual shape. When Varèse wanted to to start
from an average of 18,000hz as his upper frequency limit he was in
fact very close to reality. It is now known that the average ear can
only perceive "a sinusoidal wave if its frequency falls between ap-
proximately 15hz and 20,000hz." [3] Unfortunately for Varèse, fate
was against him, for the world was now sinking into an era of economic depression. It was a bad moment to attempt the creation of a
laboratory with such very non-commercial aims. Varèse-Gambara was
to say in an interview: "Personally, I am being brought up short
every moment by the poverty of the means of expression at my disposal. Just think, for example, it's impossible to produce a continuous
sound." [4] Attacking musical performers in the same interview, he
added: "The performer, the virtuoso, ought no longer to exist: he
would be better replaced by a machine, and he will be. We shall
find new intensities too, for the realm of sound has still been very
incompletely explored. These ideas still shock a great many people;
but you will see them become realities in the more or less distant
future. . . The composer will have improved, more flexible means
at his disposal with which to express himself. His ideas will no longer
be distorted by adaptation or performance as all those of the classics
were." Needless to say, when Varèse lashed out at virtuoso performers
like this, it was an aggressive reaction. But in fact, he knew perfectly
well that performers would always be necessary to play the music of
the classics. But he himself, how he would have loved to be able to
dispense with interpreters! Again, in the same interview, referring
to music for motion pictures, which was only in its very first beginnings then, he said: "The eye and the ear don't perceive in the
same way, and synchronized music doesn't take this into account.
They insist on recording music played by the usual orchestras,
when in fact the instrumental values are completely distorted. . . .
It is the first modern, scientific means music has so far been given
to escape from the tradition in which it is imprisoned. I myself am
waiting for my first opportunity to have a try at it."

In 1931, Henri Philippon expressed regret in his regular recordings
column that Varèse's works had not yet been recorded. He considered
him one of the three masters of modern music, along with Schoenberg
and Bartók.

On June 6 and 11, 1931, under the auspices of the Pan American Association of Composers, Nicolas Slonimsky conducted the Orchestre des Concerts Straram in two concerts at the Salle Gaveau both of which included *Intégrales*. This time, the result was a great success. Emile Vuillermoz wrote in *Excelsior*: "At last—and it was truly the apotheosis of these concerts—we have heard Varèse's *Intégrales*. Here at last is a work that poses the problem of new orchestration and composition logically. . . Despite its scientific title, this work is not inscrutable and purely cerebral. Of all those that were presented to us here, it is perhaps the most deeply human. It liberates, in effect, the lyricism inherent in pure timbre. There are magnificent possibilities there. Edgar Varèse offers us a foretaste of a new art and a hitherto unknown mode of expression. . . *Intégrales* never for a moment goes outside the enchanted circle of music." [5] Boris de Schloezer remarked: "With *Intégrales*, music acquires as it were a spatial reality, one might say that instead of unfolding in time it exists in space." [6] Alexis Remizov said, in the magazine *Kinéo*: "But what overwhelmed me was, toward the end, Varèse's 'acoustical geometry,' his *Intégrales*." [7] And finally, his friend Le Flem wrote: "There is a tragic anguish, a poignant emotion in this music which is not merely the revelation of new musical processes but also that of present-day man, whose native gentleness is at odds with the brutality and mechanical precision of his age." [8] It is apparent, in short, that the reaction in Paris was an adult one. Certain of the critics, such as Vuillermoz and Le Flem, did not stop at appearances. They were more attracted by the human quality underlying this new esthetic than by its mere novelty. In order to make this step into the Varesian universe the listener must hear the works more than once. Thus, it is clearly very important that the work should be played again, in order that the element of surprise, of superficial shock, may be allowed to fade, enabling us to go on to a higher stage of knowledge. It is only after we have reached this true knowledge that we can speak of a profound relation between listener and work; that we can speak of a manifestation of the work in its fullness, in its beauty, in its uniqueness.

The year 1931 was an important one in Varèse's development. During it, he completed a work that many consider to be one of the masterpieces of twentieth century music: *Ionisation*. Pierrette Mari was to say that Messiaen places this work "very high among the productions of the twentieth century." [9] Begun in 1929, it was completed on November 13, 1931. But is it the first work to employ only percussive instruments, as was once thought? Alfred Frankenstein, writing of Amadeo Roldan's *Ritmicas,* states that these pieces were composed in 1930, and therefore claims that Roldan, not Varèse, was the first composer to use only percussion in a work.[10] Whether this is so or not, the Roldan work is, of course, a very slight one, based on Cuban folk rhythms, and scored for only very few instruments. No. 6 of the series, for example, is based on a rhumba rhythm. So that one can say that *Ionisation* is, in any case, the first Western work for percussion alone which has no basis in folklore. Needless to say, long before either Roldan or Varèse there were compositions for percussion alone in China, in India, in Japan, or in Java. Balinese music is percussion music, after all. Eastern musicians have never had anything to learn from their Western counterparts in the matter of *sound*—quite the contrary; for it proved necessary to wait for the development of new techniques, making new universes of sound possible, before the West was able to affirm itself in this field. This is why, when Varèse conceived a work for percussion instruments alone, he was returning to an age-old tradition. What is really important is that Varèse, in 1931, should have produced a masterwork that together with his previous works, called into question the very meaning of the word *music* as Western composers had understood it until that time. For is *Ionisation* not the first truly *universal* musical entity? It has a profoundly Western logic and structure, and also a plastic beauty worthy of the Orient. That, in my opinion, is the significance and the implication of this work. However, how can we say that *Intégrales,* composed in 1925, did not already contain the same implication?

Ionisation requires an ensemble of thirteen musicians who play a total of thirty-seven percussion instruments including two sirens, one high, one low in pitch.[11] The conductor Robert Craft has analyzed the work as follows: "Each section of *Ionisation* is identified by its own combination of instruments, or range of sonority, and each important change in the substance of the sonority is also a demarcation in the form; the first entrance of the anvils. . . slightly more than half-way through the piece, and the entrance of the piano and chimes, near the end, are the most striking changes of this sort. As in Varèse's other music, dynamics are not adjunctive, but an integral part of the composition. In a piece which is in one sense all rhythmic, Varèse achieves relief by means of rhythmic unisons—the triplets at No. 7, the first loud place, and the fives between No. 8 and No. 9. . . . His achievement is in the sense of progress and development the listener feels from the first bar to the last. *Ionisation* is noble music, capable of exalting the listener. When the masterpieces of the twentieth century are enumerated, it should be on the list, not in first place, perhaps, but there, nevertheless." [12] We will return to *Ionisation* a little later, on the occasion of its first performance, two years later, in New York.

On February 25, 1932, Nicholas Slonimsky conducted the Orchestre Symphonique de Paris in a concert in the Salle Pleyel. One of the works played was *Arcana,* of which this was the first Paris performance. "After the last bar of *Arcana* had faded into silence," René Julliard wrote, "a long time passed before the audience was able to pull itself together and express its surprise and emotion in an enthusiastic and undisputed ovation." [13] Certain critics then alluded to *Le Sacre du Printemps.* Moreover, Stravinsky himself, later on, was to say: "Some of *me* shows through in *Arcana,* too: *Petrushka* at number 9; *The Firebird* at three measures before number 5; and *Le Sacre du Printemps,* at two measures before number 17, and one measure before number 24, and in the section beginning at number 19. . . ." [14] What diligent accountancy! As though a few bars of Gluck in some work by Mozart were sufficient to make the latter into the great creator we know him for! For, in fact, as my friend François Morel has often pointed out to me, the two works, as worlds of sound, are very different indeed. Indeed, pushing the comparison between them even further, we find Frederick Goldbeck, in *La Revue Musicale,* pausing to emphasize the differences between the two composers: "Musically, in *Le Sacre du Printemps,* we have simple themes which cross and quarrel with one another, flogged on by the tonal base; a contrast between the quite amiable motif and the savagery of its presentations. In Varèse, there is no trace of any 'musical psychology' of this kind. The linear material (one does not dare to say thematic) is hewn out of amelodic matter which is governed by augmented fourths, the major seventh, the minor ninth and other

ascetic intervals. Another dissimilarity, this one rhythmic: the parox-
ysms in *Le Sacre du Printemps* contradict and hammer at the square
framework of the periods with metrical punches: contradictions, added
beats, the whole dramatic dynamism of the strongly punctuated bar
wrenching at the regular sway of the rhythm. Varèse, on the contrary,
arcs the rhythmic rebound to the very limit of its tension. In place
of the Stravinskian metre, submerged, trampled, crushed by the osti-
nato, he gives us a rhythm shaken, contracted, twisted by inter-
secting vibrations and resonances, and orchestral bells. Those hackle-
raising syncopations, those arched and straining triplets, listen to
them shake at their bars like wild beasts in a cage—while Stravinsky
blows his bars up with a neatly timed flick on a plunger. . . And
these musical incompatibilities are mirrored in a spiritual divergence
too." [15] Florent Schmitt was to exclaim: "A magnificently stylized
nightmare, a nightmare dreamed by giants."[16] René Julliard perceived and conveyed the dimensions of *Arcana*: "It is a gigantic
step forward or else a return to the very origins of music. . . Varèse
is music in the pure state, the noise of gravitating worlds, the syn-
thetized projection of all the silences and songs of earth and sky. . .
A conception of such vastness is not inhuman but extrahuman. . . ." [17]
One really needs to quote the whole piece. Henri Prunières, on the
other hand, said that he found Varèse's art too cerebral to attract
his sympathy. Lastly, Le Flem observed: "Of all Varèse's works, *Arcana*
appears the most perfect, the most perfectly balanced. . . The orchestra
is carried away in this vertiginous motion. It knows nothing of repose.
The rhythm seizes it and shakes it in the most breathtaking way.
The instruments unleash their tornadoes of sonorities." [18] Again,
I wish I could quote the whole article. The version performed in
1932, and again in 1957-58 under the baton of either Bernstein or
Maderna, was slightly altered and refined in 1960. A comparison of
the two endings makes this clear. The mass of sound in the 1932 version has been cut off, as it were, obliquely. Varèse has eliminated
from his ending a certain solidity that might serve to reassure us.
He now ends the work with a quiet thrill of tension.

After Paris, Slonimsky went on to conduct the Philharmonische
Orchester of Berlin in a concert in the Beethoven Hall there on
March 5, 1932. One can only suppose that the Berlin critics and

audiences were much more conservative than those of Paris. Thus we find the critic of the *Cottbuser Anziger,* summing up the audience's impressions as follows: "At times bored, at times irritated, occasionally involuntarily amused, the audience had borne with the works of the first four composers in patience. With the sound poem entitled *Arcana* by Edgar Varèse . . . they literally flew off the handle." [19] The critic of the *Berliner-Zeitung,* more pretentious than his colleague, decreed: "What strikes one most in Varèse's *Arcana* is the overestimation of the element of sound per se. There is no doubt that music can be constructed on the basis of pure dynamic and rhythmic elements; there is no doubt that the historical evolution of music impelled Varèse toward results of this sort, but Varèse himself is not logical enough to succeed in an experiment of this nature. He abruptly yields to a dramatic and thematic tendency that compromises the originality of the endeavor, which is rather better brought off in Antheil's work." [20] Max Marschalk summed up, in the *Vossische Zeitung,* as follows: "Edgard Varèse abuses the orchestra, one might object. Perhaps he does! But if so what seems an abuse at first quite often comes to seem quite normal later on." [21] The reaction of the Berlin audience confirmed the impression expressed by Varèse himself, on December 22, 1928, when writing in reply to a letter from Ernst Schoen: "What you tell me about the situation in Germany does not surprise me. It is perhaps (certainly even) the most cowardly of all countries from the point of view of intellectual progress. It is a pity that the same spirit of adventure and enterprise that governs their industrial and business undertakings does not rule in this sphere too. . . As for the attitude of the musicians, it is dictated by their thirst for official and academic honors. Pigs racing one another to the trough. . ." It was certainly not pleasant for Varèse to write those harsh words. His severity was all the greater because he had a profound love for Germany. Moreover, at the end of the First World War he had been one of the first members of an association which was trying to achieve the resumption of cultural exchanges with Germany. Elsewhere, referring to the state of music in his country, Hermann Scherchen wrote shortly before his death that in 1933, modern music, being considered a product of Judaeo-Bolshevik decadence, was *officially forbidden.*[22] And the performance of *Arcana* in Berlin took place just one year before Hitler's accession to power. In fact, as may be guessed, that city's reaction to a composition of such power was only one of the many symptoms of the disease from which Germany was suffering at that time. How should a nation, gnawed at by feelings of inferiority, asking only to put its soul in the keeping of some incarnation of God, who would lead it to the summit of power and glory, how should such a nation not have preferred the security of those vast, evocative Wagnerian poems that were, in their eyes, such a faithful mirror of their aspirations? Although his explanation is somewhat over-simplified, Jung was to observe, having studied Germany under Hitler: "It is not without having carefully weighed the pros and cons that one dares to conceive the notion that a people can be suffering in its entirety from, as it were, a psychopathic inferiority." [23] Haunted by greatness, it prefers not to recognize it in others, so as to avoid aggravating the anxiety stirred up by its own feeling of inferiority. Naturally, it is not a question of Germany only; that was only a particular case, occurring at a particular time. Yesterday Germany, tomorrow England or France. One can always explain the failure of great works to some extent by the nature of the ills afflicting the society that rejects them. But here we are in danger of venturing out into territory mined with questions that are doubtless unanswerable in the present state of our knowledge.

13

Ecuatorial

The last address at which Varèse lived in Paris was 7, rue Bellini. It was there that Maurice Richard, from the newspaper *la Liberté,* went to interview him on the occasion of the fiftieth anniversary of Wagner's death. Varèse had this to say: "Wagner's influence? For my part, I don't think it was so disastrous. For one thing, the reaction against it gave us a composer like Debussy, and that in itself is something. Music certainly needs a new Wagner; a force that will wake it up and give it a few punches. Wagner was a very great man, you know, a sort of Michelangelo of music, despite what certain little cliques think on the subject; I can only hope that his detractors will leave music behind them with as much toughness and life in it as certain parts of his work which are still capable of disturbing us today." He then went on to deplore "the extent to which France is losing its prestige abroad," adding: "We need a great Romantic, since it is my opinion, in effect, that all great creators, in science or in art, have been Romantics: genius is Romantic. It is the work that is Classic, after it has survived the test of time." [1]

In a letter to José Rodriguez, later published, Varèse attacks the academicism of the young French school, as well as neo-classicism. Having affirmed that "American music must speak its own language, and not be the result of a certain mummified European formula," he added: "It is disheartening to see the young school here in France

113

becoming zealously academic. The neo-classical ideal does not certainly make for creative effort. It is lassitude constructing a theory by which to excuse itself and this theory has become the fashion. It is perhaps normal at a time of world-wide hesitancy to wish to escape into the categorical past, but life with its exigencies goes on and in the end will sweep away all that is static, all that does not move with the rhythm of life itself. . . . And I see no reason for young American composers coming to study over here if it is to take back a lot of old mannerisms as so many of them have done. You will understand, of course, that I do not speak of those who come to study with masters such as Schoenberg, etc." ² Varèse's attitude over this question of neo-classicism was never to change. He remained savagely opposed to all systems, and to all those who allowed themselves to be imprisoned by them.

In New York, a number of puritans had set out on the warpath against the moral dangers allegedly threatening American students in Paris. The magazine *Musical Courier* interviewed several Americans living in Paris to find out their opinions on this subject. Varèse replied: "I hasten to assure you that the present campaign led by preachers, abetted by the press, seems to me almost too childish for discussion. However, it interests you to know what I think of the pitfalls of Paris; here you are. There may be a certain wicked—if we must have the word—Paris, made up of the international derelicts, rich morons and their hangers-on, pretentious intellectuals and neurotics; I believe that its influence is nil and that it attracts only its own kind.

"Among those who condemn Paris are to be found certain sensation-mongers who, having satisfied their curiosity, can hardly find enough hypocrisy in the whole world to project their virtuous façades. But certainly they must admit that in their 'wicked Paris' they met but few Parisians. And in general the critics of Paris no more understand its true aspect than those Frenchmen, who pass pre-emptory judgment in volumes destined for sensational sales, understand America. I feel suspicious of anyone who sets himself up as a judge of other people's morals, building himself a wall of such lofty morality that one has to wonder what he is hiding behind it.

"As for misguided youth and its suicides, I think it will be found that the highest percentage of youthful suicides occur in countries

1. Varèse, with his brothers and sister (1892-93).

2. Claude Cortot, Varèse's grandfather. (A charcoal sketch by the sculptor Julio Gonzalez, 1908.)

3. Varèse's birth certificate.

PREFECTURE DE LA SEINE

Mairie
du   *Arrondissement

Coût de cette expédition : 1 F
(Décret du 6 octobre 1958)

C   N° 849758

Varèse Edgar   13e Lot — N° 14830

EXTRAIT des Minutes des Actes

de

G.B.

Le vingt-deux décembre mil huit cent quatre vingt-trois à
quatre heures du soir est né Edgard Victor Achille Charles
VARESE , du sexe masculin ./ Marié le 5 novembre 1907 à ***
PARIS I° avec Suzanne BING ./

P.E.C.

PARIS le premier avril mil neuf cent soixante-cinq ./
—/ 12 rue de Strasbourg
Approuvé ce renvoi.

4. Varèse in 1910.

5. Varèse's admission papers to composition class, signed by Fauré.

6. Cover to the first publication of the score of *Hyperprism*, 1924.

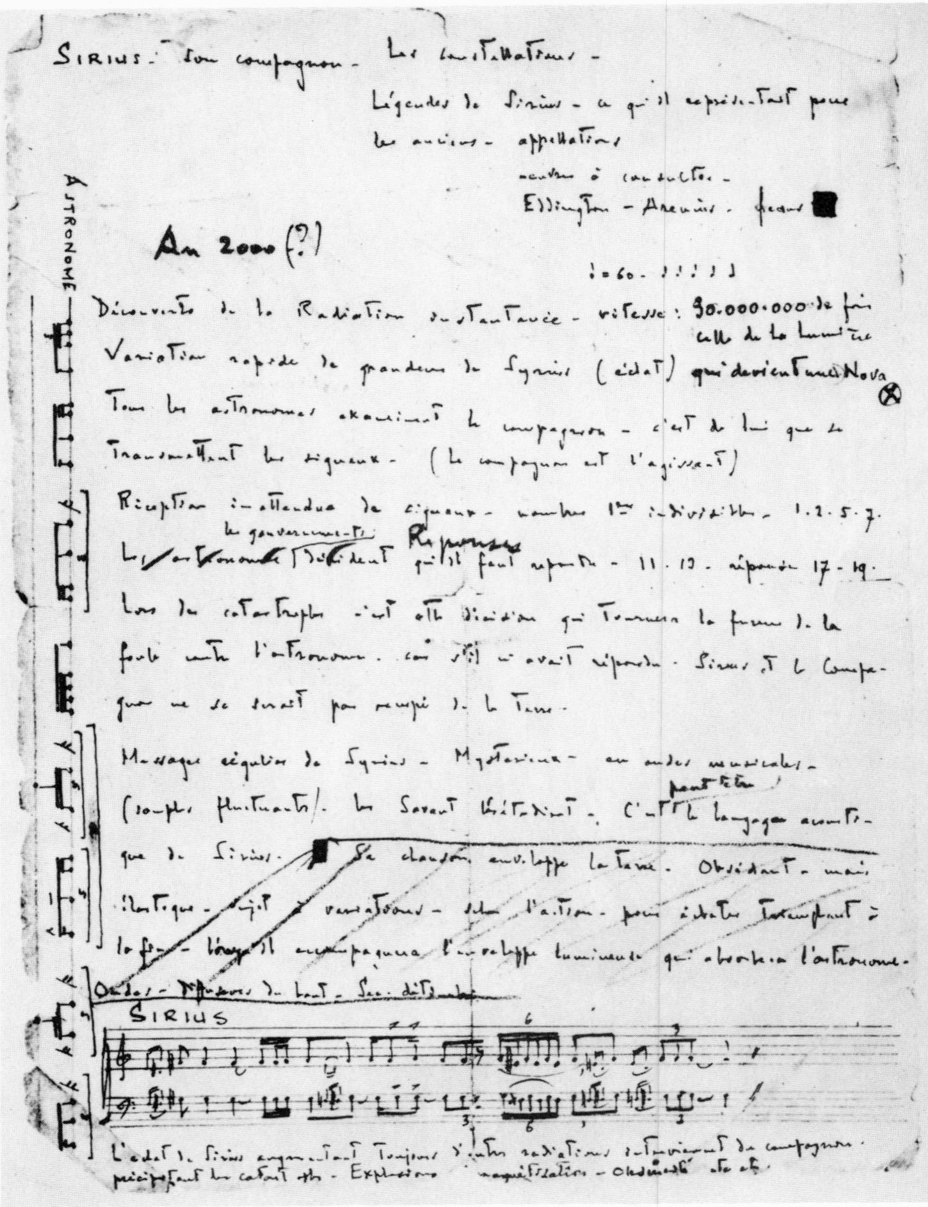

7. The first sketch of *l'Astronome*, 1928.

8. Varèse and Villa-Lobos in Paris, March, 1930.

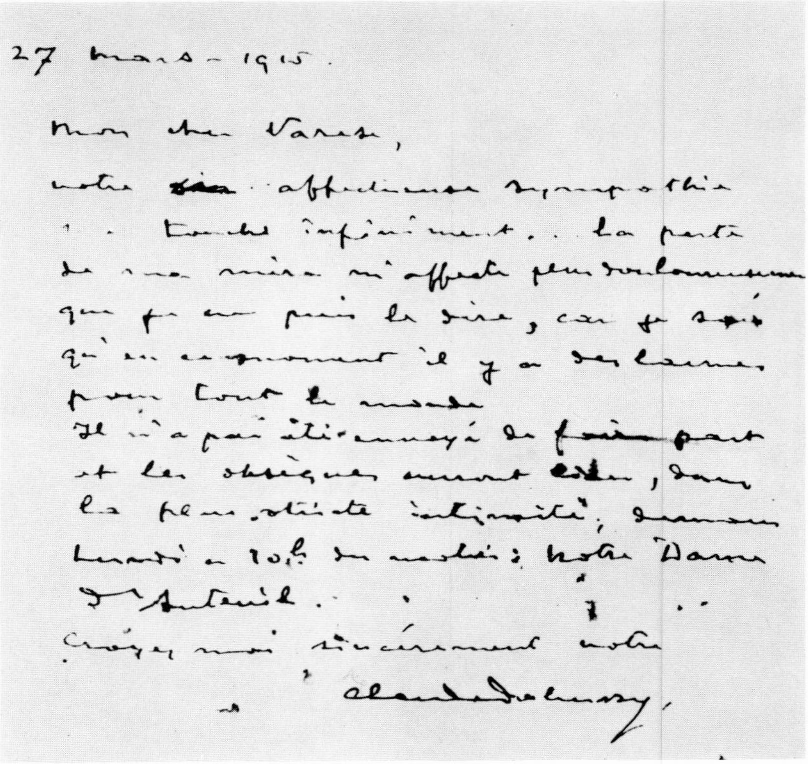

27 mars – 1915.

Mon cher Varèse,

votre affectueuse sympathie m'a touché infiniment. La perte de ma mère m'affecte plus douloureusement que je ne puis le dire, car je sais qu'en ce moment il y a des larmes pour tout le monde.

Il n'a pas été envoyé de faire part et les obsèques auront lieu, dans la plus stricte intimité, demain lundi à 10h du matin: Notre Dame d'Auteuil.

Croyez-moi sincèrement votre

Claude Debussy.

9. A letter from Claude Debussy, and a letter from Richard Strauss.

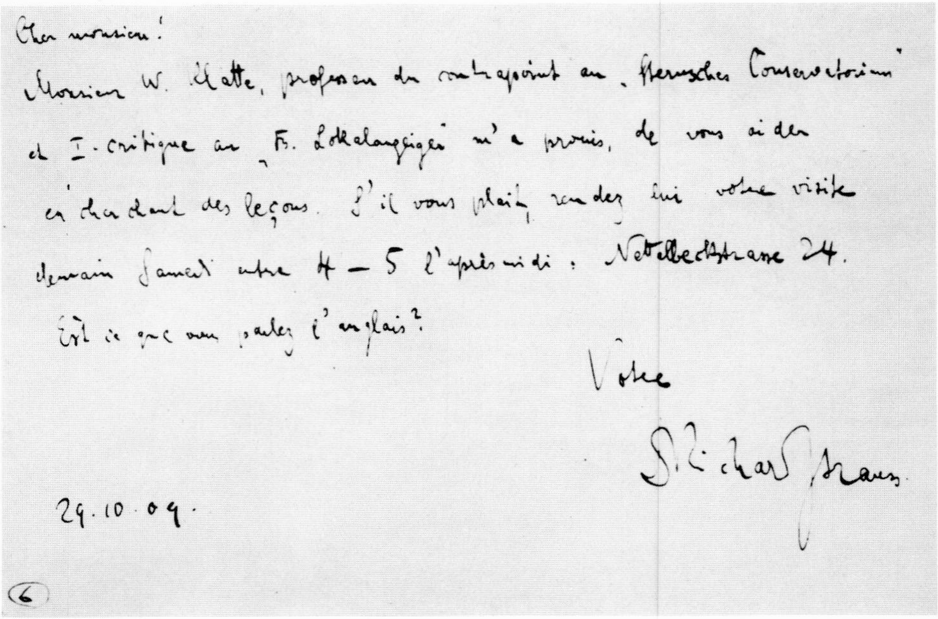

Cher monsieur!

Monsieur W. Klatte, professeur de contrepoint au „Sternsches Conservatorium" et critique au „B. Lokalanzeiger" m'a promis de vous aider en cherchant des leçons. S'il vous plaît rendez lui votre visite demain Samedi entre 4 – 5 l'après midi: Nettelbeckstrasse 24.

Est ce que vous parlez l'anglais?

Votre

Dr. Richard Strauss

29.10.09.

(6)

10. Varèse's gongs, in his studio.

11. A letter from Massenet (1906 or 1907).

12. Edgard and Louise Varèse, 1965.

13. Part of a letter from Romain Rolland.

14. Letter from Varèse to the author, February 3, 1964.

15. Varèse and the author, in front of a poster announcing the première of *Nocturnal* at Town Hall, New York, April 30, 1961.

16. Varèse in 1964.

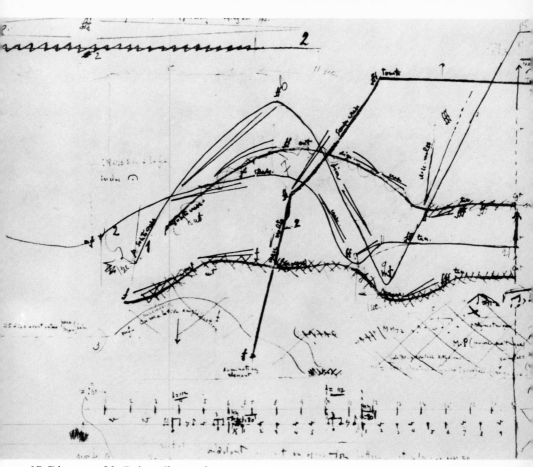

17. Diagram of *le Poème électronique*.

18. Varèse's work table, at the time of his death (1965).

where morality is raised to the rank of a state institution or a profitable business organization. As against the few unbalanced youths who kill themselves in Paris, think of the many others whom Paris has armed with confidence and given the impetus, afoot and lighthearted, to take to the open road."[3] This reply makes it clear that Varèse was of the same French polemical family as, say, Bernanos. He could not tolerate hypocrisy or mediocrity.

It will be remembered, no doubt, that Alejo Carpentier, in his article on Varèse, talked about a work on which the composer was then working and which was based upon a text by Robert Desnos and Carpentier himself. In face, Varèse himself wrote the first scenario for this project, which he entitled *l'Astronome,* as early as 1928, in New York. Was the work to have been an opera? In a sense, though, it would be better to describe it as a work conceived for the stage, or even a public place, in which visual and aural perceptions would have been very closely linked, in which the different means of human expression, such as words, dance, and music, would have been combined in a total spectacle, so that man in his totality could take part in it. Obviously, this idea of a synthesis of the various forms of artistic expression in one work was not new. Varèse had placed his action in the year 2000 A.D. As we shall see, he always remained fascinated by science, and above all by astronomy; the passionate admirer of Paracelsus and Leonardo da Vinci was still there. Varèse was a Renaissance man—a man of the new Renaissance we are living through today. In 1928, we find him jotting down the following notes: "Discovery of instantaneous radiation—speed 30,000,000 times that of light. Rapid variations in the size of Sirius (explosion) which becomes a Nova. All the astronomers examine the Companion (of Sirius) —this is where the signals are being transmitted from. (The Companion is the active agent). Unexpected reception of signals—prime numbers 1, 3, 5, 7. The governments decide they must answer 11,12. The answer to that is 17,19. When the catastrophes occur, it is this decision which will turn the fury of the mob against the astronomer, since if he had not replied, Sirius and the Companion would not have taken any notice of Earth. Regular messages from Sirius. Mysterious—in musical waves (supple, fluctuating). The Wise Men study them. Perhaps it is the acoustical language of Sirius. The brightness of Sirius is still increasing, other radiations come in from the Companion, precipitating the catastrophes. Explosions, darkness, etc." It is evident that from a certain point of view Varèse was predicting radioastronomy and radio-sources as early as 1928. In the margin of this first sketch, Varèse had written in the musical themes for Sirius and the Astronomer. For example the theme for Sirius (the wave theme) was to be scored for the ondes Martenot. Subsequently, Varèse elaborated this first sketch and gave it a more concrete form on the dramatic level.

"The sky. A summer's night. All the constellations will grow pale as Sirius grows more and more intense. Milky ways.

The height of the tower can be sensed. Low down in the distance, the city. Chorus, voices, astronomer.

A voice: The point, the point, it's getting bigger.

Shouts, circle, horizon, Equator, light of a world.

Eye! Dizziness! Red! Aldebaran!

Exploding altogether—Sirius!

Dizzying space

One light alone on everything that exists!

Distant voices—We know. We know.

Sirius and his Companion glow.

And the Companion is the master now.

And Sirius obeys.

(The Star shines. First signals. Projections of prime numbers, 1, 3—1, 3—1, 3, (at intervals).

After the catastrophes, the rising flood of stupor and fear, the mob wants its revenge on the astronomer. A voice emerges from the mob, calling for the astronomer's death. The tower is attacked, and we hear the noise of the *drill*.

Drill and cries cease. Great knell tolled in the orchestra, then further signals from the astronomer and the star's answer. Stupefied murmurs from the petrified mob.

FINAL

1. Reprise of drill, rays, and dance.

Harangue of Herald and the inspired Negro, quite short. Brief silence.

2. Second knell from orchestra. Then signals from astronomer to star—which fails to answer them.
A voice cries out: I'm afraid.

3. Threatening shouts and sound of drill again. Anger of mob.

4. The beam from the star twists down suddenly, transfixes the astronomer, disintegrates him, absorbs him.

5. The choir howls out that a miracle has happened. The mob ceases to revile the astronomer: reversal of attitude—he is made into a saint.

6. The mob is turned to stone. The spotlights are turned into the auditorium, blinding the spectators.
> The tower is empty. Universal and petrified silence. a few wax figures staring in front of them with fixed stares and no expression."

This second sketch, of which I have only transcribed the beginning and the end here, took up several pages. It was this scenario that Varèse handed over to Robert Desnos and Alejo Carpentier in 1928 as a basis on which to work. But that collaboration didn't come to anything. Consequently, in 1932, or early in 1933, Varèse entrusted his project to Antonin Artaud. Paule Thévenin has published the text of the resulting scenario in the second volume of Artaud's *Oeuvres complètes*.[4] The poet had called it: *The firmament is gone*. Apparently Artaud conceived the work in five movements, though he only finished four of them. However, Louise Varèse has since told me that Carpentier's earlier sketch was nearer to the atmosphere of "fear and mystery" that Varèse wanted to create. In 1934, Artaud had still not heard any of Varèse's compositions. Indeed, he wrote in a copy of his *Héliogabale ou l'anarchiste couronné*, which appeared in 1934: "To my dear Edgar Varèse, whose music I love without having heard it. Both because hearing you talk about music has enabled me to dream of it, and because I know that with your music in revolt we shall all be able to look forward again to a new state of the world, affectionately, Antonin Artaud." Then Varèse didn't hear from Artaud for a while. On December 28, 1935, he wrote to point this out: "I'm astonished not to have heard from you. How are you getting on with the work? I would very much like to have whatever you've already done—even if it's only the outline we sketched out in Paris—so as to have it on me when I go out—when the brain is storing things up and working them out. Think of all the changes we shall have to make in the texts—and all the time that will be wasted mailing them to and fro. The fact is, I'd like to apply myself seriously to this work in the late spring, during my stay in Mexico.

"I've already told you that it will be possible for me to have the instruments I envisage built. It is some time now since I wrote asking you to send me copies of your Theater of Cruelty manifesto by return, since I was supposed to pass them on to some people who had agreed to take a very active interest in you. No reply. A pity. Things move fast over here. Lost opportunities don't come again. They don't like things that have been warmed over. . . ." But Artaud was ill. Finally, in spite of everything, Varèse did receive a version of *The firmament is gone*. However, that version, now in my possession, is different in some respects from the text published by Paule Thévenin, which was probably a later draft.

Giacometti used to say: "A work that didn't come off, a work that did come off, that doesn't mean a thing. Failure interests me just as much as success. Weaknesses are just as apparent in successful works as in the others." [5] One might say, equally well, that the knowledge of a creator's great yearnings and great, almost unrealizable visions tells us as much about his being as the works he did in fact realize. That is why I find it strange that Brassaï was evidently unable to suppress a certain degree of amusement when recounting the outline that Varèse once gave him of this project: "One evening," he writes, "in a little café, having first insisted on my promising absolute secrecy in the matter, Varèse told me about the scenario of the opera he was going to write. The scene was an observatory, and the hero an astronomer. The latter rakes the sky with his telescope. He rakes it . . . with such avidity that as the stars grow progressively bigger and bigger so they become also more and more threatening and end up by absorbing him completely. . . But, in the final scene, when the astronomer is volatilized into interstellar space, factory sirens and airplane propellers were supposed to come into action. Their 'music' was to be as strident and unbearable as possible, so as to terrify the audience and render it *groggy*, as he put it. At that moment, he told me, the powerful spotlights supposedly raking the sky up on stage would be turned abruptly down into the auditorium, blinding the audience and filling

them with such panic that they wouldn't even be able to run away." [6]
This dream of Varèse's was never realized. But by reading Artaud's
published scenario we can gain some idea of what the work might
have been from the dramatic point of view. We shall never know what
the music would have been for that dialogue between the man,
threatened by the mob, and Sirius, who, to protest him, distintegrates
him by drawing him up into his beams so that he can then "ressusci-
tate" him. There is an end-of-the-world, apocalyptic atmosphere about
this idea that can only be felt on the level of terror, of mystery. How
can one not think of that "shadow" on a wall in Hiroshima, the
shadow of the man who was disintegrated by the bomb: only his
shadow remained, for the wall had been protected by the man's body.
Thus, almost twenty years after Varèse's "dream," men were indeed
disintegrated. Nonetheless, it is questionable whether the necessary
technical means then existed to enable Varèse's music to attain its
esthetic aims. The work would have required at least the same quality
and power in its technical means of expression as was available for
the *Poème électronique* in Brussels. In 1930 or 1935 we were still a
long way from that kind of quality, and electronics was still in its
infancy.

In 1933, Diego Rivera offered Louise and Edgard Varèse one of
his houses so that they could settle for a while in Mexico. However,
they decided to go back to New York, to their house on Sullivan
Street. It was Trotsky, some while later, who moved into Rivera's villa.

On August 3rd, Varèse left Paris with Jolivet for Barcelona, where
he stopped to visit his friend Miró, and then to Madrid. Louise Varèse
had decided she would rather spend the summer in Grenoble. At the
end of the summer, she embarked on the *de Grasse* and was rejoined
by her husband in the Spanish port of Vigo. They then sailed on to
New York, which they reached, after a short stopover in Lisbon, on
September 27th.

On March 6, 1933, while Varèse was still in Paris, Nicolas Slonimsky
conducted the first performance of *Ionisation*, in Carnegie Hall,
New York, under the auspices of the Pan American Association of
Composers. Paul Rosenfeld immediately grasped its implications:
"*Ionisation,* the wonderful, terrifying new composition by Edgar
Varèse appears to have been not at all fantastically named by its

composer. By reason of their excessive hardness, excessive indeter-
minacy and other points of dissemblance from the more humanly
vibrating sonorities of string and wind instruments, the tones of the
forty-one percussion and friction pieces . . . in themselves do suggest
the life of the inanimate universe. The illusion, if illusion it be, of
an analogy between the music and events or processes in the physio-
chemical fields, is re-enforced by the volumes of the extremely simpli-
fied, skeletalized form, which explosive, curiously timed and curiously
responsive to one another, further suggest incandescent manifestations
of material entities in space. . . . The new work is a complete if
singular piece of music: as complete a one as any of the best of its
prodigious elder brethren, Varèse's compositions for mixed orchestra;
and *their* solidity, let it be here affirmed, is by no means apparent only
to members of what will vulgarly be called Varèse's clique. . . ." [7]
But Rosenfeld was an exceptional critic. I have the impression, having
read the only other criticism I have been able to unearth, that the
audience was deeply bewildered; the critic from the magazine *Musical
Courier* wrote: "Varèse's latest effort (played twice) contains almost
nothing of traditional tonal quality, being scored for various Gatling
gun species of percussion, a dolorous and quaintly modulated siren,
sleigh bells and an ingenious instrument that imitated the voice of an
anguished bull. Toward the end of this strange work, which moved
even earnest devotees of the musically esoteric to smiles, there was a
slight undercurrent of the lyrical in some muted tones of a piano
and a celeste." [8] All that the *New York Herald Tribune* critic had to
say was: "What with the vicissitudes of attending simultaneous musical
performances at different points, the reviewer unfortunately missed
Mr. Varèse's first new work to be made public here in several
years. . . . " [9] Doubtless that eminent gentleman had preferred to
settle for the security of a concert given by some great star conductor.
But we must not be unjust. Who could really be equal to the task of
evaluating a work of this scope, so radically original and of such importance in the history of music? *Ionisation* set living forces in motion
whose effects will never cease to be felt. And indeed, it is in its very
essence a fresco of movement, of the great word of movement. Anyone
who neglects its epic dimension, during the performance, allowing
himself to be hypnotized by numbers, does not know how to subject

number to poetry, and without poetry *Ionisation* no longer exists, life
no longer exists.

After this first performance in New York, Slonimsky conducted
Ionisation again in Havana, in late April of 1933; then Henry Cowell
conducted the work, in July, in San Francisco. The critic of the
San Francisco Examiner, Redfern Mason, exclaimed: "Atonal phan-
tasmagoria. So striking. So novel and, at the same time, so beautiful
that it catches your breath." [10] The critic sent from the *Los Angeles
Times* wrote: "Not one serious listener would have missed the im-
pressiveness of this work in which form, expressed in phrasing and
dynamics, was as finely followed as in one of the classic conceptions
of a countrapuntal master. Moreover, the work is significant in its
pure concern with the methodic possibilities of percussion instruments, heretofore regarded as incapable of such functioning. Emotional depths are touched by *Ionisation* as by a sculptural masterpiece
of geometric abstraction." [11] It is evident that one must sometimes go
outside the great metropolises, such as New York, in order to find a
simpler, more lucid, more generous receptiveness.

In 1932, there appeared a French translation of *Legends of Guatemala* by Miguel Angel Asturias, the Guatemalan poet and novelist.
The translation was by Francis de Miomandre, and Paul Valéry had
written a preface to the volume. Asturias knew Varèse. He had even
expressed his impressions of *Arcana* in an article entitled *"En la Jaula
de la Torre Eiffel."* [12] It was for this reason that he sent him a copy of
the French translation of his book with this inscription: *"To Edgar
Varèse, Maestro—mago de los sonidos estas Légendes de Guatémala,
con toda mi admiración y afecto, Asturias, 1932."* The great novelist
was then living in Paris, as was the Cuban Carpentier, and the
Chilean poet Huidobro. Varèse was wonderstruck and shaken by the
Popol-Vuh texts Asturias had chosen. He was particularly taken with
a great prayer of supplication that was to become the foundation text
for his own work *Ecuatorial*. However, Varèse knew Spanish quite
well. He therefore used the original text.[13] Few pieces of writing could
have suited him better, could have corresponded more closely to his
own tragic nature than this vast and noble Mayan incantation which
rolls forth in the same accents as David's Psalms. It is the prayer

of a people who stand upright, at once respectful and proud, as they address their gods. They ask for sons and daughters, for maize, and for peace between men. They ask that evil, moral as well as physical, shall be kept from them. They do not ask for riches, they ask for peace. They mention only their elementary needs, the only essential ones. We should not forget that at the time when Varèse was inspired by this sacred text, the depression was still at its height. At a time when so many men were going hungry, Varèse was struck by this prayer because it gives men an authentic sense of values. Thus, the choice of this text takes on the character of a revolt against the robot world, against the power wielded by the sharks of the financial world. This is truly, as Artaud put it, "music in revolt." And this is the work that Varèse was to complete in the United States, after his five-year stay in Paris. *Ecuatorial* is perhaps for Varèse what *Socrate* was for Satie. In the case of both works, one can certainly speak of austerity, of starkness.

Varèse was to write to Odile Vivier: "*Ecuatorial* was a title that had a fairly geographical connotation, suggesting to me as it did the regions in which the Pre-Colombian arts had flourished. I wanted to give the music a little of that rough-hewn and elemental intensity that characterized their strange and primitive works. It should be performed as a drama and an incantation, guided by the imploring fervor of the text, and following the dynamic markings of the score." The work is dedicated to Varèse's wife. It is composed for a choir of bass voices (though for the last performance in his lifetime, confronted with a choir's lack of sensitivity, Varèse chose to go back to the solo bass voice of the original 1934 version), four trombones, four trumpets, piano, organ, two ondes Martenot, and a percussion section comprising kettledrums, drums, two tom-toms, cymbals, including one hanging cymbal, "temple blocks," and side-drums. The choir sings in unison throughout. In the first version, as I have just indicated, he had conceived the choir part as sung by a solo bass voice amplified by means of a megaphone. In that version he also used two ondes Teremine. For the first time, according to Odile Vivier, he was to attain "sounds as high as eleven thousand five hundred cycles per second." [14] Despite this, however, the ondes Teremines used then were still rather primitive instruments. One can imagine the audience's reaction at the first performance. *Ecuatorial* is a great work, austere and dense, as befits an incantation and a cry to the gods. The directions given in the score as to how the choir should perform it are particularly noteworthy.

The first performance of *Ecuatorial*, and the only one for more than twenty-five years, took place on April 15, 1934, in New York's Town Hall, with Slonimsky conducting. The soloist was Chase Baromeo. The conductor had also planned *Ionisation* as a part of the same program. The critic from the magazine *Trend* gave proof of great intelligence in his reaction to *Ecuatorial* when he wrote: "No description could convey an idea of the unusual instrumental coloring achieved with this combination, or convince anyone, who has not heard it, of the primordial cataclysmic power of the work. Certain imperfections in the still new theremins marred the ensemble now and then and technical difficulties muddied an occasional passage. But these were faults in the performance and not in the conception, and will be eliminated in the course of time." [15] If only all critics had enough intelligence, imagination, and humility to suspend their anathemas when faced with a composition which, for strictly technical reasons, is able to attain its full effect only with time! The true creator must take risks—and does take them! Throughout the history of music, daring has been a sign of genius. Risk is one of creation's dialectical elements. Even Mozart, often misunderstood, did not hesitate to write works of total beauty for Franklin's newly invented glass harmonica. And the risk Varèse took was immeasurably greater, since his revolution was a radical one, since he was attacking music's basic equipment, its very means of expression. This meant that he was inevitably bound to employ at least some instruments that had not yet been perfected in performances of his works. He knew that the instrument which would fulfill the intentions of his score would be invented one day. To return to the impressions of some of the critics, W. P. Tryon, an admirer of Varèse since 1922, as we have seen, had this to say of *Ecuatorial:* "Perhaps Mr. Slonimsky misconceived its latitude somehow and got mixed about the unusual score. He may have been too explicit and literal with the unusual score. . . . No doubt he overemphasized detail and so tended to destroy the main effect. After the manner, again, of early Wagnerian conductors, he permitted the instruments to cover the voice." [16] Here is another critic's reaction: "Mr. Varèse has written music that has power and atmosphere. It is sometimes unclear: a welter of sound obscures any central meaning in such pages. The theremins gave the work an unearthly quality at times; in some passages they were mere caterwauling. . . . As for Mr. Varèse's *Ionisation*, it suggested possibilities, but in itself it could hardly be called music." [17] The *New York Herald Tribune* critic remarked: "The music, however, seemed more fitted to a text more miniatory than the one to which it was set." [18] Doesn't that seem extraordinary? Varèse had been inspired by the Popol-Vuh text, without it there would have been no *Ecuatorial*, and now someone tells him he chose the wrong text. . . As for the reporter from *Musical America*, he was indignant at the "raucous cacophony that almost drowned the fine voice of Mr. Baromeo." [19] The failure of *Ecuatorial* could not help but force upon Varèse's attention yet again the extent to which he was being paralyzed by the slowness of technological progress. He was being impelled to go on fighting with a crossbow or an old bronze cannon when what he needed were ballistic missiles!

In the spring of 1934, Michael Sperling devoted a long article in the magazine *Trend* entirely to Varèse. The composer was given the opportunity of saying what he thought about various questions. Sperling introduced him in this way: "Of medium height, but powerfully built, with a shock of steel wool for hair, he displays in every gesture, in every expression of his mobile, swarthy face, the restless energy that animates him. Such an energy is indeed needed in a man who can be the impulse behind a new form of expression, who can, so to speak, set it on its feet and give it propulsion. For it is Varèse more than any other who had the boldness of spirit and the conviction of mind to play a light, for America, on modern music." On the subject of star-performers, Varèse delivered himself of what was at that time a very courageous judgment: "There was change—witness Cézanne and Picasso—but in the art of the ear there were the obstacles of the virtuoso and the conductor, men like Toscanini who used music simply as a means of self-glorification. It was in their power to decide what to play and how to play it—always with an eye to showing themselves off in the best light, regardless of the intention of the music." Then Varèse gave an explanation of the aims of the Pan American Association of Composers: "The Pan American was begun because I realized that Europe was drifting back to neo-classicism, or rather what is so-called, there really being no such possible thing. You can't make a classic; it has to become one with age. What is called neo-classicism is really academism. This influence we wished to combat is a vicious thing, for it stifles spontaneous expression, and we could combat it by performing work that was alive, that spoke for itself forcefully and truly, even if awkwardly. . . . In this connection it is interesting to note that for the first time in the history of the world it is the youth that is reactionary." Next, Varèse gave his opinions about Stravinsky, Schoenberg and dodecaphonic music: "I think that Stravinsky is finished, and I believe that Schoenberg is of much greater importance. But on the other hand, while Schoenberg's music will undoubtedly leave its impress on the future, his 'system' is not likely to, it being to music what the Cubists are to painting. This 'system' of atonality simply does not exist; it is a fallacy of thought, for we feel a tonality whether or not we deny its presence. It is not necessary to have a tonic with its third and fifth to establish tonality—for what is this chord but a fundamental with its second and third overtones? Whether he is called an atonalist or not, Schoenberg is a romanticist in conception and an impressionist in execution; while Debussy is in conception a symbolist but in the working out of his composition an impressionist." (In about 1960, in conversation with the German critic H. H. Stuckenschmidt, Varèse was to say: "You still have dodecaphonic music over there? You're so academic, you Europeans, aren't you?") Then Varèse gave his opinion on the importance of music and architecture: "Music and architecture are the only arts alive today— architecture because of the need of it, and out of which an aesthetic sense will grow; music because it is the one art capable of reaching the masses. Architecture, however, does not necessarily crystallize the tendency of the day. In present-day architecture, it is mass, planes and volume that count." He ended with a few reflections on orchestration: "The orchestra, in the present sense of the word, like the virtuoso, is finished. Therefore orchestration, as we call it, must revert to its original meaning; must become part and parcel of the substance itself. From this it follows that Rimsky-Korsakov was a poor orchestrator and Brahms a good one. The composition itself is the orchestration. You can't write a piece of music and then say that you will orchestrate it; both processes must be accomplished in the one stroke, for orchestration is the response to the musical content of the work." [20]

14

The Abyss

1935 . . . The historian Maurice Baumont characterized this period briefly as follows: "Everywhere the individual self is handing in its resignation, and the emphasis is being placed on 'the man in the street,' on the tastes of the 'average citizen.' Freedom of thought is no longer fashionable. . . . It is the masses that are imposing their desires and their tastes on culture. . . . Nonconformity is treated as treason. . . . The individual is being 'brought to heel'. . . ." [1] Then he quotes Paul Valéry: "The situation and credit of thought have never been so much reduced or so much disputed." [2] Needless to say, the diffusion of "culture" among the masses is a step forward. At last, and perhaps for the first time in history, whole peoples were able to attain a consciousness of the spiritual light that irradiates humanity, were able to draw sustenance from it and set forward into the future. The individual was obliged to call his individuality into question, to consider the deep roots of his sociality, of his existence, as essentially a question of relationship. He was, if you wish, a center of gravitation within gravitation. It was therefore natural enough that this awakening to new and more complex values should have led to confusion or even in some cases, such as that of Fascism, to disaster. This is why we are now witnessing a phenomenon of "massification," a process of reducing everything to uniformity through the intermediary of the great new methods of communication—the *mass media*. It is natural that the individual should have sensed his fragility, become aware of his vulnerability in a society in the throes of an economic crisis which was in no way organized, structured, to deal with its real social problems. But what is, in my opinion, a degradation is to try to act in accordance with the tastes of the masses as such, and to consider them as normative in the realm of art, which is essentially and above all the realm of creation and of liberty. Even Trotsky understood that perfectly well. One cannot, for example, create proletarian literature. The masses, by definition, have neither will nor vision. That is why to take them as the foundation of new values is to kill the mind and its expansion into works of art by means of creation, in other words, its expansion into the universe. It is in this sense that 1935 was a dangerous time for creation and for creators in all realms of subjective expression. The bonfire of "mass culture" threatened to consume everything. On another level, Roosevelt was launching his program of social and economic reforms known as the New Deal. It was at this critical moment that there began what one may call a period of crisis, of depression, in Varèse's life. (Needless to say, such an event in the deepest levels of any man's life cannot be neatly bounded by mere dates. All we can say is that the thing occurred at about this time.) This man who was a creator, an individual in the fullest sense of the term, found himself in opposition to a social organization and to a mentality which were in fact contradictory to the meaning of his life and came near to destroying him. He would have nothing to do with the inertia of the men who prefer "intellectual comfort," the slow assimilation of what has been, instead of the risk inherent in the necessary mutations that all living beings must face up to. And lastly, the most tragic part of all, Varèse as a creator was at the same time haunted by a vision of what a musical work should be and also perpetually prevented from making that vision into a reality by the indifference of those who enable technicians, inventors, scientific researchers, to live. For the capitalist is his own servant, or else the servant of the image he has of the "average man", an image which is doubtless nothing but the projection of his own vision of what the world should be. Baumont, referring to this figure, was to say: " 'the average man,' no matter what class he belongs to, has set ideas about everything. Made confident by his own mediocrity, he knows nothing, meddles with everything, and has an answer for everything. Stuffed with all the facile ideas into which he has been initiated by the democratization of culture . . . the stultifying simplicity of slogans . . . This herd member . . . robot. The mass, daughter of modern techniques, has all the rights, and everything is sacrificed to it; it has replaced quality in the same way as the organization has replaced the individual." [3] And even though one has to be wary of this concept of the *masses*—now that we are acquainted with the findings of microsociology and social psychology—there is some truth in what Baumont says. It was against this "average man," this fossilized creature, sometimes in the guise of a company director, sometimes in that of an advisory member to some foundation or other, that Varèse undertook to struggle from 1932 onward. For his true problem as a creator was that he no longer wished to compose, at that time, for old instruments. He said so categorically in a letter to Professor Teremine: "I no longer wish to compose for the old instruments played by men, and I am handicapped by a lack of adequate electrical instruments for which I conceive my music." [4] This is why all his efforts were now to be directed towards facilitating the invention of new instruments. He was being devoured, as it were, by his own inner and unappeasable vision. He could not free himself from the sounds that were inflaming his soul. It was only later, after he had found the way to that new universe of sound and been able, after much suffering and sifting, after many years, to make it a reality, that he was to return, like one new born, to traditional musical instruments.

In 1932, he got into touch with Dr. Fletcher, director of acoustical research in the laboratories of the Bell Telephone Company. He wrote to him on December 1st: "It gave me great satisfaction to know that you are so entirely in sympathy with my ideas and that you too feel that there is a real need of an organization for the type of work I outlined in my application. I am perfectly convinced that any concern willing to set up such a branch, where I could work in collaboration with its own scientists, would be fully repaid for its investment (negligible where there is already an acoustical laboratory installed) not only from the point of view of art and science but also materially in the application of the results obtained.

"You saw by my outline that my objectives are two-fold: acoustical research in the interest of pure music and the working out and application of certain results for the improvement of the Sound Film—

with other ramifications, radio, etc. It is naturally along the latter lines that I look to gain the interest of any organization in my collaboration.

"As I told you, it is in order to continue, at least for one more year, my work both of research and composition, that I applied for a Guggenheim fellowship. As things are now I shall be forced to earn a living entirely outside music. And my preoccupation is the fear of having to go into something where I should no longer have the time nor opportunity for the work in sound which is of such vital importance—to say nothing of my composition. That is why I am looking to find a situation in a company organized for the sort of work in sound where my collaboration would have value and be worth a pecuniary return. To make money does not interest me. I only desire to have sufficient for my actual needs so that not having to worry about money I can give all my energy to work.

"May I ask you frankly whether you think that your own company or any other with which you have connections could be brought to consider my proposition. It would be a great joy to me to be able to collaborate uninterruptedly with you. Will you be so good as to consider seriously my request and let me know your opinion." [5] Then, without waiting for this reply, Varèse also applied to Henry Allen Moe of the John Simon Guggenheim Memorial Foundation. The latter replied on January 23, 1933, asking him for further details and explanations. Varèse then wrote again, on February 6th: "The acoustical work which I have undertaken, and which I hope to be able to continue, in collaboration with René Bertrand, consists in experiments which I have suggested on his invention: the Dynaphone. The Dynaphone (invented 1927–28) is a musical instrument of electrical oscillations somewhat similar to the theremin, Givelet and Martenot electrical instruments. But its principle and operation are entirely different, the resemblance being only superficial. The technical results I look for are as follows:

"1. To obtain absolutely pure fundamentals.

"2. By means of loading the fundamentals with certain series of harmonics, to obtain timbres which will produce new sounds.

"3. To speculate on the new sounds that the combination of two or more interfering Dynaphones would give if combined in a single instrument.

"4. To increase the range of the instrument so as to obtain high frequencies which no other instrument can give, together with adequate intensity. . . .

"The practical result of our work will be a new instrument which will be adequate to the needs of the creative musician and of the musicologist. I have conceived a system by which the instrument may be used not only for the tempered and natural scales, but one which also allows for the accurate production of any number of frequencies and consequently is able to produce any interval or any subdivision required by the ancient or exotic modes." It is scarcely necessary to add that the venerable Guggenheim Foundation did not even begin to understand Varèse's proposals, and that it must have found such precoccupations strange, to say the least. After all, it later refused a request from Henry Miller. Moreover, it also goes without saying that no commercial firm had any desire to engage itself in research of this nature at a time when the "average man" had so many other needs to be attended to. If one wanted to make money, there were so many other ways. So it was that Varèse found himself truly paralyzed, inasmuch as his creative requirements were for timbres and sounds that only those new instruments could have given him. Besides which, these rejections, this indifference, could not help but be—and were—psychologically disastrous. He was to remain thus torn between his needs and the meagerness of his means. Even without the unwritten *Astronome*, we have *Espace* as a sort of testimony to this long despair—which was to result in Varèse's twelve years of silence. At that time, *Espace* meant another agonizing tussle with traditional instruments at the very moment when he began to despair of ever seeing his acoustical dreams take on reality. This dialectic between aspiration and means was all the more terrible in that it was experienced by a creator of the utmost power and lasted for so long a time. That is why this inward rift was even to manifest itself in a physical illness, and above all in the temptation to kill himself, in a veritable obsession with suicide as the struggle reached its peak of intensity. Thus both mind and body, in their own ways, were to rise in revolt against the intolerable constraint being imposed upon them. Varèse destroyed all his sketches, refused to compose, and wanted to change his *trade*. And at the same time as he was was subjecting himself to this ruthless purge, his previous works either slid into oblivion or were laughed at. He was fifty-two.

Varèse first had the idea of a work entitled *Espace* in Paris, in 1929. It was then that he sketched out the argument that Dorothy Norman was later to publish in *Twice A Year*, 1941, in a more fully worked-out version. It was this text that Henry Miller reproduced in his *Air-conditioned Nightmare*. I also included it in *Visages d'Edgard Varèse*, though erroneously entitled *Déserts*. In fact, the piece is a sort of scenario with all the intensity of a manifesto. The words are obviously meant to be spoken, to convey the rhythm and sense of forward movement that were to charge the work with a sort of electrical energy

"Theme: TODAY. The world awake! Humanity on the march. Nothing can stop it. A conscious humanity neither exploitable nor pitiable. Marching! There is only going. Millions of feet endlessly tramping, treading, pounding, striding, leaping.

"Rhythms change: quick, slow, staccato, dragging, racing, smoothe. The final crescendo giving the impression that confidently, inexorably the going will never stop . . . projecting itself into space. . . .

"Voices in the sky, as though magic, invisible hands were turning on and off the knobs of fantastic radios, filling all space, criss-crossing, overlapping, penetrating each other, splitting up, superimposing, repulsing each other, colliding, crashing. Phrases, slogans, utterances, chants, proclamations. China, Russia, Spain, the Fascist states and the opposing Democracies all breaking their paralyzing crusts.

"What should be avoided: tone of propaganda as well as any journalistic speculating on timely events and doctrines. I want the epic impact of today stripped of its mannerisms and snobbisms.

"I suggest using, here and there, snatches of phrases of American, French, Russian, Chinese, Spanish, German revolutions like shooting stars, also recurring words poundingly repeated like hammer blows or throbbing in an underground ostenato, stubborn and ritualistic.

"I should like an exultant, even prophetic tone, the writing, however, lean and bare, active, almost like the account of a prizefight, blow for blow, the audience kept keyed-up, tense and unconscious of the style of the announcer.

"Also some phrases out of folklore, for the sake of their human, near-the-earth quality. I want to encompass everything that is human, from the most primitive to the farthest reaches of science." [6] It is evident that Varèse had a vision of the world, of humanity's oneness, similar to that of a man like Teilhard de Chardin. It has an epic grandeur that calls to mind Beethoven's *Ninth Symphony* or Eisenstein's slow frescoes. Varèse had imagined a performance of the work being broadcast simultaneously in and from all the capitals of the world. The choirs, each singing in its own language, would have made their entries with mathematical precision. The work would have been divided up into seconds, with the greatest exactitude, so that the chorus in Paris—or Madrid, or Moscow, or Pekin, or Mexico City, or New York—would have come onto the air at exactly the right moment. All men could have listened simultaneously to this song of brotherhood and liberation. It was with this immense idea that Varèse was to struggle, in silence, in despair, until the war rose, in 1939, like the red and terrible wall of reality to block that demiurgic vision. It was then that Varèse was to say to Miller: "I'd like something that gives the impression of the Gobi Desert." Thus it was war that brought about the metamorphosis or transition from *Espace*, a work celebrating brotherhood, to *Déserts*, a work that is like a cry against all that is barbarous, savage, and absurd. *Déserts* is indeed a black and terrible Passover. But this time there is no freedom from slavery first: only the entry into the wilderness.

In December, 1936, the New York newspapers began to show an interest in *Espace*. The version they wrote about was the one for chorus and orchestra preoccupying Varèse at the time. We are thus able to gain some faint idea of the way in which Varèse envisaged the work being performed—and consequently of his conception of it—from these articles. In the *New York Times* of December 6, 1936, we read: "Mr. Varèse's particular interest is in composing rhythms in space as well as rhythms in time. No startling achievements toward this end can be realized until means are developed for transmitting musical sounds electrically from the instruments to different sections of the auditorium.

"Today, with the technical means that are readily adaptable, the differentiation of the various masses of the different planes, as well as these beams of sound, can be made discernible to the listener by artful placing of loud-speakers to reproduce faithfully the tones in diverse parts of the hall, accompanied by other acoustical arrangements. . . .

"Mr. Varèse will entitle his new composition 'Space.' It is a symphony in one movement taking about fifteen minutes to play. It will be played conventionally, without the bizarre electrical appliances he foresees, but he hopes it will suggest the possibilities of the space element when he finishes it in the Spring.

"Another development he anticipates is that of exploiting scientifically the fractional note. Our present chromatic scale of halftones can, with the aid of electricity, be broken down into almost infinite gradations of vibration, he said. This could revolutionize symphonic effects." Needless to say, Varèse was obliged to forgo the use of such electrical instruments as existed at that time: their imperfections could only have marred the work's sound quality, at least in most cases.

In March, 1937, André Malraux spent some time in New York soliciting support wherever he could for the Spanish Republic. At one point, he spent a whole evening and night in the Varèses' apartment on Sullivan Street reading the manuscript of *Espoir*. Varèse, fired with enthusiasm, envisaged a collaboration between Malraux and himself. Malraux was to write a text for the chorus of *Espace*. The result was that the New York newspapers began to talk about their "Red Symphony" or their "Symphony of Revolution."

On March 3rd, Varèse and Malraux gave a press conference on their projected collaboration at the Hotel Mayflower. (In fact, though there is nothing surprising about it, this piece of publicity had been organized by Malraux's New York publishers, Random House.) Next day, the reporter from the *New York Times* wrote:

"Since the choir is to take part in a revolutionary symphony, Mr. Varèse said it would include Negroes. Mr. Malraux added that it would also include Russians, and that he had no doubt the symphony would be performed immediately anywhere they might wish in Russia. . . .

"For Mr. Varèse, he (Malraux) will become a poet, rewriting lyric passages of 'Days of Wrath,' reflecting what goes on in a communist's mind in the face of death for the cause. These will be the words for the chorus in the third and closing movement of the symphony.

"To convey the natural aspirations of the hero for the good things in life, the terror of death and the final exaltation of consecration to the cause, Mr. Varèse will call upon new electrical instruments, he said, and will have sections of the orchestra and chorus wired to amplifiers in different sections of the auditorium so that the music will at times hit the hearer on the back of his neck."

Apparently Varèse's idea for a performance of *Espace* given by performers in several countries linked by radio came later, between 1937 and 1939. At least, that is what I believe is to be deducted from my conversations with him on the subject. Varèse also entrusted me with the text (in English) of a very brief analysis of this work as he conceived it in the version for chorus and orchestra. It reads as follows:

"ESPACE, for orchestra and Chorus in 3 movements to be performed without interruption.

"1st movement, 12 to 15 minutes duration for full orchestra. It is built on the shifting play of planes, volumes, masses in space; very dynamic, abrupt in its statements, devoid of all rhetorical and pedantic developments.

"2nd movement, very short, 2 to 3 minutes; lyrical, for strings only, to serve as a kind of shock absorber between 1st and 3rd movements. A relaxation.

"3rd movement: Plan and suggestions for choral text. Duration, 18 to 20 minutes; for full orchestra and a large chorus to be used to the full extent of its possibilities: singing, humming, yelling, chanting, mumbling, hammered declamation, etc.

"Theme: TODAY . . . Marching humanity."

As we know, Varèse was going through a period of crisis at that time, and so *Espace* was never finished. Nevertheless, this long labor was to be useful for *Etude, Déserts* and the *Poème électronique.*

From 1935 to 1940, with the exception of *Densité 21.5,* he was to work on no further compositions. He did battle with *Espace,* from town to town. He did battle with himself, and against all the forces that were trying to silence him, the exterior ones as well as the interior ones. One spark of hope survived: silence could not be his fate.

We still have one heart-rending reminder of the crisis that Varèse underwent: his *Densité 21.5.* This work was composed in January, 1936, at the request of the flautist Georges Barrère, for the launching of the latter's platinum flute. The title is of course derived from the specific gravity of platinum at that time (it is now 21.45). For me, *Densité 21.5* is one long cry. Only *Déserts* (or *Etude pour Espace*) was later to attain this same tragic intensity. *Densité 21.5* achieves such purity that one can truly qualify it as Mozartian, even though the conception of song that animates it is at the antipodes of Mozart's. For this is truly a song-cry. In Mozart, the cry is a piercing explosion within the song, but in Varèse it becomes the very substance of the song: it makes the song possible. Mozart begins from the song and allows it to explode into a cry. Varèse begins from the cry and transmutes it into either song or silence. This is why the tension is so strong. In Mozart, the tension is a peak; in Varèse, silence is an abyss that cleaves the tension like a crevasse. These moments of relaxation are to him what tension was for Mozart. They are two conceptions of tragedy. But Varèse's conception, like Webern's, is certainly more in conformity with the age of Nazi concentration camps, thermonuclear bombs, and interminable and savage civil wars.

Odile Vivier was to write of *Densité 21.5:* "It is a pure melody which rises around certain pivotal notes, employing scoring in which the reversed chromatics alternate with very disjunct intervals. The rhythmic values, which are extremely varied, set short notes against long, held ones, making subtle use of the triplets that have been erroneously termed 'irrational values.' The use of the flute's different registers is particularly noteworthy in that they are combined with very different and very subtly varied intensities. In certain passages, the attack and the intensity change with every note. The effect of an echo, or more exactly a sensation of space and depth, with definite and receding planes, is created by register changes linked with contrasts of intensity; a high pitched *fortissimo* is followed by a sudden mid-frequency *piano,* or a rising *forte* in the mid-bass is succeeded by a *piano subito* on a high note, which is then repeated three times after a little ornament. The listener has the impression that there are several instruments answering one another. And I do mean 'several instruments,' not 'several flutes,' for certain percussive effects in this piece (the keys striking the flute while the performer blows very softly) exceed the acoustical possibilities customarily expected of a flute. . . This scoring is characteristic of the use to which wind instruments are put in Varèse works." [7]

The first performance of *Densité 21.5* was given by Georges Barrère on Sunday, February 16, 1936, in Carnegie Hall. This was the first time that Barrère had played his platinum flute (valued at $3,000 by the *New York Times*). The occasion was a gala benefit concert given on behalf of the Lycée Français in New York. Such artists as Lily Pons and Lucienne Boyer also appeared, and Carnegie Hall was besieged by two thousand people. Many newspapers gave this musical event coverage, but there were no reviews of Varèse's work.[8] In April, 1946, Varèse revised his score before publication. A little later, the composer Marc Wilkinson was to make an exhaustive analysis of *Densité 21.5*.[9]

15

Travels and Lectures

After June, 1936, Varèse went to live for some time in the southwest of the United States, for the most part in Santa Fe, New Mexico. Santa Fe is, of course, the oldest city in the United States after St. Augustine, Florida. It is to the south of the desert.

On June 15, 1936, the *Santa Fe New Mexican* announced Varèse's arrival. In his first press conference the composer spoke about the "movement of sound masses," "transmutation," and "sonic beams." On August 21st, in the same newspaper, he had this to say on the subject of Beethoven: "It was really a blessing that Beethoven was deaf and, being so, isolated himself from the world. He heard with his inner ear . . . and really wanted the effects that can be had today. I believe he returned to the quartet because he imagined beyond the physical possibilities of his time." But though Varèse was outwardly speaking of Beethoven, it is possible that it was unconsciously to his own isolation that he was referring. It was not by chance that he had moved physically so close to the desert at that time. The desert was becoming the symbol of the reception that was being given to his boldest ideas, to his dreams, to his inner world, to his works. It was because Varèse felt himself living in a desert that he moved to the desert. He felt the need for some harmony between the nature surrounding him and the despair he felt within. The desert one finds in a city such as New York is of another essence. It is the desert of multiplicity, of paroxysm; it can make emptiness manifest, but never the vastness of distance, never silence. But the real desert was to become the physical and symbolic site of his *Passion,* of his suffering—as we say the Passion of Christ. It was there, in that desolation, face to face with the dryness of the world, that he was to think seriously of suicide, that he was to allow himself to be devoured as it were by the darkness. The glaring desert light, in alliance with the sand, benumbed him, plunged him into a torpor that urged him on to self destruction. At least that is the impression one receives from a photograph of him taken that year in Santa Fe. His face is tormented as it has never been before. He is crushed by the light against a whitewashed wall, his eyes riveted to the flagstones of the patio, one hand open in a waiting gesture, but passively, almost indifferently.

In the newspaper article mentioned above, which appeared on August 21st, the writer noted: "Varèse returns time and again to Beethoven's *Ninth Symphony* in illustration of various points, referring to its 'colossal majesty' and calling it 'the greatest choral work.' " The writer then added: "All the contradictions of music are felt by this composer, who says: 'Music is the most abstract of the arts and also the most physical. . . . Music is under two signs, the stars and wine.' He gives three principles at the base of all composition, 'inertia, force, and rhythm,' with their further contradictions." At the very outset of his piece, the reporter commented on the impression this interview with Varèse had left him with: that Varèse knew more about the history of music than most of his contemporaries.

It was natural that Varèse should have taken such an interest in the *Ninth Symphony* precisely at the time when he himself was working on *Espace*, since the latter work was to include a chorus in its last movement. As with Mozart, Beethoven, or Schubert, it was at the moment when he was sinking most deeply into distress that Varèse had the vision of a work celebrating brotherhood and freedom. It is a thing that remains a paradox in the human soul and one of the qualities of the great creators. They return to life only through the still unformed work that draws them toward it, despite themselves, and forces them to live again. They are saved by their profound innocence.

Varèse seems to have given his first lecture in Santa Fe on Sunday,

August 23rd, under the auspices of the Society for Indian Affairs. The event took place at the Mary Austin House, and the composer spoke on "The Music of our Time." Next day's *Santa Fe New Mexican* reported some of his speech. For example: "A work of art must make the rules; rules do not make a work of art. . . . On the threshold of beauty, art and science must collaborate. . . . I tell people I am not a musician; I work with rhythms, frequencies and intensities. . . . Tunes are merely the gossips in music. . . ." And the writer of the article concluded: "In a sphere where vibrations successively become electricity, silence, heat and light, he exposed the feeble inadequacy of the human ear and futility of human fingers." After the lecture there was a reception in Varèse's honor.

We know that Varèse returned to New York late in November, 1936, and that he arrived in Santa Fe for a second stay on April 17, 1937. These facts are recorded in the little notebooks Varèse used to note down his movements from time to time—when he thought of it.

In July, almost certainly after talking it over with Malraux, Varèse organized a committee in aid of the Spanish Republic. The primary objective of this committee, of which Varèse was president and Dr. William J. Crookston secretary, was to collect together enough money to pay for an ambulance. On July 12th, Varèse sent a message to all the newspapers advising them that he had just learned that almost ten thousand soldiers and civilians were evacuating Bilbao and Santander, among other cities, that many were dying of gangrene, and that there were no drugs, antiseptics, anaesthetics, or vaccines for them. In short, men, women, and children were dying in the most agonizing pain. In the Santa Fe region alone, Varèse had before very long collected $1,316.92. He even succeeded in persuading Monseigneur P. F. Mahoney to speak in favor of this campaign even though it was on behalf of men on the side of the "Reds." Monseigneur Mahoney accepted on condition that he be allowed to request aid only on behalf of the women and children. This anecdote gives some idea of Varèse's powers of persuasion.[1] Despite appearances, however, it was at this time that Varèse was most filled with despair and began to talk of committing suicide. He even made inquiries of a doctor friend, though cloaking his true reasons under the pretext of wanting to know which were the most efficient poisons. In spite of everything, however, Louise Varèse did not at any time seriously believe that he would be able to kill himself. After all, it was precisely during this crisis period that he was able to forget himself sufficiently to "commit" himself, to give himself to others. Varèse was a profoundly magnanimous man, and it was doubtless that very generosity of soul which prevented him from killing himself. A man so affected by the wretchedness of other men—men suffering so far away in Europe —cannot kill himself. A living being with such a nature may well be momentarily drawn to death, but his passion for life and other living creatures is too deeply rooted for him to will his own destruction.

Beginning on Tuesday, August 10, 1937, Varèse was to give a series of classes in orchestration for both professional and amateur musicians. The classes were organized by the Arsuna Galleries in Santa Fe. Varèse entitled the series as a whole: "Music as Living Matter." Over a period of six weeks, Varèse examined the woodwinds, the brass section, the strings, percussion instruments, and the harp, without forgetting the acoustical point of view. His examples were chosen primarily from the following works: Beethoven's *Fifth* and *Seventh Symphonies*, Brahms' *First Symphony*, Ravel's *Bolero*, and *Ionisation*. Thanks to the faithful *Santa Fe New Mexican*, some few scraps of these classes have survived. Thus on August 25th, the day after the third class, we read: "What is music? Something that must come out by sound." Then the reporter goes on to tell us that Varèse talked about the various instruments as though they were children, living and breathing creatures. He summed up Varèse's reflections on the individual instruments as follows: "It is the most articulate of instruments (soft brass). It can compete with the woodwinds in velocity, produce a beautiful staccato, and it is unbelievable how long a tone can be held on it." On the subject of Wagner's use of tubas, he notes: ". . . Beautiful on paper, but in use always out of tune with the orchestra. . . . When really played well, of course they are in tune and achieve a magnificent effect. Wagner uses these in the 'Ring' only, and Strauss uses them excitingly in 'Electra.' " Speaking of the bassoon, he says: "It is very powerful in bass but loses its personality, growing thinner as it goes up, as opposed to the horn which is more powerful the higher up it goes." Summing up his impressions of the brass instruments, Varèse emphasized their life-giving energy: "They are full of sun. . . . They can rise from pianissimo to tremendous power immediately; can make a great attack, then drop to piano right away." On August 31st, Varèse studied the strings. Mentioning Mozart, he observed that he was "the iconoclast who first put the clarinet into the orchestra." Having demonstrated the analogy between certain string instruments, in some registers, with the flute and the oboe, for example, doubled with a violin, he defined the character of the violin's strings, the various types of bowing, their characteristics and their functions. He called the viola a "bastard instrument." Then he went into the history of the cello and the double bass, clarifying their functions in the history of the orchestra. He referred to the risk the strings run of being absorbed by the woodwinds if the latter become dominant. After a discussion period with the audience, Varèse ended by observing that "Orchestration can be taught in an hour. But after a lifetime of study you are just beginning to know a little bit. The more you study, the more possibilities you see." [2] On Tuesday, September 7th, Varèse talked to his audience about the harp and the percussion instruments, drawing his examples from the recording of *Ionisation*. He quoted a few remarks of Stravinsky's on the subject of *Ionisation*. In conclusion, he tackled the role played by percussion instruments in the works of Beethoven, Rossini, Meyerbeer, Berlioz, etc.[3]

Though Varèse was a born storyteller, he was not a talkative man about himself. He refused to justify himself. He was a man of lapidary expression. Here, for example, are the thirteen aphorisms he had published in the magazine *Eolus* under the title *By the Dozen*:

"There are two Infinities: God and stupidity."

"Beyond a certain degree of intensity, all our passions are resolved into the same dynamism."

"Sometimes one sees so far that expression refuses to follow as though it were afraid."

"A man is culpable in the eyes of society when he escapes from the jurisdiction of its mediocrity."

"I have known fierce and uncompromising traditionalists who proclaimed the unchanging dogmas of schools that were. Each trafficked in a corpse. Yet when business began appreciably to fall off, they would quaintly admit that the time had come for the dead to die."

"The Bourgeoisie calls the cowardice which holds it paralyzed in sordid beatitude, prudence."

"Talent does what it will; genius what it can."

"Each new work should have as a means of expression, a fresh technique, appropriate and flexible, in no way thwarting the free yield of the conception."

"The dead govern us. Their lives, their laws, their traditions, their works weigh us down, poison and enervate us. Fear, ruler of the mob, bows to their decrees, strengthens their power and sterilizes any individual revolt against them."

"Each age of man requires a change of set."

"One must know how to exhaust adversity."

"Pleasure has only rights."

"The word *chance* expresses only our ignorance of causes."

In the *New Mexico Sentinel* of September 21, 1937, he offered these eight further aphorisms:

"Beauty seems to affect some people as a personal affront."

"Men set themselves a goal, and having attained it, are satisfied and grow paunches. In their complacency they forget that their only future now is death."

"There comes a moment when those we have hitherto despised arouse our pity. An easy wasy, perhaps, of balancing our accounts."

"No matter how consummate a work of art may seem, it is only an approximation of the original conception. It is the artist's conciousness of this discrepancy between his conception and the realization that assures his progress."

"The significance of a social change is part of the content of art in every age. An artist is never a precursor. He only reflects his age and stamps it on history. It is not he who is ahead of his day, but the general public that is always behind the times."

"The beginning of art is not reason. It is the buried treasure of the unconscious . . . that unconscious which has more understanding than our lucidity."

"An excess of reason is mortal to art. You cannot raise beauty out of a formula."

"It is imagination that gives form to dreams."

He was to return to this penultimate thought later on, when he confided to Stravinsky: "I rather like a certain clumsiness in a work of art." [4]

Varèse's last lesson, on September 21, 1937, was devoted to an account of possible new instruments, in particular electrical ones. He alluded to instruments as *sound producers* as opposed to those instruments which are merely *sound reproducers.* He predicted the quality and the wealth of sounds that these instruments would eventually be able to provide. Then he gave a quick sketch of the history of orchestration from Monteverdi up to the present day.[5]

Varèse also founded a Schola Cantorum in Santa Fe. The nucleus of it was formed by forty already known singers; but Varèse was aiming at a chorus of a hundred. The few rehearsals that took place were held in the St. Francis Auditorium in the Art Museum. The aim of the Schola was not to give concerts but to bring together all those who loved the works of the greatest choral composers of all ages and liked to sing them together. But Varèse was obliged to abandon the project after only a few rehearsals.

Toward the end of September, 1937, a concert was given in the Art Museum auditorium in order to buy a piano for the museum. Varèse introduced the program. He began with these words: "Of all the arts, music is the one communal art. It requires for its existence extensive co-operation and organization. . . Singing together the greatest choral music of all time is the surest way of developing in a community that sense of quality and reverence for beauty, which is the basis of a musical culture. . . . Entertainment has its place in life just as candies and cocktails have, but health is not built on such a diet alone, nor culture exclusively on amusement." [6]

On November 8th, Varèse was in Albuquerque, en route to San Francisco. He had abandoned the desert for the ocean and the great city. Gently, the sun was coming out again. He found a place to live on Washington Street. It was there that Jehanne Bietry-Salinger from the newspaper *Courrier du Pacifique* (published in French) went for her first interview with the composer. "They had just moved in his piano," she wrote, "which it had been necessary to haul up with the aid of sizeable pulleys, over the gutterings, and then push across the large, unfenced roof from which one looks out over the steel bridge with its orange colored Gothic arches that runs over the entrance to the Golden Gate, linking the low plain of the Marina to the leap-frogging hills of Marin county on the other side. . .

"Varèse, standing in the narrow frame of the open doorway, seemed bigger than the landscape. He talked to me about his work, his work 'on the stocks,' as he says, for he talks about his music like a manual laborer.

"His black, bushy, electrified hair, seemed to writhe like coils of wire. Hands pressed to his temples, he gazed out over the bay, his eyes heavy with thought, his dilated nostrils sucking in the heady sea air in a gluttonous stream.

"The face is etched with deep, sculpted lines, the mouth is wide and full of life, the nose slightly aquiline. Everything about him indicates great strength, and the perpetual nourishment of the head by the heart, of the heart by the idea, of the idea by experience." Then Varèse spoke enthusiastically about *Espace,* and about the text he was still waiting to receive from Malraux. At that time he was working on the idea of a composition for performance in an auditorium, but "he was going to insist on the use of loudspeakers, which by producing echoes and amplifying the sounds would make a maximum of acoustical efficiency possible." "As Varèse was talking to me," the writer went on, "sometimes in a very low and almost oppressed voice, sometimes loudly, his words hurried and tightly packed, it seemed to me that his thought and his words had assumed a musical form. . . Varèse's voice fell suddenly silent. He bit his lips, which seemed to be still talking. His eyelids became redder than before. The giant had halted on the threshold of infinity. His conception was about to infringe the boundaries of what is possible. . . There was a great gust of wind, and a young woman emerged onto the roof with its covering of tarred paper. She took down her washing, which was hanging there in the mist and the smoke. Varèse looked, smiled, came inside his studio and sat down. The tuner was still plucking at the strings of the darkened piano that tomorrow was to become the composer's principal tool. In his thick-ribbed corduroy smock of beige velvet, worn over a thick, turtle-necked, gray wool pullover, he sat there now and talked to me about tea and honey." Suddenly, seriously, Varèse said to his journalist visitor: "My work is in the future, I've barely begun." [7] After the moving, and somewhat romantic picture just painted for us, these last words from the composer seem like an irruption of reality. He had the feeling that he was beginning all over again; that was why the struggle was so terrible. There is no doubt that this feeling was a product of his vision of a new musical universe much more than it was of his despair.

In an interview given to the *San Francisco News,* he declared: "Today is an age of speed, synthesis and dynamics. Consequently we expect contemporary forms to reflect those qualities." [8]

On February 15, 1938, *Offrandes* was performed at the San Francisco Community Playhouse by the Sinfonietta Orchestra under the direction of Giulio Minetti. Varèse's composition was evidently the sensation of the evening. It aroused the crowd's curiosity and attracted them to the performance; it was loudly applauded and the second section was encored. After the concert—which Pierre Monteux attended—Varèse told a journalist from the *Courrier du Pacifique* that it was "just a very small scale work, a purely intimate piece." The same journalist observed that this was the first time in the history of the orchestra that the auditorium of the Community Playhouse had been absolutely full. Then, speaking of the composer, he added: "In Varèse's presence, only the greatest of the great can survive without damage the shock produced by his personality and his originality. The great, in the realm of music as in all others, are few and far between."

In February, 1938, Varèse suddenly fell ill and was obliged to undergo an operation. Louise Varèse hurried to his side. After two months of convalescence, he went to spend a week in Santa Barbara with the Eichems. Then he and Louise Varèse went together to Los Angeles, early in May. They were to stay there until the fall of 1940. It was there, too, that Varèse, with the help of an electrical engineer, was to make several attempts at recording sounds at different pitches by varying the speed of a turntable.

In 1939, at the invitation of the University of Southern California, he gave one of his most important lectures. That evening, Varèse was able to state categorically: "Unhappily the conditions of freedom, necessary for the vigorous growth of music and the spread of its influence, do not exist today. . . . It is obvious that the America of today cannot be culturally affected by the music of today, since even the music public, to say nothing of the great masses, is kept in almost total ignorance of what living composers have to say. . . . Unfortunately it has been the experience of composers in free democ-

racies, that freedom to write as they please does not bring with it
the right to be heard, to say nothing of the right to live. Our present
administration which has been a Big Brother to the plastic artist
has done nothing for his counterpart in music, the composer. Only
performers have, as far as I know, been benefited by the Federal
Music Projects. . . . And as for material benefits, the Federal Music
Budget has entirely ignored the natural needs of the composer who,
I assure you, enjoys eating just as much as a violinist, a drummer
or even a conductor! . . . I believe because the nature of music is
not fully understood, that music has not gone forward with the other
arts today, but still turns around and around like a squirrel in a
cage. . . . At different times and in different places, music has been
considered as an Art or as a Science. In reality, music partakes of
both." Then, Varèse went on to elucidate the relationship between
music and acoustics: "When you listen to music do you ever stop to
realize that you are being subjected to a physical phenomenon? Not
until the air between the listener's ear and the instrument has been
disturbed does music occur. . . . In order to anticipate the result, a
composer must understand the mechanics of the instruments and
must know just as much as possible about acoustics. We are all
familiar with the term 'paper music'—music that can be read but
fails to say anything in sound. But music must live in sound."

Then, after quoting Brahms' definition of composition—"the organization of disparate elements"—Varèse went on to attack the neo-
classicists and the return to Bach, or to Mozart, or to Debussy: "I
am pretty sure that if Debussy returned to the world today, after
hearing the Debussyists, he would change his name. . . . The very
basis of creative work is irreverence! The very basis of creative work
is experimentation . . . bold experimentation. You have only to turn
to the revered past for the corroboration of my contention." Varèse
then quoted some remarks by Lawrence Gilman, who had compiled
various pearls of criticism directed against composers now considered
as classics. A great Berlin critic once wrote of Chopin, for example:
"He (Chopin) is indefatigable, almost inexhaustible in his ear-split-
ting dissonances . . ." Then, in refutation of D. C. Parker, who
had written that "pioneers and experimentors are seldom first-rate
creators," he added: "There has never been a creator of lasting importance who was not also an innovator. The links in the chain of

tradition are formed by men who have all been revolutionists." And later, Varèse was to say, in effect, that tradition isn't supposed to mean just fifty years of *bad habits*. Considering the social aspect of creativity, he said: "In every domain of art, a work that corresponds to the need of its day carries a message of social and cultural value. Preceding ages show us that changes in art occur because societies and artists have new needs. . . . It is the artist who crystalizes his age . . . who fixes his age in history." Returning to his reflections upon the instruments and new requirements of his art, he exclaimed: "We composers are forced to use, in the realization of our works, instruments that have not changed for two centuries. . . . Although for convenience and profit in our daily lives we have found something better than the hand pump, we still blow with effort into wind instruments. And the arbitrary, tempered system to which we still cling is not capable of setting down even as much as our obsolete instruments are capable of playing. . . .

"Personally, for my conceptions. I need an entirely new medium of expression: a sound-producing machine (not a sound-reproducing one). . . .

"Whatever I write, whatever my message, it will reach the listener unadulterated by 'interpretation.' It will work something like this: after a composer has set down his score on paper by means of a new graphic, similar in principle to a seismographic or oscilographic notation, he will then, with the collaboration of a sound engineer, transfer the score directly to this electric machine. After that anyone will be able to press a button to release the music exactly as the composer wrote it . . . exactly like opening a book.

"And here are the advantages I anticipate from such a machine: liberation from the arbitrary, paralyzing tempered system; the possibility of obtaining any number of cycles or if still desired subdivisions of the octave, consequently the formation of any desired scale; unsuspected range in low and high registers, new harmonic splendors obtainable from the use of sub-harmonic combinations now impossible, the possibility of obtaining any differentiation of timbre, of sound-combinations, new dynamics far beyond the present human-power orchestra, a sense of sound-projection in space by means of the emission of sound in any part or in many parts of the hall as may be required by the score, cross rhythms unrelated to each other, treated simultaneously, or to use the old word, 'counterpuntally,' since the machine would be able to beat any number of desired notes, any subdivision of them, omission or fraction of them—all these in a given unit of measure or time which is humanly impossible to attain." So, once more we find the recurrence of the idea of a kind of music similar to taped music. Moreover, Varèse was very aware at this time of the necessity for a new type of scoring, a new method of notation. The works he meant to entrust to his machine were all preconceived and thoroughly organized ones. He had no intention of collecting samples of sound merely in order to stock a sound-library. He conceived works, then searched for the means to express those conceptions. Varèse was first and foremost a creator, a poet. This sound machine was for him no more than a means, as the violin was for a Vivaldi. If someone had agreed to provide him with a laboratory in the early thirties, then we should have been able to talk about concrete music or "electronic music" as early as that. There would have been no need to wait until 1948. Varèse lacked the necessary technological progress: developments in electronics, magnetic recording tape, etc. Messiaen has already said that Varèse was "the man who created electronic music with real instruments." This is something that a Dr. Fletcher or a Henry Allen Moe could not be aware of in 1932. Moreover, even in 1948 no one dared use the word "music" in this context. The expression "concert of sounds" was cautiously employed, and with reason, since there was no musical work attaining the level of art involved. It was not until 1950 that Schaeffer and Henry were to talk of the *Symphony for Solo Man*. And it is apparent from this title that though the means were new, the spirit organizing the sounds was perhaps less so. Then, in 1952, Schaeffer was to publish his book on *"musique concrète."* That same year, in America, the first performance of "tape-music" was given at Columbia University, New York. The following year, which is to say in 1952, Stockhausen composed his *Etude no. 1* in Cologne. Varèse had begun *Déserts* in 1950, and in 1952 he had already finished the instrumental part of the score and was starting on the tape insertions. In 1959, the musicologists Boris de Schloezer and Marina Scriabine quite rightly observed: "From now on, like the painter, the musician is going to produce his work by performing it, which means, in his case, by putting it into the form of sounds; it will come into being in the course of its sonorization. So that the role of electro-acoustical devices is not the same as that played by instruments: one composes *for* the latter, taking into account all their particularities, but one composes *with* the former, since their function is factural." 9 This is what Varèse had meant, almost thirty years beforehand, when he made his distinction between the machine that produces sounds and the machine that reproduces them. Thus, little by little, the world was inevitably catching up with his conceptions. Varèse had spoken of "an unlimited number of cycles," of "the formation of any desired scale," of an "undreamed of scope of registers," of "unprecedented intensities beyond anything that can be produced by our orchestras," and lastly, of "a projection of sound into space" by broadcasting it from any given part of a concert hall, etc. . . . One only has to re-read the transcription of his words on this subject published in the magazine *Bifur* in 1930. In his book *Music in Germany*, published in 1957, H. Eimert pointed out that "electro-acoustical methods do not enable us to create 'music' in the traditional sense of the word. When electronic instruments attempt to do so, the performance always consists only of substitute music. . . . The new means of sound production in fact demands new and creative ideas about composition, and those ideas cannot be derived from anything other than the sound itself, from the 'acoustical new material' . . . The composer is no longer concerned today merely with 70 or 80 sounds, with 6 or 7 intensities ranging from *pp* to *ff*, with halves, quarters and eighths of tones, but with electrical frequencies ranging from 50 to 50,000 hz, with more than 40 precisely calibrated degrees of intensity, and with a multiplicity of durations (measured in inches of magnetic tape) lying wholly outside our present customary framework of note values." 10

All this makes it possible for us to grasp the importance of this lecture, given in 1939, in which Varèse went more deeply into various ideas that he had begun to express and elaborate at least as early as 1916. It is as well to keep these facts in mind when we speak of *"musique concrète,"* or when we find a critic, such as the one signing himself R. L., attacking Varèse after the first performance of *Déserts*. Moreover, Eimert's remarks can also help us to understand why certain composers, extremely lucid and advanced in other ways, were unable to accept the *Poème électronique*. Boulez' attempt in

Poésie pour pouvoir was a failure, doubtless because he had not had the benefit of the long and profound meditation on these new techniques which had been preoccupying Varèse over so long a period of time. Varèse had prepared himself inwardly, in spirit, for his confrontation with magnetic tape. And this was not, or is not, necessarily the case with even very intelligent composers such as Boulez. Of course, he is not the only composer, far from it, who has not been successful in his confrontation with this new universe. After all, the available electronic techniques are still not perfect, and indeed were unable to match the subtleties that even a musician as experienced in their use as Varèse could hear and was attempting to express. But the day will come . . . It will be understood eventually that Varèse was right, even in the *Poème électronique*.

When war broke out, in late August, 1939, Varèse was still living in Los Angeles. This proximity to Hollywood—where he was in fact to live the following spring—aroused a hope in him that his ideas might be of interest to the motion picture makers, and that they might provide him with the means of realizing those ideas. Having settled into his new residence at 1338 North Sierra Bonita, he sent a long letter, on April 22, 1940, to André Dumonceau, a Hollywood producer. In this letter he put down the essentials of his thought on the relationship between sounds and images, particularly insofar as it affects "music" for the motion picture. Then he wrote an article for the magazine *The Commonweal* which was entitled: "Organized Sound for the Sound Film." This article must serve as a foundation for any examination of Varèse's thought in this field. "Being master of the greatest range of sensations and emotions, from the most physical reactions to the most abstract conceptions, *organized sound* may be called on to intervene at the point where the spoken word has reached the limit of its efficacy, and where the precision of the image only tends to limit the flight of the imagination. . . . There is a discrepancy between the events and interests of our epoch and a sound commentary produced by concert instruments which had already reached their climax in the eighteenth and nineteenth centuries, and whose texture cannot possibly suggest the sounds we expect to find surrounding the action or the visually logical source of these sounds." After stating that he is, of course, not dealing with purely musical films or historical or ethnic ones which have their own special musical requirements, Varèse continues. "However, when on the screen we see a tremendous outburst of nature—for instance a tornado—the accompanying commentary by a large symphony orchestra is too apt to evoke in the hearer not this particular, real drama of nature, but rather a gesticulating conductor leading his men through a tempest of 'William Tell' or 'The Flying Dutchman' or any other too well-remembered chromatic program music. Why not startle the imagination into a realization of the reality of the unfolding drama (whether of nature or of human lives) by the use of combinations of sound possible today but which never before today could have been produced? We now are in possession of scientific means not merely of realistic reproduction of sounds but of *production of entirely new combinations of sound,* with the possibility of creating new emotions, awakening dulled sensibilities. Any possible sound we can imagine can be produced with perfect control of its quality, intensity and pitch, opening up entirely new auditory perspectives. And these sounds must not be speculated upon as separate entities for sporadic, atmospheric effects but taken as thematic material and organized into a score standing on its own merit.

"Between this sound score and the dramatic continuity, the relation must be one of intimate and interacting connection: a relationship of unity, of form and of rhythm. But this weaving together of the disparate sonorous and visual elements which will make of a film a unified whole cannot be achieved by the device of an imitative repetition of the visual. Although certainly unintentional, there is something very comical, even of the nature of parody, in the usual musical procedure: the music scampering to keep up with the action, increasing in volume and tempo in an impossible effort to express exactly the same thing in the same way. . . . Often the most exciting moment of a dramatic situation will be far more enhanced by an abrupt, timely suspension of all sound than by any musical outburst. The simultaneous opposition of dynamics is a most effective device and I wonder that it is so seldom used. . . .

"It seems to me that the motion picture industry might profit (even in the dollar sense in the end) in having a laboratory or a department for the study of the problem of a more complete and understanding use of the sound apparatus. . . . There should be a co-ordinating department where composer, or *sound organizer*, and electrical engineer work together." [11]

As we have just seen, Varèse never ceased to return to his definition of music as "organized sound." In this article, Varèse rebels against the notion of music as a mere accompaniment to the motion picture. He wants a truly complementary relationship between image and sound. Claude Samuel, in his book entitled *Panorama de l'Art musical contemporain*, remarks: "Whereas the motion picture is discontinuous movement, a sequence of moving images, music represents (or could represent) a unifying element; it is able to underline an effect, suggest an emotion, create an atmosphere, and discreetly but profoundly modify the whole meaning of a film." [12] We are not far here from Varèse's notion of complementarity. Some twenty-five years later, approaching film music in his turn, Pierre Boulez was to say: ". . . Film music should be non-recorded music, created by artificial means. If you introduce an instrument distorted by electro-acoustical techniques, or purely acoustical music, into a film, one can sense that it is fulfilling its purpose. Because the sound has been transformed, as long as it has been so deliberately." [13] Here again, we find that Varèse had understood the real problem involved: the necessity for transforming the sounds, for getting away from direct imitation, for suggesting. Thus it comes as no surprise to hear that Hollywood promptly closed all its doors to him. After this last disappointment, this latest installment in the world's perpetual incomprehension, Varèse returned to New York, tired, very tired, if not broken. The war had taken over now. In the world's laboratories, for other ends than musical creation, the scientists were perfecting the process of tape recording; electronics were to develop prodigiously. Before music could attain a freedom such as it had never known, war had to lay whole countries waste. But that accords only too well with the dialectical character of human history. The war brought about an acceleration in scientific discoveries, but the price was a heavy one. Varèse, in silence, was also to pay for these discoveries, even though they were the answer to his ceaseless, thirty-year quest.

16

Silence and Rebirth

Times of war are not particularly propitious for creation, and particularly for the creation of musical works. Today, what do we have that was composed in the years 1939–45, if we except Webern's *Cantatas*, his *Variation op. 30*, and one or two works by Bartók? And even then, was it not perhaps their approaching deaths that accorded Webern and Bartòk this privilege? It is therefore not surprising, when we consider the external conditions, and particularly the profound state of crisis Varèse was experiencing, that he should have been plunged into a silence in which his only companions were his old friends of the School of Burgundy, and men like Monteverdi, Victoria, Schütz, and Marc-Antoine Charpentier. True, Varèse still continued to talk of *Espace*, but everything was against its completion. He confessed to Professor Theremin, as I noted earlier: "I have just begun a work in which an important part is given to a large chorus, and with it I want to use several of your instruments—augmenting their range as I did for those I used in my *Ecuatorial*—especially in the high range. Would you be so kind as to let me know if it is possible to procure these and where . . . and, in case of modifications, in what they consist. Also, if you have conceived or constructed new ones, would you let me have a detailed description of their character and use." [1]

In October, 1940, Varèse returned to the Pacific coast. A year later, on October 8, 1941, the director of the American Film Center, Donald

Slesinger, was to make some inquiries of his friend Frank Blum, who had spoken to him about Varèse. But nothing came of it.

Varèse, it seems to me, was always surrounded by friends who loved and admired him. Indeed, very often the veneration they felt for him, the respect they had for his genius, kept them at a certain distance. Louise Varèse told me that at the time of Varèse's deepest despair no one would ever have suspected what he was feeling. He would make them all laugh in order to hide his distress. Varèse was a man of the profoundest modesty in everything that concerned himself. He didn't like to talk about his *self*. My *self* is of no interest to anyone, he was inclined to say. That was why he was so stubbornly taciturn in everything that had to do with his private relationships and his own tragedy. I believe it was the Duchesse Edmée de la Rochefoucauld who said in her preface to a book about Valéry that the latter could never see anything of interest in a biography other than the subject's place and date of birth. Those two facts were all he needed in order to situate a writer in time and space. This attitude, however, is only justifiable if one is only considering those determining factors, such as the social ones, that are external to the creator himself. But no creator is wholly the product of such causes. In order to understand him as a man, even if not as a creator, the story of his inner being is of primordial importance; his silent struggles, the great blows in his life, his loves, his own aggressiveness—all that has shaped the inward being, and that being cannot seriously be dissociated from the man as creator. Nevertheless, Varèse had the same conception of biography as Valéry, and it is a point of view that can also be defended. This is why it would be impossible for me really to approach the subject of the man as he was to his friends, in all his generosity and wealth of spirit. I can do no more than provide indications, scattered here and there along the path of his real life, his profound life, his life "as it was in itself." It is as though a sign of the sun should glow feebly through thick cloud. I talk to you of signs, by means of signs, but the sun is beyond all words.

It would be impossible for me to list the names of all the friends who sat down to eat at Varèse's table, from Claudel to Henry Miller, from Fernand Léger to Miró. Let it suffice for me to say and the reader to know that his house on Sullivan Street was always open to all those who were either visiting New York or who lived there. Sometimes it would be young composers seeking his moral support, sometimes writers, sometimes painters, who loved his company, his Burgundian verve, his deep and radiant warmth. Yes, that is the word. Varèse was radiant. When Miller mentions the *angel* when writing about Varèse it is doubtless this luminosity, this radiance that he was thinking of. But in any case, whenever he was not working, Varèse loved to be surrounded by friends. Doubtless he needed to be ceaselessly reassured by the presence of others, above all by the presence of those beings in whom he could sense a real and outgoing sympathy towards him.

And what sensitivity and generosity where his friends were concerned! One day as we were walking home from Washington Square after standing to watch the chess-players there for a while (a daily habit with Varèse), we stopped for a moment in front of the window of a handbag boutique. We were both particularly struck by the beauty of one of the bags and by the texture of its honey-colored leather. Without thinking, I exclaimed: "How my wife would love that bag!" Two weeks later, my wife received that very handbag as a gift. Another time, on one of my birthdays, he sent me a first edition score of *Ionisation* with an inscription in it, as well as a tape of *Arcana*. One day, when we were in Stratford, Ontario, where Varèse was attending a meeting of composers from all over the world, a very famous Canadian musician came up to the "master" to ask him up for a drink, without even deigning to glance at Varèse's companions, who happened to be myself and another friend. Varèse replied very firmly: "Of course! Provided my friends are invited too!" He had a way of preferring our company to that of the celebrities, which must have shocked a great many people. In general I think that deep down Varèse had a great desire to charm people. He was a born charmer. He was always going in to chat to a lutemaker who lived just a few doors away from him; always stopping people he knew slightly in the street to inquire after their healths, their wives, etc. He was interested in everyone, except the vain and the mediocre. He was interested in everything that had life. A recent anecdote conveys how fascinating people found him. After the death of Charlie Parker, the great jazz musician, the latter's wife came to see Varèse to tell him that her husband had followed Varèse up and down the streets of Greenwich Village for two years without even daring to speak to him. Evidently he even said to his wife: "He's the only man I'd willingly be a servant to." I am not surprised that the creators of jazz should have been influenced by the timbres and rhythms of Varèse's works. A little later, he himself was to join a group of musicians in trying out some pieces of jazz *à la Varèse*. I have heard some of the improvisations they recorded. There is no doubt that, on the level of sound quality and timbre, jazz could enrich itself and achieve a profound renewal by exploring the Varesian universe.

Saint-John Perse came to visit Varèse shortly after the latter's return to New York. On a copy of T. S. Eliot's translation of *Anabase*, he wrote: "For you, Varèse, born in the country of the *'Téméraire,'* and to whom the sirens of New York harbor were dedicating so noble a song of strength and solitude, in your 'no-man's-land' on Sullivan Street, that evening. Manhattan, December 21, 1940, Saint-Léger Léger." On a copy of the first edition of *Eloges*, dating from 1911, he was to write: "To Edgard Varèse so unexpectedly and so sympathetically, *Eloges,* with all my friendship, infinitely older than its birth certificate: 19... New York, Alexis Saint-L. Léger." Later, of course, Louise Varèse was to make the first English translation of *Eloges*.

Varèse met Einstein several times, but was alway disappointed to find that so great a mind could only talk about Mozart. Moreover, Busoni's passion for Mozart appeared equally incomprehensible to him. Varèse did not belong to that spiritual family. I do remember discussing Mozart with him for a whole hour, one day when we went out to buy a pizza. If he was willing to discuss the subject for that length of time I suppose he must at least have had some doubts.

Henry Miller first heard of Varèse from his wife Mona (June Smith) at the time when—as Miller's readers will remember—she was selling poems in Greenwich Village bars, in 1926 or '27. In a letter, Miller says: "The first time I went to Paris (1928), with my wife (Mona), I met him through her. She had met him when she was there alone, the year before. It was a very brief meeting. I knew no French then—not a word. I do remember how he looked—a striking figure, handsome, alive, full of humor. A man you would notice in a crowd. . . .

"Then, on my return to New York, in 1940—and in '41, I believe, I saw Varèse a number of times, at his work place and at the home of a Hungarian doctor, a friend of his. Knowing some French by this time, I could savor his wit and humor to better advantage. Whenever we met I had to laugh. He was a marvelous mime and storyteller. He also cooked, if I remember. Seems to me I had several meals—excellent ones—at his home in Sullivan Street. . . . The man himself will ever remain in my memory, as a great, good, warm-hearted, understanding man, fully alive, never properly appreciated, a true Burgundian in every sense of the word." [2] (I remember a *boeuf bourguignon* that Varèse once cooked especially for me. What a dish! And what a master-cook too, I might add!) Miller, as his readers may perhaps remember, also mentions this first encounter between Varèse and Mona in *Nexus,* though he describes it as taking place in Paris rather than in New York.[3] Such details are unimportant, however; no writer was to be so generous toward Varèse as Miller. He has written some magnificent pages about him in his *Air-conditioned Nightmare.* There must be a great many people who discovered Varèse through that work. I myself, after reading it, felt a hunger for Varèse's music as one feels a hunger for sun in autumn, when it seems as though the gray cold will go on shrouding us and penetrating our bones forever. So I set out to meet a joy, some marvel that was my due and that I had been deprived of. I wrote to Varèse, who immediately sent me the first long-playing record of his work. I could never have imagined such things. The works were vaster, stronger than all my deaf man's dreams, for it was then that I first became aware that I didn't know how to listen, it was then that I discovered what the true beauty of sound is. I had been hearing music for years, for my parents were musicians, but now I was like a blind man who has suddenly walked through into the light. I had just been born into the world of sound, and even to that of Oriental music. My ears were virgin. And I discovered how many "composers" were equally deaf. People were managing to write music without ears. What a challenge! As though it were enough to be able to decipher lines of notes, to write a score, and living creations of sound would spring from nowhere. It was then I saw how Varèse's works are in fact mighty battlements, defenses against all caricatures, all lies, dooming everything in man's spirit that is merely death to annihilation.

A friend of Varèse's, Waldo Peirce, in a note of thanks written to Louise Varèse on January 16, 1942, conjured up the joy that their company gave: "Thanks so much from both of us for your fine party . . . It was really grand . . . We must get together again and rouse the spectre of Jean Arthur (Rimbaud). . . with a few Marius and Olive stories for seasoning . . . as delivered by Edgar du Vieux Port. . ." Reading those lines, I think of the red and blue dining-room, its long table, Varèse's pictures all around, and especially of Varèse, at the end of a meal, devouring clusters of green grapes like a true Burgundian. I think of Calder's mobile, spinning like a word of silence in the drawing-room, of the alcove in which Louise Varèse worked, of the round table from India, of the portrait in oils of Varèse's mother, painted when she was still a little girl. I think of the workroom in the basement, with the piano, the gongs, and a thousand other instruments taking up all the space; of the drawings on the wall, the letters hanging at the end of strings, the Mirò paintings, the NO SMOKING sign (for Varèse was afraid of fire—though one did smoke down there, albeit with the greatest vigilance), the portrait of Claude Cortot drawn by Julio Gonzalez, the antique armoire in which all the precious letters from Debussy, the Busoni scores, etc. were kept. And I know what it means to say that a house is alive. And I envy men like Carlos Salzedo, or Thomas Bouchard, or Paul Rosenfeld, all of whom visited Varèse there so often.

Late in 1940, Rosenfeld had an important article published with the title: "We Want Varèse." In it, he wrote: "The most savage of the composer-prophets: possibly the last of the great romantics; not only because of his tendency to seize life in terms of the monstrous and elemental."

The harpist Lucile Lawrence, who was married at that time to Carlos Salzedo, has sent me an account of one or two anecdotes she remembers from the forties.

"Talking about composers who write commercially and those who write 'seriously,' Varèse said: 'You can't be both a virgin and a whore.'

"One day, he remarked to a young musician that one had to be a masochist to be a composer. Then he added: 'Remember, nobody asked you to compose.'

"People often ask why Koussevitsky, who played so many new works, never played Varèse's compositions. Some years ago Koussevitsky had an apartment in Paris where he went at the end of the Boston Symphony season. Salzedo had tea with him there one afternoon, and was surprised to see scores of *Amériques* and *Arcana* on the piano. Salzedo asked Koussevitsky if those works interested him. Koussevitsky replied that they interested him very much. 'Why don't you play them?' asked Salzedo. Koussevitsky replied: 'The day Varèse dedicates a work to me, I'll play that one and all the others.' Salzedo immediately cabled Varèse to dedicate a work to Koussevitsky. Varèse flatly refused to do so." Apparently Koussevitsky had heard that Varèse had dedicated a work to Stokowski . . .

In 1941, Varèse founded a choral society which was called at that time the "New Chorus." Greenwich House, at 46 Barrow Street, became its rehearsal room. Stokowski announced that he was deeply interested in the newly formed choir and in everything that Varèse did. The latter recruited his singers from all classes of society; but because of the war it was difficult to find enough tenors and basses. He was obliged to reorganize the chorus and call it "The Greater New York Chorus." Bartòk, Schoenberg, Villa-Lobos, Carl Ruggles, and others lent him their support; they all became members of the advisory committee. But it was not until the fall of 1942 that Varèse was able to resume his rehearsals. His first concert was given on April 24, 1943, at the Washington Irving High School, under the auspices of Geneviève Tabouis's newspaper *Pour la Victoire,* and as a benefit for the "Coordinating Council of French Relief Societies." Varèse had included some motets by Victoria, etc., as well as some folk songs in the program, and it was an enormous success. As Varèse explained to Michael Singer of the *Daily Worker:* "In this time of crisis, it is of the greatest importance to do our best to preserve cultural values, even more important, to forge ahead and build up new realities. The function of The Greater New York Chorus is to preserve, to disseminate and to build." There is no doubt that the sense of life which emanates from the works of the Renaissance, for example, provides a catharsis which makes it possible to rediscover the fundamentals. Varèse was fighting against the war in his own way. Not only because he derived no pecuniary gain from these concerts, and was thus helping France, his occupied native land, but above all because in the very midst of that tragedy he was offering men reasons to go on hoping in the greatness of the human spirit. It was in this spirit that Varèse himself said, at that time, that "war is a destructive and chronic accident, and art a living, permanent force." Moreover, for himself, at the deepest moment of his crisis, perhaps this was a way of returning to *his* origins, to his little Romanesque church in Villars, a way of drawing up fresh sap.

Subsequently, in the "Pageant of Liberation," Varèse gave a "masterly performance" of the Berlioz *la Marseillaise*, with his chorus. It was a revelation, even for the French people present. The following week, in an interview given to the newspaper *Pour la Victoire*, he talked about Berlioz and about the role of his chorus. Having recalled the fact that Wagner looked upon Berlioz as "the savior of the musical world" and that Heine called him a "titanic nightingale, a lark with the dimensions of an eagle," Varèse added: "He was the creator of the dramatic symphony and the inventor of the modern orchestra. If he were living today, he would certainly be one of the first to deplore the stagnation of music and to wish for new instruments and new means of sound production." On the subject of his chorus, he said: "First of all, I should like to augment it, because I very much want to make the great choral music of the past, which has been too much neglected, known to all those worthy of it, and not just to a handful of music fanciers. Above all, I want to rescue all the marvels of our French choral music from oblivion, the primitive masters, the fourteenth century ones, those who made up the School of Burgundy, in fact all those who have paved the way up till our own day . . . for this music has always belonged to everyone, and still does. But for that, we need big halls. I have lost too many chorus members because of the war to think of it for the moment."

On June 5, 1946, in a church, Varèse presented a concert for the benefit of the American Friends Service Committee, for the relief of the children of France. It was an association supported by all the French celebrities and others living in New York. The program consisted of pieces by Titelouze, Susay, Ferdinando de la Torre, Victoria, Schütz (*Dialogo per la Pascua*), Marc-Antoine Charpentier (*Pestis Mediolanis*), etc. Varèse's repertoire was vast. Several of these works were being performed in New York for the first time.

In recognition of all the services he had rendered his native country, Claudel obtained the Légion d'honneur for Varèse, and wanted to present it to him himself. But Varèse refused, despite Claudel's insistence.[4] At the same time, a remark of Varèse's, reported in the June 11, 1945, issue of *Newsweek*, gives us some idea of his state of mind at the time: "I haven't made enough money from my compositions even to pay for my funeral." In effect, it seems probable that it was only thanks to his wife's work as a translator and the help of a few patrons that he was able to subsist through the long years of that difficult period. During those years, Louise Varèse translated *la Joie* by Bernanos, Rimbaud's *les Illuminations,* Baudelaire's *le Spleen de Paris,* Julien Gracq's *le Château d'Argol,* Proust's *Plaisirs et regrets,* several novels by Simenon, and later on, *Eloges* by Saint-John Perse. It was at the time of the International Composers' Guild, during the period when he had least material worries, and when his works were being performed, that Varèse composed most of his works. The tranquillity of mind he enjoyed at that time had enabled him to make music as a whole take a gigantic step forward, especially since he was then in the prime of life. But the progress on to *Déserts* could only be accomplished in solitude, in sickness, and often in despair. All that he was to give the world in 1947 was his *Etude d'Espace.* For *Espace,* as he had at first conceived it, was no longer possible.

During these postwar years, Varèse's words were often bitter. For ten years he did battle with the impossible, often refusing to write even a single note, cursing music. But though his words were hard, they were not unjust. His sufferings had earned him the right to say what he felt about the richest country in the world, the country which had just allowed Bartòk to die in poverty. (Later, Arthur Lourié was to write, referring to Bartòk's funeral: "Varèse and I found that we were the only musicians present.") Thus we find H. C. Schonberg, in the *Musical Digest,* reporting these words: "There is nothing for a true composer. People who are not composers make money. Hollywood. A stupid thing. You will see—this country will die because of the middleman. Here in America it's always an excitment to see who's coming next. Always the manager, the middleman, will try to make a discovery—a new virtuoso, a new singer. Conductors, they are anxious to get first performances, and then never play the music again. What *is* it, a first performance? What does it mean? The tenth, the twentieth performance—that's the important thing. Unfortunately for the majority in America, art is only tolerated. It is not a necessity. We must draw a line between entertainment and art. Art is from the shoulders up, the other from the hips down. And the poeple who contribute most to the low quality are those in radio and motion pictures. You can say this for me: I am fed up with 'give the people what they want.' What the people never get is a chance to choose. There is no choice. The big shots are very poor experts in knowing what the people want because they themselves have not yet caught up with the people." [5] Indeed, Varèse was to vent his spleen more than once on the impresarios; "always the middleman," he would cry in anger. (He hadn't read Dale Carnegie.) He was to say: They talk about a divorce between modern music and the public, but there can't be a divorce between them, because there's never been a marriage. And also: How can people know that they don't like these works when they don't know them? In the June, 1946, issue of the magazine *Listen* he gave his opinion of performers, virtuoso and otherwise: "A composition is only a blueprint, a graph, which awaits mechanical means for its sonorous realization. The responsibility of a performer is thus very great. But he cannot go beyond the work. Sometimes a masterly execution of a familiar composition so stirs an audience that the performance appears as a 'revelation.' The listeners in their enthusiasm attribute what seems to them a metamorphosis entirely to the virtuoso. He has, however, simply brought to life what the work contains, but which other performers have failed to find or failed to project. . . . It is evident that even a performer who tries sincerely to respect the letter as well as the spirit of a work cannot function, cannot do it justice, unless given a certain latitude. The music must be allowed to speak. I am always a little suspicious of scores too meticulously marked, with too many indications, as of an overly finicky performance where each note is a fatal affair, and the least detail intellectualized to the detriment of the general line, the sweep of the work as a whole. . . . Naturally, each performer has a different approach, a different rendition, of the same work resulting from all that has gone to make up his personality—temperament, natural gifts, attainments, conditioning, cultural baggage—determining the reflexes which come into play in contact with the work.

"I must say that my preference goes to the present trend of the younger generation of performers: the objective, realistic, business-like way they attack and present a work, bringing its architecture into strong relief, sticking to the dynamics the work and the composer demand, and doing full justice to details and episodes without exaggerating them. A solid, precise technique permits them to dispense with virtuosic exhibitionism. . . . As for those performers who are afraid that, unless they use a work as a soapbox—or a sidewalk—their personalities will be diminished, let me point out that respect for a work and complete submission to its will cannot fail to exalt an interpreter's personality. For when he and the work become one, his stature is increased and that of the work as well.

"With Bach comes to a close a period in which he was not only the dominating figure as a composer but also the most rigorous planner, organizer and codifier. Whether the destiny of music called for the severity of his regimen or not is questionable, but the fact remains that there is no mystery, and never has been, about what Bach demands in regard to the performance of his scores." The magazine *Listen* had invited four people, considered as the leaders in their particular fields, to give their opinions on the question of interpretation; the four were Varèse, Maggie Teyte, Arthur Schnabel, and the musicologist Gustave Reese.

After the dissolution of The Greater New York Chorus, Varèse entered into a collaboration with the New Music Society, which had a chorus of twenty-two voices. Then he completed his *Etude* in February, 1947. This work is composed for two pianos, percussion and mixed chorus. Perhaps for the first time in the history of music, Varèse dispensed with a coherent text having a meaning of its own and instead selected various phrases from different languages, none having any meaning in relation to the others, and perhaps not even in itself, since one would at least have to know all the languages to begin with. Thus Varèse began from the principle, which he had already expressed, that a chorus must have concrete words to bite into, that consonants are necessary, and that it cannot therefore be given only vowels or diphthongs to sing. The chorus speaks, declaims, and becomes, so various are the sonorities of its words, a sort of percussion section. In addition, the chorus also performs a melodic function, since Varèse employs it, in certain sections, in its full polyphonic capacity. We should remember, therefore, that the use he makes of the chorus in *Etude* is very different from that found in *Ecuatorial* and much closer to what we find in *Nocturnal*, though the semantic dimension has not been suppressed in the latter as it was in *Etude*. The use of the percussion is also very solid, with some unique inventions. This is why, even though this work was never played again during Varèse's lifetime, it deserves to be published like any of the others. The criterion of its singularity is to my mind quite sufficient justification for this. It is a work in which the composer's suffering abruptly explodes after his long silence and struggles in the desert. The aggression in its percussive attack hits one in the pit of the stomach. And the search for some infinity, expressed by the chorus, is very clear in certain sections. The first and only performance of *Etude* took place at the New School for Social Research on February 23, 1947. The twenty-two-voice chorus, made up of amateurs, was certainly inadequate. I am lucky enough to possess a tape of the only 78 r.p.m. records of it (three sides) that Varèse preserved. Since the composer also conducted the work himself, this recording is also the only document that has come down to us of his conception of how to conduct percussion and chorus, even though the chorus was not powerful enough, at least on the recording. Later, Varèse used two or three excerpts from *Etude* in his *Poème électronique,* though they were so transposed and filtered as to become unrecognizable. He also used the soprano's cry in *Nocturnal,* though "skewering" it with a piccolo. However, the acoustical atmosphere of *Nocturnal* is in fact very different. It doesn't seem important to me whether or not *Etude* and *Nocturnal,* for example, are masterpieces. They both move me profoundly, and each, in its uniqueness, contributes essential elements to our knowledge of Varèse's world of sound. That is what is important. Varèse himself looked upon his work, performed in 1947, as an *Etude,* so that we too must look upon it as such, in the same way that we accept being moved by a painter's sketch. The final page of *Etude* was moreover published as a photograph in the 1947–48 winter issue of the magazine *Possibilities.*

On March 30, 1947, with the same chorus, Varèse conducted a concert entitled "Modern Music of the Sixteenth and Seventeenth Centuries." The program consisted of works by Nicolas de Grigny, Couperin, Monteverdi, Marc-Antoine Charpentier, Frescobaldi, Schütz and Grandi. The best critics in New York attended. Kurt List commented in his article: "Varèse's great contribution to early Medieval, Renaissance and Baroque music has been his approach to it. At no point has it been a dusty pilgrimage into antiquity to him. Varèse's performances of pre-Bach music are totally kindled and

historically precise as plodding presentations elsewhere never are."
Olin Downes, of the *New York Times,* emphasized Varèse's musical
sense and his very deep knowledge of the great music of that period.[6]
It is thus evident that Varèse was often more appreciated as an
initiator into music of the past than as a creator. I shall always feel
a nostalgia for Varèse conducting Monteverdi. How regrettable it is
that no recording of those marvelous moments exists. Varèse was a
born chorus-master. Ever since his days at the Schola Cantorum,
when he was twenty, he had been deepening his knowledge of this
music, which he preferred above all other kinds. It was a profound
joy to him to conduct those works. And that joy and love could not
fail to communicate themselves to the listener in a kind of dazzlement.
One felt the atmosphere of the hall filled with a kind of angelic
radiance—even after the concert was over.

But let us return to Kurt List's article, for he also went on to
discuss Varèse as a creative artist: "Varèse's music of the twenties is
literally clairvoyant—presaging physical discoveries which extended
beyond theory only two decades later. . . . He realized that scientific
systems spring from concepts just as philosophy and art, and therefore hinged his music on conceptual rather than physical qualities of
motored operation. He side-stepped both the primitive mechanism of
futurist noise-makers, and the emotional retrospection of certain works
by followers of Arnold Schoenberg. In this manner Varèse alone has
been able to take a modernly percussive route and reach a distinguished and relevant style. . . . Varèse has carried his awareness of
modern activity beyond composing, and into his work as a conductor
and organizer. No style is too abstruse for precise projection at his
hands. . . ."

During the summer of 1948, Varèse was invited by Columbia University to give a series of classes in composition. In addition, he was
asked to prepare a series of lectures on twentieth century music.
Varèse had necessarily to limit himself in his choice of musical examples as well as in his choice of the composers to be covered. Having
sketched out a plan for the whole series, he wrote to each of the
living composers he wished to discuss. (But since he would almost
certainly be giving a lecture on American music, he was also obliged
to write to the majority of living American composers). For ex-

ample, in a letter to Dallapiccola, dated May 10, 1948, we find
Varèse asking the Italian composer to state his beliefs as briefly as
possible and to send over any documents that might be helpful in
the elucidation of his intentions, whether technical or esthetic. He
also asked the following questions: (1) which work, of all those recorded, do you consider as most typical, as most representative of
your work? (2) can you send me, together with a copy of the recording and the score of the work you choose, your own analysis of that
work? (Schoenberg's reply included a twenty-page account of his
esthetic.) Among the composers studied, not all, of course, living,
were Satie, Debussy, Ravel, Schoenberg, Webern, Bartòk, Stravinsky,
Krenek, Dallapiccola, Messiaen, and Alois Hába. This procedure on
Varèse's part makes it clear how much he respected the conceptions of
other creators, and there is no doubt that it enabled him to expound
the thoughts and works of other composers with the greatest objectivity.
His first step was to put himself humbly at each composer's service.
Then afterwards, with equal simplicity, he was able to give his own
very subjective opinion. He would first explain the other composer's thought, thus running less risk of distorting it, and only
then take up a personal position which was all the more clearcut
and original for his being himself a creator of the first rank, with a
profound knowledge of music, individual intuitions, and individual
tastes. All of which was recognized by the critic Olin Downes in an
article that appeared in the *New York Times* of July 25th. In speaking
of Busoni, Varèse criticized neo-classicism in these terms: "To Ferruccio Busoni must be given the credit for the inception of this idea
around 1917. It was taken up later in the twenties by such composers as Hindemith in Germany and Stravinsky in France.

"With Busoni it was originally a protest against the late nineteenth
century Romanticism, a tendency he disliked. For Busoni, who ador-
ed Mozart, neo-classicism was a return to clarity, elegance, logic, a
return of ideals of the eighteenth century.

"Now, in spite of the very fine works which have been done by
gifted composers who have chosen to limit themselves by this formula,
it is, it seems to me, a dangerous and pernicious principle. For, good
or bad, it seems to me that it looks in the wrong direction. It takes
the parkways and not the lonely and uncharted roads through the
wilderness; it gives up adventure, effort, research, experimentation.

It is a real menace to the progress of the art and science of music. . . .

"Neo-classicism has been called a style. It might be called a style in the sense of being a fashion—comparable to a product of the garment industry. There is too often, in this return to Bach, Scarlatti, Pergolesi, Couperin, Mozart, and so forth, a mixture of superficial musicology and intellectual sycophancy or pure indolence.

"When music or any other art begins to look back over its shoulder it is because it is out of touch with reality. It refuses to face the problems of its own day. . .

"Leaving a concert of contemporary music one is forced to conclude that most composers are deaf or that their perception is limited to the sounds that orchestras have been making for a couple of hundred years." [7]

At the end of a letter to Dallapiccola, Varèse told the Italian composer that he had heard his work *Due liriche di Anacreonte* and that it had given him great joy. Dallapiccola himself has since written to me: "His first letter was an event for me; you mustn't forget how difficult beginnings can be . . . and that particular work was my first to be performed in the United States. . . What joy, shortly afterwards, to receive a letter from the Maestro whom I admired so much." [8] In another letter, Dallapiccola gave me his own reaction to neo-classicism: "I remember that in my country people were writing (without even blinking an eye) that 'Germany has only one great composer: Paul Hindemith.' The latest work by Hindemith or Stravinsky always constituted the 'sensation' in our concert halls." [9] Moreover, as Dallapiccola recalled, it was not until 1946, in Venice, that a work by Webern, the *opus 21,* was played for the first time in Italy. Varèse was to wait even longer.

In the last month of 1948, Varèse was confined to his bed by illness for five weeks. It was at this time that the conductor Frederic Waldman was preparing a concert that was to be given, under the auspices of the League of Composers, as a tribute to the memory of Paul Rosenfeld, a great friend of Varèse's, who had just died. This concert was to take place on January 23, 1949, in the auditorium of the Museum of Modern Art in New York. Waldman had chosen *Hyperprism* as one of the works to be played. Having made certain inquiries as to Varèse's intentions, Waldman then discussed with him, at the same meeting, the long-playing record of Varèse's work that

Waldman was later to conduct, and which was to be brought out by E.M.S. Waldman was to write later of the man he met in 1949: "At that time Varèse was known as having reached maturity, and as having shown the way to a new generation willing to take over and follow his line. I expected to meet the sedate Olympian, settled with contentment, proud of the proficiency of his past. Instead I was delighted to find a man full of progressive ideas on music and with a mind open to the new. The tragic symptoms of the aging revolutionary who has exhausted himself were not evident. Varèse has spent a lifetime pursuing new aspects and possibilities and at no time has he ever been satisfied with repeating himself on the basis of a recent success." [10] The composer Virgil Thomson wrote, after having heard *Hyperprism*: "It is a real 'modern music' of twenty years back, and it still makes its point. . . . The sounds that Varèse makes in this piece are handsome in the abstract; and with no cue as to the work's particular meaning, your listener found it absorbing, convincing, beautiful and in every way grand. . . I know, it is great music." [11] Thus, little by little, the critics were to arrive at a second stage of acquaintance with Varèse's works. The more clear-sighted of them were no longer to write in the same fashion as during the twenties. War works profound, even unconscious transformations in men. They awaken suddenly to find values they had supposed solid and alive lying in ruins all around them. The "pupils" that Varèse was to find visiting him were to be much more exacting as musicians, and much more aware of the true problems. It was they who were to rediscover Varèse after his long silence, and not the electrical engineers, as one critic has claimed. In 1949, for example, the Chinese composer Chou Wen Chung, who had first arrived in the United States in 1946, came knocking at his door. (It was Chou Wen Chung who, after Varèse's death, was to have the privilege and the extremely heavy task of going over even the very smallest fragments of *Nocturnal* and *Nuit*, the compositions on which Varèse had still not finished working. And in the case of *Nocturnal*, at Louise Varèse's request, he was to search until he found extracts which would permit the completion and publication of the work. He had already for some time had the intention of writing a book on Varèse's work; now, happily, he will be able to base his work on Varèse's own manuscripts, thus making it possible for him to compare them with the published scores, in order to make certain that no inaccuracies have slipped into them.) Many others were to follow, from Japan, from Canada, etc.

In Buenos Aires, the composer Juan Carlos Paz wrote a long article on Varèse's work which he entitled: "Varèse's contribution to experimental music."[12] In Sweden, Olaf Stakenberg offered a study in the *Expressen* of July 9, 1949. In Germany, Stuckenschmidt and Josef Rufer wrote asking Varèse for an article for their magazine *Stimmen*.[13] In the United States, the magazine *Possibilities* published the questions of eight composers (Robert Palmer, Adolph Weiss, Milton Babbitt, Kurt List, Henry Cowell, John Cage, Harold Shapero, and Jacques de Menace), together with the answers of Varèse and Alexis Haieff.[14]

It is regrettable that the conductors then at the height of their fame, like Stokowski, should not have programmed Varèse's great compositions, such as *Arcana* and *Amériques,* afresh at this stage. They could have done a great deal to make those works known to a wider public. Only Waldman and Slonimsky were to remain faithful at this time. But despite these reservations, in 1949 it was genuinely possible to talk of a renaissance, of a new and growing awareness, of a new audience. From that year on, Varèse himself was to continue his forward progress of the twenties. His true destiny was beginning, one might say, paradoxically. Henceforth it was to become possible to understand and love him as he was in himself, in all his miraculous individuality. He was sixty-five years old.

17

Varèse's Originality

Jack Skurnick, a record producer whose products were sold under the E.M.S. label (Elaine Music Shop, which was on 44th Street), asked Sidney Finkelstein to introduce him to the most important living composer still not represented on records. Finkelstein named Varèse, and Skurnick, full of enthusiasm, decided to record Varèse's entire output. But unfortunately he died after the appearance of the first record (EMS-401). Frederic Waldman was chosen to conduct the Juilliard Percussion Orchestra and the New York Wind Ensemble. René le Roy performed *Densité 21.5,* Finkelstein wrote the sleeve notes, and by an unfortunate error gave the date of composition of *Ionisation* as 1924. For the first recording, five works had initially been selected; however, in order to avoid compromising the technical quality of the recording, which meant keeping the amount of music recorded below fourteen minutes per side, it was finally decided to record only *Intégrales, Densité 21.5, Ionisation,* and *Octandre.* This record was of enormous importance, not only because of the compositions it made available, but also because of the quality of recorded sound achieved by the sound engineer, Robert E. Blake, who had Varèse himself as advisor throughout. For ten years, this was the only Varèse recording on the market, if we except one other recording of *Densité 21.5.* It was through this recording that the majority of young composers discovered Varèse's works—in most cases long before they were able to hear any of them in a concert, and even before they were able to study them in score form. Varèse's name had been forgotten. It was not even known. In 1950, in Paris, for example, he was known only to a very few initiates. At that time, Olivier Messiaen evidently remarked to the composer Iannis Xénakis that "the greatest living French composer was Edgard Varèse, who is unfortunately unknown and misunderstood." [1] The distribution of this record was to enable Varèse, little by little, to break through the wall of silence surrounding him. And from that point on, nothing could stop the expansion of his musical universe.

Varèse began composing the instrumental part of *Déserts* during the summer of 1950. But he was invited to visit Germany that year, and was consequently obliged to interrupt his work.

He arrived in Frankfurt on July 27th. Darmstadt is scarcely more than a thirty-minute journey from there, and Varèse had been invited partly by Wolfgang Steinnecke to give a course of lectures in Darmstadt, and partly by the American High Commission to lecture on his "theories" of music in the various "America Houses" in the principal West German cities.

Wolfgang Steinnecke had been trying to make Darmstadt into "the place in Germany where living music shall be reborn from the ashes of stupidity and oppression." [2] First, having obtained the castle of Kranischstein from Ludwig Metzger for the purpose, he founded the Kranischsteiner Musikinstitut in 1946. Among the students Varèse taught in 1950 was, for example, Luigi Nono. At the end of the course, Hermann Scherchen was to say of Varèse: "This man of sixty-five has suddenly appeared on the horizon of the musical world, not as a twilight-shrouded figure but rather as a living torch burning with creative musical ideas." Varèse left Germany on September 23rd.

In June, 1951, Dallapiccola was invited to teach a course in composition at the Tanglewood Berkshire Music Center. It was there that he met Varèse for the first time: "Very difficult to describe my impression to you," he has since written to me; "a giant, violent and very witty in conversation; a prince who enjoys dealing with the people. You should have heard him talking tbout Paris . . . and that whole Parisian world; you would have been in stitches too. And when one went out with him one got the impression that he was the King of

Greenwich Village: he knew all the bars; he chatted with everyone. . . A miracle of simplicity hiding beneath one of the most complex personalities it would be possible to imagine." [3]

After hearing the E.M.S. record, Henry Miller wrote to Varèse: "Last night my wife and I had the first chance of hearing your recordings—chez des amis ici, deux musiciens. Tout le monde était ravi. In fact, 'knocked out.' I had the definite impression that 25 or 35 years before the horrible discovery of the powers of the atom, you were already in the new age. No one crossed the frontier with the courage and the integrity which your music reveals. My wife who is by no means a connoisseur of music remarked that the music reminded her of the title of a Greek poet's famous (and as yet unknown) work: *Proauakrousna*, or 'A Knocking to Awaken.' We were really awake, I tell you—and more—electrified. . . . How pale and feeble your imitators sound! You are a healthy man, alive to the finger-tips. The music confirms it. Now and then I thought I heard sounds from ancient Tibet, Japan, Siam—and the Polynesian world. It is gay too. Ah! The gay wisdom, as Nietzsche said. . . . It was like a joyous electrocution. The martyrs of old often went to the stake singing. . . No one goes thus to the electric chair. Dommage." [4] Yes, Miller was right when he said he thought he could hear "sounds" of Tibet. . . Later, when sending Varèse a copy of *Plexus,* he enclosed the following note (written in French) : *"Varèse*. The name has really gotten into my guts. Your face, your mouth, your voice. Unforgettable. Stay there with the angels, dear maestro."[5] It was with this same generosity of spirit and enthusiasm that Miller poured out those extraordinary pages in his *Air-conditioned Nightmare.* And let us not forget that those pages were published in 1945. All that Miller could have heard, at that point in time, were the 78 r.p.m. recordings of *Ionisation* and (possibly) *Octandre.* And it was this same recording of *Ionisation*, made before the war, that first enabled the young Boulez to hear a work by Varèse—in about 1944, and doubtless through the intermediary of Messiaen.

During the single year 1951, *Ionisation* was played in several cities. After a performance at the Festival of Illinois, Virgil Thomson was to write: "The Varèse *Ionisation* . . . I fancy, about to become a classic. This composer, once thought outrageously advanced, has of late been coming into general acceptance by musicians." [6]

But this judgment of Thomson's was premature as we shall see. The battles were beginning again. Two years later, in his book *Rhythm and Tempo,* Curt Sachs was to say: "This (*Ionisation*) is a truly extraordinary piece in extraordinary rhythms and counter-rhythms, and perhaps the greatest rhythmic inspirations ever materialized." [7]

In 1951, Schoenberg died. Varèse confided to Dallapiccola on October 21st: "It is sad that Schoenberg is no longer with us. His success gave me great pleasure, and you know my friendship and admiration for him." In 1953, Varèse was to say to Fred Grunfeld in the course of a radio conversation, that Schoenberg, Webern and Berg were great *despite* their system. But he was much less respectful of the dodecaphonists, their imitators. He was to emphasize this attitude in a letter to Dallapiccola written on December 7, 1952: "I'm working a great deal—especially in the sphere of 'sound' which for me is the solid base of music, my raw material. The intellectualism of the interval is a factor which for me has nothing to do with our age and its new concepts. As obsolete as the artificial versification of a Banville. (Not to be misinterpreted. This doesn't apply to artists like Schoenberg, Webern, you and a few others—but to those clever-clever fellows who need crutches—and who, since they lack talent, do not know that talent is not something conferred upon one by any amount of professional trickery, but that it stamps its mark upon a successful work by brushing aside all the pedantic routines of the musical mass-producers). Do you know this passage from Valéry? 'In all the arts there is a physical aspect that we can no longer consider or deal with as we have in the past. Neither space, nor time, nor matter any longer represents for us what it has always represented before. We must accept that all these changes necessarily transform the techniques of art, influence even the faculties of invention—influence them deeply enough to modify the conception of art itself.' "

In 1951, the magazine *l'Age du cinéma* announced that Varèse was to work on a film entitled *le Minotaure,* to be directed by Hans Richter.[8] As far as I know, however, this film was never made.

Varèse's first collaboration with his moviemaker friend Thomas Bouchard dates back to the early forties. During the war, as was well known, Fernand Léger stayed in Bouchard's house, 80 West 40th Street. Bouchard began making a film about the artist and his work in

1942, and finished it in 1945. Now Varèse and Léger had known each other for many years. Indeed, they had belonged to the same French army unit during the First World War. Bouchard asked Varèse if he would choose extracts from *Octandre, Ionisation, Intégrales,* and *Hyperprism* for the sound track of his film. The first official showing took place at the Sorbonne on April 5, 1946. For the second film, which was about Kurt Seligmann and was called *la Naissance d'un tableau,* Bouchard suggested to Varèse that he should select and arrange a series of excerpts from music of the baroque era. This second film was finished in 1950. But Varèse's most important collaboration with Bouchard was on the latter's film *Around and About Joan Miró,* which was shot in color and lasts some sixty-six minutes. The first showing of this took place early in October, 1955, at the Fogg Museum in Cambridge, Massachusetts. For the sequence called *The Procession of Vergès,* which was shot in black and white, Varèse provided a soundtrack he had recorded himself, at home, and which was ultimately a combination of four different tapes. Moreover, this work was carried out over a period of time also taken up with his research into the sounds he would require for the taped interpolations in *Déserts,* which we shall return to later. Needless to say, Varèse had to work with rudimentary equipment, since he had no sound studio at his disposal. Despite this, the music he produced is very striking. According to the description of the filmed sequence sent me by Thomas Bouchard, what one sees on the screen is a Good Friday procession which begins at midnight in a little village some sixty miles outside Barcelona. In the narrow streets—lighted solely by the flickering glow emanating from shells stuck to the walls of the houses —we see boys and men walking towards us, dressed in blue and white tights, and with their faces hidden behind death's head masks. They dance and dance, as though bewitched by the Gregorian melodies sung by tall, cowled figures. Following them are the young girls, gliding slowly through the shadows, and grief-stricken penitents, all chained together and accompanied by a statue of the Virgin Mary wearing a crown of lighted candles. Lastly, come soldiers in Roman-style armor surrounding a fourteen-foot-high wooden figure of Christ. It is easy to imagine the atmosphere. Such a sequence of images was bound to fascinate Varèse, who had once lived in a Romanesque house, and exalt his imagination. The track of organized sounds lasts two minutes, forty-seven seconds. But Bouchard, in order to make this film, had to live for five months with Mirò in Spain in order to impregnate himself with the light and the colors that are inevitably mirrored in Mirò's works.

Varèse was also chosen to work on a film entitled *Carnegie Hall*. We know from Lucile Lawrence what happened: "When Boris Morros filmed his picture, *Carnegie Hall,*" she recalls, "Varèse was asked to compose a special work for the film, for which he was paid. The day came for the rehearsal, and Varèse went down to listen. When he heard the liberties they had taken with his music, he said, 'Here is your check. Give me my score,' and departed." The check, one imagines, must have been fairly enormous. Was the work in question *Etude pour Espace?* Varèse was often asked to write musical comedies for Broadway. He would answer: "I can't, it takes a talent I don't have."

His interest in films was doubtless related to his equally strong passion for painting, which dated back to his early youth. We must not forget those years when Varèse used to take his glass of *rouge* with Modigliani and other painters. He had even painted pictures himself—the canvases that used to decorate his dining room. The painters he admired most were Cimabue, Giotto, El Greco, Rubens, Goya, Picasso, Chagall, Dubuffet, the Tachists, and the early works of Kandinsky and Klee. Needless to say, Julio Gonzalez was among the sculptors he most admired, as was Giacometti, who also entertained great respect for Varèse.

Varèse began composing the instrumental parts of *Déserts* in the summer of 1950, and completed them late in 1952. Then, with the help of a technical assistant, he began recording the noises to be used in his taped interpolations of organized sound, most of which he gathered up in the ironworks, sawmills and various factories of Philadelphia. In this way he continued to build up his own sound-library until the summer of 1954. But the rumor was already current in Paris, before 1952, that there was a composer in New York who had a conception of percussion that was consistent with the direction then being taken by the new, so-called "concrete" music. In his book published in 1952, Pierre Schaeffer, speaking of Varèse, said: " (He) has devoted himself to that poor relation of the orchestra, the per-

cussion section. He has promoted it to the rank of 'orchestra.' He
has added to it, here and there, various effects provided by American
studios (sic). I do not know the details. More or less electrical
'Varinettes,' bellowing sounds produced by some unknown means,
but occasionally in every way similar to ours. Varèse speeds across
France without touching down. This Frenchman has not had the
ill luck, as we have, to be a prophet in his own country. . . And the
strange thing is that Varèse, who has continued, though with improve-
ments, to make use of the orchestra, who does not use a 'prepared'
piano as Cage does, composes music which occasionally bears a singular resemblance to *musique concrète*." [9] The Varèse evoked in these
pages appears in the guise of a sorcerer, a sort of alchemist working in
some hidden room at the heart of an imaginary laboratory. Nothing
is really known about him. No one knows what to imagine. Thus
it is that the false legends have sprung up that are so difficult to
uproot. Of course one can say and write, if one wishes, that Varèse's
compositions have a resemblance to *musique concrète*. But, in fact,
there is no comparison. Varèse's works, conceived long beforehand,
and ripened over a long period of time, have a much more considerable esthetic import. They cannot be reduced to that superficial
element of originality represented by the technique—which however
new it may be is still in the end, as we ought to remember, no more
than a technique—of employing sounds recorded on magnetic tape.
Varèse's compositions possess a beauty of sound and structure far ex-
ceeding the effects obtained by the seekers of so-called *musique
concrète*. (Though I do not wish to minimize the importance of their
researches in any way here: I am concerned only with re-establishing
the perspective of values). Varèse's esthetic has a place for *all music,*
including *musique concrète,* "tape music," "electronic music," or whatever you choose to call it; his vision of the universe of sound trans-
cends such limits. He employs such techniques insofar as he needs
them as elements in a given composition. Like Monteverdi, his ultimate passion was for the finished work: an authentic work of art
impregnated with imagination, sensibility, structure, and humanity.
We know how intransigent he was on this point. (One has only
to think of *Etude pour Espace,* and later *Nocturnal.*) All the rest
is mere cardboard fakery. This was why, as we shall see later, with
the very first of his works in which he incorporated taped inter-

polations of organized sounds he far surpassed in beauty, in power, in tragic depth, everything that anyone had been able to produce in the various sound studios. Varèse made no experiments and wrote no experimental music. He was a composer of genius who had already foreseen the possibility of these new directions thirty years before. He had had the time to know what he wanted, to represent to himself what it was he wanted *to hear*. All he then desired was that music should attain to the most total liberty. I believe that at the very moment I am writing these lines one can truthfully say of the majority of the "works" produced by the experimenters in studios what Paul Valéry once said of our progress in science: "A stage has been reached where our means of investigation and action have left our means of representation and comprehension far behind them." [10] Whereas in the case of Varèse, who was a genius, his means of representation and the depth of his comprehension far surpassed his means of action. For electronics, even in 1965, were still not sufficiently developed to express his inner music in all its fullness and sublimity of sound. Existentially, he could not but be caught in a ceaseless conflict between his "dreams" and the technical means of making them manifest. This fundamental dialectic could not fail to distress and exasperate him, to stretch him on a sort of perpetual spiritual rack. That is why, when considering his development as a composer, I refuse to let myself speak of Varèse as a precursor of *musique concrète*. Varèse was a creator in his own right, a visionary who was able to incorporate everything into a work. He thought only of the work in hand, like any artisan; he thought only of how to express himself, like any creator; he thought only of how to communicate the inaccessible, like any genius. For as he himself often insisted, the machine can give back only what man gives to the machine. Without a brain to feed it, even the most complex of computers is nothing. But I shall return to *Déserts* later on. The first copyright of this work was taken out in 1953. Frederick Prausnitz was to give the first performance of the instrumental sections in June, 1953, but the project fell through. Varèse was to tell Dallapiccola: "Our June concert—and my latest work—had to be cancelled for lack of a blessing from the union. You know its omnipotence and the control it exercises over the country's sixth industry: music." [11]

During a visit to New York in 1952, Pierre Boulez met Varèse for the first time. In 1953, Scherchen conducted *Ionisation* in Rome. Varèse wrote to Dallapiccola on September 29th: "In case he (Scherchen) has difficulty in obtaining some of the instruments the work requires, please advise him to approach some of the American *jazz bands* (they must abound in Rome) and he will certainly find what he needs."

On December 13, 1953, the New York radio station WQXR devoted a program to Varèse entitled *Mind over Music*. He told the interviewer at that time: "I think that what we need in the musical world is more spirit." Then he went on to discuss Debussy, and observed that "in *Jeux,* we find a higher state of tension than in any work before it." During this period, Varèse was slowly emerging in all his profound originality. To some, his works now seemed the most original since those of Debussy and Schoenberg, the most expressive of our age. After the war years, after the Korean war, there was little musical discourse that could stand up to a confrontation with history, with the age of concentration camps, the H bomb, civil wars, and persistent famine. War creates a void in which few works are able to preserve their validity. And silence is always preferable to lies, unless one is content to take refuge in a dead and sometimes intolerable past.

18

Déserts

On February 8, 1954, André Malraux made a great effort to persuade Varèse that he should go back to Europe: "That you should come over to Europe," he wrote in his letter, "there can be no doubt. Your works intrigue all the young musicians here, fascinate those who know them, and give those who have heard only a part of them the feeling that there is something imbued with true pathos going on there; something for which our sensibility is at last ready, and which would doubtless find the sudden audience so long awaited by Satie. The topicality provided by the presence of their creator would crystallize within a month all that now remains scattered, and which is ready to cease being so. From the point of view of the United States, in the realm I know best, that of painting, it seems to me that the legitimacy of the aid which should be accorded to creations such as yours would be very easily understood. Whether John Marin is American or not, his work is part of the expression of this country. It bears witness to it. Your music written in New York harmonizes with that city by means of underlying voices that will be recognized for what they are immediately. The United States has the privilege of defining itself in part by what it gives rise to, as the Netherlands once defined themselves by the hospitality which they accorded to liberty of thought. And for posterity, the Frenchman Descartes is no mean ambassador of the Dutchman's honor. After all, when the plaque is put up on that little house in Sullivan Street, there will be no way of not recognizing that it is indeed in New York.

"Both here and in Germany you will find many musicians and writers who will be happy to support your work; and some who will be proud to do so. Come. . ."

In fact, Varèse had been thinking of visiting Paris for some time at this point, since he had already received another invitation, this one from Pierre Schaeffer, to go and finish his taped interpolations for *Déserts* there. On January 8, 1954, he mentioned this in a letter to Dallapiccola which finished thus: "MUSICA LIBERA." But on April 10th, he wrote again: "Caro Maestro and amico. Since I am going back to work on my German and Italian, perhaps I shall be able to enter into a bilingual correspondence with you one of these days." Then he explained why he had delayed so long in replying to a letter: "The blame must be laid on work—work that is going to keep me here for another 2 or 3 months—and in consequence force me to postpone my trip to Europe. But it only means that the pleasure will be postponed until early September. I shall do everything I can to try to come to Italy, which I don't know, and if it can be arranged you will be one of the first I shall visit. I shall in any case give you warning of my arrival and keep you informed of all my plans."

We know from an article by Abraham Skulsky in the January 24th *New York Herald Tribune* that by the beginning of 1954 Varèse was already very far advanced in the composition of a work commissioned by the Louisville Symphony Orchestra. The work was apparently to be entitled *Trinum*; it was divided into three sections to be played without a break and was based upon three fundamental elements: tension, intensity, and rhythm (treated as an element of stability and not as meter). The texture was created by intervals that occurred, for the most part, in groups of three. Though it was written for orchestra, Varèse was to transform this work, after the first performance, into "organized sounds on tape," so that it should not be limited by the tempered scale system. There is no doubt that the three sections of this work became the three taped interpolations in *Déserts*. However, this does not necessarily mean that it was not until 1954 that Varèse decided to incorporate interpolations of taped organized sounds into the orchestral work he had entitled *Déserts*. The development of those interpolations from

Trinum makes this seem probable, but the matter still remains in doubt.

As I have said, Pierre Schaeffer invited Varèse to Paris so that he could complete his interpolations of organized sound at the Radio-Télévision Française research center. The first performance of *Déserts,* we must remember, was to be broadcast by the R.T.F. Orchestra. (Though Schaeffer was to say later on, in *les Lettres Françaises* on June 16, 1965: "I didn't like that work. . . ." He would have liked to have been able to dissuade Scherchen from compromising himself in this venture, which he himself had doubts about "occasionally.")

Varèse arrived at Le Havre on October 5, 1954, bringing his sounds and his diagrams with him. He then set to work in the research studio organizing, filtering, and metamorphosing his noises. It was a great moment for him. At last some of his dream images could take real shape—though still very imperfectly as yet. In Paris, the Concerts du Petit-Marigny (later to become the Concerts du Domaine Musical) presented *Densité 21.5* and *Octandre* under the direction of Scherchen.

But before we go any further, it is important that we go back for a moment in order to investigate the very conception of *Déserts.* Varése himself explained to Abraham Skulsky of the *New York Herald Tribune* that it had been conceived originally as the concert version of a film that was to be called *Déserts.* The film itself was to be made *after* the musical score. Varèse's intention was to create a film that would be truly original in its conception of the relations between image and sound. Visually, the film was to reveal several aspects of the desert or wilderness: the deserts of earth (sand, snow) ; the deserts of the sea; the deserts of outer space (galaxies, nebulae, etc.) ; but particularly *the deserts in the mind of man.* Varèse also said: "Visual image and organized sound will not duplicate each other. For the most part light and sound will work in opposition in such a way as to give the maximum emotional reaction. Sometimes they will join for dramatic effect and in order to create a feeling of unity. Such contrasts achieved through the synchronization of simultaneous, unrelated elements would create a dissociation of ideas which would excite the imagination and stimulate the emotions."[1] Though the musical part of the work subsists, the film itself, on the other hand, was never made.

We know what Varèse meant by the title *Déserts*. But let us not forget that this work had been ripening in his unconscious since 1936 or 1937. Varèse had set out from the physical desert of New Mexico, that desert of sand in which his body was being consumed, to cross a fifteen-year wilderness of the spirit, the desert of solitude and silence, the desert of both physical and moral suffering. The desert is a hard school. Remember how the majestic theme of brotherhood, to be expressed in *Espace*, was little by little devoured by a tragic vision of the world reflecting the infinite disaster of the Spanish Civil War, the Second World War, and then the Korean War. The tragedy exploded first in *Etude pour Espace*. Then the vision was further amplified until it reached its paroxysm in the taped interpolations for *Déserts*. One thinks of Miguel de Unamuno's conclusion to his work of fire and sword, *Del Sentimiento Trágico de la Vida en los Hombres y en los Pueblos*: "But the desert hears, though men do not hear, and will be transformed one day into a forest of sound. . ." [2] With Varèse, the desert was transmuted into disaster, into the sounds of despair. A forest of din and of even more terrible silences. . . After hearing *Déserts* for the first time, I wrote to Varèse to tell him of the shock it caused, of its effect as a great cry comparable to Picasso's *Guernica*, (a comparison also made by Leonard Bernstein, in 1964, before a performance of *Déserts*). So many years of horror; the absurd nightmare of the concentration camp world, cities reduced to ashes, Hiroshima; so many men petrified in their solitude, so many men broken, so many minds consigned to the desert. The victorious Prometheus of *Arcana* had become a witness to all these things. And Prometheus in Auschwitz could only suffer, howl, and be silent. Suffer for those who no longer are: our bodiless dead, as I wrote then. The suffering there was too great for any revolt to rise and confront it.

Zarathustra is a white shade that dissolves into vapor as soon as it approaches the cry from the abyss. *Déserts* is not an anecdote, *Déserts* is not a description, *Déserts* stands beyond events. It is *suffering, horror, and desolation themselves* that Varèse is expressing, insofar as any work of art can take such things upon itself. This music has its roots in the archetypes of the great terrors, the great agonies, the profound anxieties that man has retained in the very heart of himself since those immemorial times when he lived in fear of the thunderbolt, the dark, volcanoes—in a word, Nature, forever laying him low,—and other men, the animals, and spirits. . . In the work itself, Varèse left to the organized sounds recorded on tape the task of expressing all those devastating, ruthless forces, the last nightmare of one already on the scaffold, the last panic terror of a man being thrust back into the water, the final shriek that death breaks off. In the instrumental sections, man was to advance, gradually, toward the sun, however distant that sun, in order that tomorrow he may be, may hope, may love again; in order that through him Life may shine. Few musical works produce so strong an evocation of Life and Death, since none has ever had such terrifying methods of sound production at its disposal before, or has had to express spiritual disasters, absurdities, and destructions of such horror.

The orchestral sections of *Déserts* are written for two flutes, two clarinets, two horns, three trumpets, three trombones, two tubas, a piano used as a resonating element, and five groups of percussion instruments. The taped interpolations of organized sounds are recorded on two tracks, since they are intended to be played back stereophonically. Varèse was to say that "the tapes are interpolated into the musical development at three points in antiphonal form." Then he was to add of the work as a whole: "The work progresses in opposing planes and volumes. Movement is created by the exactly calculated intensities and tensions which function in opposition to one another; the term 'intensity' referring to the desired acoustical result, the work 'tension' to the size of the interval employed." Then he concluded his notes by saying: "I am entirely on the side of invention and the application of new tools, of new means of expression, on condition that those tools and those means of expression, do not become mummified into doctrines, into safe dogmas. (I also believe that as soon as one gives up the struggle one begins to die. I belive that we should 'live dangerously,' that we must accept risks and their consequences)." (One is reminded of *In Praise of the Dangerous Life* by Blaise Cendrars.)

It was Pierre Boulez who introduced the first performance of the work to the public. (The reader may already know that Boulez, like the young Varèse, had studied mathematics and gone against the wishes of a businessman father to become the composer he is today.)

Having first described the evident structure of the work, he went on to say this of the musical language of *Déserts*: "The musical language given to the instrumental ensemble may be said to be evolved in opposing planes and volumes, the oppositions between them being manifested by the spaces maintained between the different pitches of sound, though without being founded upon any fixed system of intervals, such as a mode, a tone-row, or any sort of scale whatever. Then what is to provide them with movement, these aggregations of sound, true sound-complexes rather than chords in the traditional sense of that word? Their movement will be created by the dynamics, by the tensions. . . . This immediately means that we cannot use the word 'nuances,' for the term *dynamics* applies much more accurately to the acoustical effect desired, and obtained by means of the classic terms *piano* and *forte;* in the same way, the word 'tension' is more efficaciously applied to the magnitude and quality of the interval employed. These 'sound objects,' as it were, provided by the human potential of the orchestra, will be contrasted with the 'organized sounds' produced by a series of electro-acoustical links. . . . If you wish to provide yourself with a general idea of the construction of *Déserts,* you must remember that there are four sections of varying length developed by the instrumental forces; between these four sections there occur three interpolations of 'organized sounds' recorded on two-track magnetic tape. The shorter the sections are, the more they will be intensified and contracted into a state of extreme concentration. Thus we find Varèse showing himself once more to be a precursor in realms where contemporary music still has a great deal of unknown territory to explore. Any composer today cannot, in effect, not give his attention to two principal questions: one, the actual state of acoustics, which is presently calling into question all the notions on the subject codified since the eighteenth century, the other, the use of electro-acoustical and electronic methods. Is the possibility of some synthesis of these two orders of ideas yet perceptible? Varèse points out the path for us; better still, he has given us an example, a work." In effect, it must not be forgotten that this was the first time a composer had interpolated sections of organized and taped sound into an orchestral work. Moreover, the composer in question was soon to celebrate his seventy-first birthday.

As for the tapes, the R.T.F. studio had provided them in three different forms. The first consisted of "two superimposed tracks recorded at 38 centimeters a second"; the second of "two separate and appropriately marked tapes each corresponding to one of the playback channels and recorded at 76 centimeters per second"; and the third of "a single 76 cms.p.s. tape with the signals from both channels already mixed." These notes refer to the *first* version of the interpolations. Three other versions were to follow between the first performance and 1962, each an improvement on the one before, thanks to the progress of electronic technology.

Hermann Scherchen conducted the first performance of *Déserts* in the famous Théâtre des Champs-Elysées, where the riot provoked by *Le Sacre du Printemps* had taken place forty years before. On this occasion, which took place on December 2, 1954, the concert including *Déserts* was given by the Orchestra of Radio-Télévision Française and broadcast stereophonically, using the Bernhardt-Garret system. It was the second experiment of this kind made by the O.R.T.F. The first had been in 1950, when the work played was *Une larme du diable*, directed by René Clair. Since the audience present in the Théâtre des Champs-Elysées was increased so many fold by the broadcast, one may well say that the scandal provoked by Varèse's work that day was certainly to exceed all the previous scandals of musical history in its extent.

Déserts was played between Mozart's *B flat Overture* and Tchaikowsky's *Pathétique Symphony,* which was obviously a psychological error. The audience's reactions may be imagined. It should be pointed out that since this concert was being broadcast, and given by the National Orchestra, the audience present had not paid for its seats. During the twenties, Varèse's works had been the cause of more than one uproar. Now, thirty years later, the same composer still had the same power to shock. Could there be any better proof of the advance, of the progress of his work? What astonishing energy he must have possessed to have been able to upset the applecart all over again! The *Express* was able to write: "It was the finest scandal this auditorium built by Perret has known since that far-off night in 1913 when Monteux conducted the first performance of *Le Sacre du Printemps.*"

"The audience contributed generously to the event," the critic of *Le Monde* wrote. "Murmurs at first, then, crescendo, waves of vociferous protest mingled with wavering applause, baritones and tenors hurling shouts of 'That's enough,' 'Shame, shame,' etc., lady-like cluckings. The seats in the Théâtre des Champs-Elysées are, thanks be to heaven, solidly screwed to the floor." [4] That fine musicologist Jean Roy observed that "a certain number of people (who had not paid for their seats. . .) felt that they were being attacked in their stupidity, and protested noisily." [5] In order to form some idea of the audience's reaction and the lowness of some of the critics there are two documents in particular that the reader should be acquainted with. The first, entitled *Broadcast Cacophony,* is a very good expression of the affinity, of the unconscious collusion existing between an audience and a critic, or at least between the audience as seen by this particular critic. "Some thoughtless fellow who presides over the working out of the programs committed what we would like to believe was an imprudence: the sandwiching between. . .of a work written by a madman, grandiosely christened an 'electro-symphony' including a great deal of saucepan banging and solos for flushing toilets with fanfares for stock cars. . . . The discussion continued out on the sidewalk. . . 'This Monsieur Varèse ought to be shot out of hand. He's the Dominici of music! No, what am I saying! That would make even more noise, he'd be delighted. What our 'electrosympho-nist' needs is a trip to the electric chair.' " [6] Meanwhile, another critic, a well-known musicologist, was going even further: his review reads more like a case for the prosecution, and the savagery of his attack makes one wonder whether he was not perhaps afraid that the Vare-sian Bomb was going to demolish for good the mummified system of which he himself wished to be one of the pontiffs. "It is with certain composers as it is with a great many other things," he wrote: "they get themselves talked about simply because they happen at the right moment. . . ." Then, having mentioned A. Bruneau and d'Albert, and comparing them to Wagner, the critic went on: "Such may well be the case with Edgard Varèse, who, after having lived in retirement for more than thirty years, has now arrived back among us (at a moment when the battle of contemporary music seems to be on the point of being won), equipped with all those 'dernier cri' qualities required by our distinguished musical 'avant-garde.'

"For thirty years, in fact, Varèse's fame has scarcely spread beyond the very restricted circle of those who were interested in even the most secret and intimate aspects of contemporary music . . . and it was known that he was applying himself to researches of which the principal audacity resided in a sort of deliberate attempt to evade everything that constituted the most concrete reality of the times. Everything was therefore in order: the evasion of his musical responsibilities (sic) having been combined with an evasion of his responsibilities in the wider sense, things would probably have stopped there, if, meanwhile, a certain number of individuals with similar preoccupations (among whom are to be included several 'polytechnicians' and other men of science) had not decided to make common cause with Varèse. In fact, Varèse may well pass, in certain respects, as a precursor of concrete and electronic music, so that it would not be surprising to find him playing an important role at heart of 'musical' activity as it exists at the present time.

"His latest composition, *le Désert,* has provoked, as is only right, that careful admixture of 'for' and 'against' that constitutes 'good taste' in all authentic avant-garde manifestations. To tell the truth, there was much matter for delight there, since the work contained something for everyone: dodecaphonic techniques (absolutely indispensable at the moment, of course) , 'primitive' rhythms and variable meters, sudden interruptions of the orchestra by recorded electronic music played through loudspeakers—in short, all modern conveniences on all floors of musical composition." [7] In charity, one must assume that the injustice of this piece was mainly the product of its author's total ignorance of the facts; though even that could not excuse his contemptible attitude. Tomorrow "man will lose his reason," Cendrars wrote in 1919. But let us attempt to forget such vagaries and turn to the words written by human beings who were capable of love, of admiration, and of humility in the expression of their doubts.

Antoine Goléa wrote in *Express:* "The violence of the hostile reactions, which were immediately opposed by enthusiastic applause, is proof of the daring and the vital energy of the work that aroused them." [8] However, even for Goléa *Déserts* was "an extremely daring synthesis." Claude Rostand observed for his part: "I imagine that many people took him to be a young hothead of twenty-two, whereas Varèse is in fact a man of seventy summers." [9] Jean Roy, still in a state of shock brought on by the performance, noted: "The work roughs us up, in fact, annihilates us. We have no power over it: it is the work that takes possession of us, crushing us with the blows of its terrible fist." [10] There were several celebrities in the audience: Malraux, Michaux, Jolivet, etc. Also among them was the dadaist poet G. Ribemont-Dessaignes, who wrote an article on Varèse for the *Gazette de Lausanne*. After making it clear that this concert was "the musical event of the year" and deploring the fact that "creating something new no longer interests us," he added: "Music is always lagging behind. Only now has it achieved its full power of revolution. With Varèse. . . Varèse creates both space and the beings to occupy it, which is to say, a world owing nothing to the known world, but serving it in the office of a mask. A mask as real and alive as the reality we know." [11]

It is by no means the first time that a writer has been the first and profoundest critic of a work of art outside his own field. We have only to think of Kierkegaard analyzing Mozart's *Don Giovanni*, of Baudelaire, of Apollinaire, of Pierre-Jean Jouve, etc. One might also mention Goethe, Miller, and so many others. But Dallapiccola also, himself a composer, understood clearly too, when he heard *Déserts* for the first time from a recording. "In 1957," he has written to me, "he (Varèse) played me a recording of *Déserts*—that wonderful score— a score in which the taped music makes its entries with such spontaneity and takes its place in the midst of that large orchestra with such unprecedented ease. I went to visit him a few months ago and begged him to let me hear *Déserts* again. My impression on this second hearing was even stronger than on the first; I am convinced that in this case we may fearlessly employ that awesome term *masterpiece*."[12] And the man who does not hesitate to use that word in reference to *Déserts* is himself one of the greatest living composers. Igor Stravinsky himself has observed to Robert Craft: "Varèse's music will endure. We know this now because it is dated in the right way. The name Varèse is synonymous with a new intensity and a new concretion, and the best things in his music—the first seven measures from No. 16 in *Arcana*, the whole of *Déserts*—are among the best things in contemporary music. More power to this musical Brancusi." [13] Needless to say, such judgments carry more weight than the taunts and verbiage of any number of so-called critics and musicologists.

After that memorable concert, Varèse went on to the apartment of the composer and architect Iannis Xénakis: "He came to a hotel room in the 15th arrondissement to listen to the amateur recording I had made of his concert. He admitted quite simply that he had forgotten to eat lunch, and was glad to accept an improvised tea which my wife prepared for him." [14] Then, Varèse went on to spend a large part of the night at the research studios, no doubt working at improving his tapes.

On December 3rd, Varèse left Paris for Hamburg, where Bruno Maderna was to conduct a performance of *Déserts* on December 8th. On the same program: Stockhausen's *Kontra-Punkte*. Varèse cabled to Yves Tinayre: "Great success in Hamburg. . . . Hope return New York late January." [15] On December 13th, Maderna conducted the work again, in Stockholm, though Varèse was not present at that performance. He had returned to Paris, on December 9th, in order to record a series of conversations with Georges Charbonnier for the famous R.T.F. series *Entretiens,* on which such names as Colette, Claudel, Cendrars, Léautaud, etc., had already appeared. I was able to hear the two programs, which were broadcast from Paris, the first one on March 5, 1955. All those who heard him were struck by Varèse's frankness, vitality, and simplicity. The Parisian critics did not fail to appreciate those qualities. The critic of *Le Monde* wrote: "He is not like his work (sic). . . . He never loses his good humor, and the refinements of speculative research do not seem to be in his line at all. He is sure of himself, as solid as a rock. . . . He doesn't believe in undiscovered geniuses. . . ." [16] As for Robert Thill of *Combat,* he wrote: "Conformism has become so much the rule in radio, where the order of the day always seems to be: 'Don't rock the boat!' that one is quite surprised to hear a voice whose tone cuts right through the customary amiable mumbling." [17] Georges Charbonnier himself was to write in the Brussels weekly *Les Beaux-Arts*: "Every age, every epoch, 'sounds' in a particular way. Our age 'sounds' like the music of Edgar Varèse. Mingled with the rending, brutal, definitive sound that is the sound of Edgar Varèse, that exhausts our very selfhood, that scrapes us to the bone, there are sounds full of a nostalgia for our age: it is for our age of machines that dodecaphonism weeps, it is our age of machines that it is trying with despair to approach, it is from that effort that it draws its life—but it is Edgar Varèse who offers us that which is truly unheard of." [18]

Varèse assumed our age as it is, and lived it in its totality. That is why his music is much more tragic than it is nostalgic—tragic as no other modern composer's work has been, in my opinion, with the single exception of Webern's, in its own different way. And there is no analogy between a tragic vision and a nostalgic impulse. Bartók came near to this level of an unbearable vision in flashes, but he was unable to maintain it. With Varèse, one is able to speak of a passion of "the spirit that exists in sounds." In the third taped interpolation in *Déserts*, for example, the long cry reaches a final paroxysm in which, no longer able to continue as a cry, it becomes silence, that silence being its ultimate state, its fulfilment. (The same had already been attempted in *Etude*.) There is certainly nothing like it in the whole history of music, because no composer could ever have reached that particular intensity with the tempered-scale system and with traditional instruments. Of course there are other composers who have hurled themselves into the same abyss—I am thinking of the Schubert of the *String Quintet in C major, op. 163,* and certain lieder, and of some works by Mozart or Beethoven—but none has expressed the *tragedy of an age* so forcefully. Schubert cries out the tragedy of Schubert, which, needless to say, also expresses the tragedy of man. But throughout *Déserts*, what we hear is not only the tragedy of man but also the tragedy of the elements, of the animals, of the plants, of the stars; it is an expression of all that is *suffering, evil, despair, nothingness*; it is the expression of what in the being of beings is alienated, frustrated of its fulfilment, of its fullness, of its goal. Varèse does of course express his age, in the sense that Mozart also expressed his. But we must take care not to reduce him to the status of the composer of the machine age, of its mere externals, of the superficial qualities of its beings, as Mozart was at one time reduced to being the composer of an age of galanterie, periwigs, and minuets, etc. We must beware of falsifying the reality, the truth, and the beauty of Varèse's work. For our epoch is not merely a machine age—far from it.

The first version of the taped interpolations for *Déserts*, completed at the R.T.F. studio, was far from satisfactory as far as Varèse was concerned. It was to take him almost eight years to achieve a version that was satisfactory both as to its expressive content and its technical quality. Two further versions were to be used in concerts before this final one was reached, the one that he himself considered as definitive, in view of the progress of electronic technology. It is this final version that is used in the 1962 Columbia recording of *Déserts* conducted by Robert Craft. These interpolations, together with the *Poème électronique*, are the finest example of living music as Varèse conceived of it. There is no interpretation involved, and consequently we have the work in itself, without distortion, without any intermediary, just as the creator imagined and heard it in its essential movement and its acoustical power. Conductors ought to spend a long while meditating on these taped compositions before conducting Varèse's orchestral works. There is no better testimony as to exactly what he was seeking, what he wanted. I never cease to be astonished when I hear certain interpretations that are at the antipodes of Varèse's own thought. It was inevitable, of course, that Bach, for example, should have been unable to leave behind him so immediate and living a testimony to his conception of music. But why do conductors not listen more to Varèse's work on tape? It is the first time in the history of music (if we except the recordings of Debussy, Busoni, or Manuel de Falla playing their piano works) that we have been able to hear such a living body of work without its having first been filtered through the subjectivity of an interpreter, of a particular age: a body of work that expresses Varèse as immediately as a Renoir painting expresses Renoir. (Debussy may well have played his own works badly.) For no interpretation of Bach can ever be so profoundly an expression of Bach himself as the *Poème électronique*, for example, is of Varèse.

In May, 1955, *l'Age nouveau* published a special number on *Music and the World of Sound*. At Georges Charbonnier's request, Varèse contributed an article entitled: "The Instruments of Music and the Electronic Machine." In the very first paragraph of this article he reminds us of a truth that is no doubt elementary but which we in the West have forgotten: "In matters of music," he writes, "what we must never forget is that the listener, in order to hear music, must before all else be subjected to a physical phenomenon; which is to say that, until a perturbation, an atmospheric disturbance between the sound-producing course and the listener has taken place, there can be no music." [19] Those who were fortunate enough to hear the *Poème électronique* in Brussels, or *Déserts* in New York, when Varèse himself regulated the intensities and volume to be emitted by the loudspeakers, will know what Varèse meant by that phrase "be subjected to a physical phenomenon." The sounds did, in fact, do violence to the listener's body. The sound was concrete, and present, no longer a thing of chiaroscuro but a wave displacing air in order to strike us. That is why, for Varèse, there was no appreciable difference between a traditional instrument and an electronic instrument or sound recorded on tape. For him it was a question of intentions, of a sound's power and quality. For him, these new methods were of interest insofar as they could be employed as expression. As he himself said: "Ceaseless progress, ceaseless evolution; neither have modified in any way the problems confronting the composer—as far as the production of sounds is concerned—or his way of envisaging those problems." [20] But though Varèse was in favor of the unceasing development of sound-producing machines, this did not mean that he wished traditional instruments to disappear. "I even consider it desirable," he wrote, "that we should revive the instruments for which Monteverdi, Lully, and their predecessors actually wrote, and that their works should be presented in the original versions. The use of airplanes does not prevent us from riding on horses. . . . On the other hand, there exist sounds of which we are aware and which none of our instruments is capable of reproducing, including the electronic instruments we now possess. Which means that new instruments, or new machines, whatever name we choose to give them—will always be welcome." [21] One might say that Varèse took the part of Aristoxenes against Pythagoras by accepting the notion that the ear should be "the unique and final authority in determining what is dissonance and what is consonance," [22] and not the intellect or abstract numbers.

Immediately after arriving back in New York, Varèse set out once more to take part in a conference on the arts being held at Bennington College. On May 16th, he gave a lecture containing the same ideas expressed in his article for *l'Age nouveau*. It was the day after that, which is to say May 17th, that the first performance of *Déserts* in the United States took place. The concert was given in the National Guard Armory under the direction of Frederic Waldman. (Incidentally, Waldman was without doubt the conductor most faithful to Varèse until the very end.) The work was even played twice. The critic of the *New York Herald Tribune* recorded that "Vermonters and everyone else might well cheer, as they did. *Déserts* is a noble work of a remarkable musician." [23] But before any more significant reaction was forthcoming it was necessary to wait for the first New York performance. However, Henry Cowell was present at the Bennington concert, and he later wrote: "*Déserts* builds to a tremendous climax dynamically and in intensity towards the end. . . . This is the best work, the most mature, the largest and the most integrated, by a composer who holds a unique position among the world's creators. We predict that *Déserts* will be held as a masterpiece by those who follow tape and percussion music with devotion." [24] It would have been more accurate to write: "follow music," but let it pass. For the critic of *Harper's Magazine*, the unity that Varèse had achieved between the orchestral sections and the taped interpolations was an "astonishing tour de force." Then he went on to say: "*Déserts* is, I think, an epoch-making piece in the experimental sense. Most taped music has so far been little more than intriguing experiment with the strange sounds of the new medium. . . . Varèse, like Monteverdi in the seventeenth century, is the first big musical mind to take up the materials of a new musical experiment and put them to really serious uses. . . . Perhaps a qualitative comparison between these two is premature, by a century or so. But there is no doubt Varèse brings to his 'organized sound' not only dauntless originality but a musical technique, particularly a command of orchestration for percussion and of rhythmic organization, that is outstanding among all twentieth century composers of whatever school. He ranks far ahead of most other tape experimenters and, whatever we may think of his music, we must accord him full musical 'big league' status." [25] With this review, written by Edward Tatnall Canby, one feels that Varèse's time had at last come.

The first public performance of *Déserts* took place at New York's Town Hall on Wednesday, November 30, 1955, under the auspices of the Camera Concerts. It was conducted by the young Jacques Monod. Despite some boos, the result was "unlimited applause." J.S. Harrison of the *New York Herald Tribune* exclaimed: "It is a mammoth musical explosion." [26] However, everyone was not ready to accept the new work. The critic from *The New Yorker* for example, wrote: "I was much impressed by the composer's ingenuity, but I couldn't help noting that, for his purposes—which involved the creation of an extraordinary variety of screeching, tooting, clanging, explosive, and other nerve-shattering acoustical effects—the two stereophonic transmitters that he employed in solo roles were far more efficient than the human instrumentalists who accompanied them. This clearly indicated to me that Mr. Varèse's next logical step is the total elimination of human performers, a step that would remove his activities from the concert hall, thus finally freeing him from music and music from him. . . ." [27] In his next work, Varèse did, in effect, free himself from those "human factors," though in the work after the *Poème électronique* he was nevertheless to return to the orchestra. Varèse was essentially a free creator. What the reporter from *The New Yorker* was really afraid of was the disappearance of institutionalized music, with its traditional auditorium, its stage, its conductor mopping his brow and burying his head in his score, its soloist flipping up his tails to sit down, or arranging his violin carefully under his chin. But all that is merely a matter of ritual observances: it has nothing at all to do with music, that art par excellence of man's purest sensibility.

After the event constituted by these first performances of *Déserts* in Paris and New York, a new day had begun to dawn on the horizon of the musical world. After *Déserts*, no composer could remain ignorant of the power of sound or of the possibilities offered by new techniques. Nonetheless, the majority of them, despite everything, were to go on writing out their scores and lining up notes on their staves, since most of them do not know how to hear and have no world of sound by which we can identify them; most of them are writers of scores and not creators of organized sounds.

19

The *Poème électronique*

In the autumn of 1956, the E.M.S. recording was reissued in France under the *Boîte à Musique* label. Jean Roy was asked to contribute the liner notes. He wrote: "Very rarely, it happens that a composer will keep to the same time schedule as the painters and poets. Which is always enough to guarantee his being christened a 'precursor' and forbidden access to the status of masterpiece. Even the notion of 'work' is sometimes refused;. . .the word 'experiment' is used. . . . Twenty-five years ago, Varèse was spoken of in the same way as one would speak of a charge of dynamite. Today, Varèse's work is still loathed by those who prefer (and it is their right) a more comfortable or less vigorous kind of music (it is also permissible not to like Fernand Léger) ; but his existence and his vitality can no longer be questioned. The composer's extraordinary personality has become only too evident, and at the same time, Varèse no longer appears as totally isolated as he once was. . . . Moreover, our present growing acquaintance with the music of the Far East and the resurrection of mediaeval polyphony—for which the phonograph record is largely responsible—teach us that Edgar Varèse's daring rests upon eternal conceptions, and that music, whether as the language of feeling or the reflection of a moving world, as the caress of harmonies or as contrapuntal dialectic, is also an art of timbre, an art of rhythm and a structuring of acoustical space. . . . Edgar Varèse's scientific pre-occupations and his ever-increasing knowledge of the laws of acoustics both help to give his work, not the esoteric significance that his titles might lead one to suppose, but a solidity, a concrete reality, a fresh-ness, an efficacity which ally themselves in his rough-hewn originality with a return to the earliest sources." [1]

In 1956, M. Kalff, the artistic director of the Philips plant at Eindhoven, Holland, paid a visit to Le Corbusier. He had come to suggest to him that "he create the Philips pavilion at the World's Fair" which was to be held in Brussels in 1958. Whereupon Le Corbusier replied: "I won't create a pavilion; I will create an 'Elec-tronic Poem' together with the vessel that will contain it. The vessel will be the pavilion, and there will be no façade to this vessel." [2] Le Corbusier then told me how this idea had come to him: "It was as I saw M. Kalff standing there (about six foot three inches tall) in front of me, that there suddenly and spontaneously sprang into my mind, out of the unknown, this notion of an 'Electronic Poem,' which is to say, of a work capable of profoundly affecting the human sensibility by audio-visual means. Hollywood has been in existence for a long while now, as have symphony concerts, opera, books, photography, moving pictures, but I nevertheless had an obscure sense that some-thing could be brought into being on the creative level using the perhaps prodigious means offered by electronics: speed, number, color, sound, noise, unlimited power. Such was the sudden idea! If you should ever happen across someone who can explain the reasons for the birth of an idea—a phenomenon outside time and the human will—you must send me a photograph of him." [3] And together with this idea, this sudden wonder, came the ineluctable presence of Varèse, "Sounds, noises, unlimited power. . . . A new creation opening all before it. . . . Immediately, I thought of Varèse, with whom I had had no dealings for nearly 25 years. My feeling about this was so strong that I was forced to say I would not undertake this task except on condition that Varèse should create the music. They said: 'We have our own musicians; we have our own composers.' I said: 'You must take it or leave it, as you wish. And moreover, I also make it a con-dition that Varèse shall be accorded a remuneration worthy of him.' It was rather upsetting for a huge firm like Philips, since they're not used to that sort of thing, but M. Kalff had understood well enough." [4] There is something fantastic in this sudden determination on Le Corbusier's part to insist on Varèse's participation in his project; it is as though, in a flash of lightning, he had been given the intuition, the revelation, that Varèse was the only man able to create the sounds he needed. His respect for Varèse was so great that he imposed no scenario or conditions of any kind upon him. "You will do just as you wish," he wrote to him, "I shall leave you quite free, thinking of your music as a presence surrounding a man reading, for example, some book or tale and whose ear catches noises from outside (a barrel organ, a brass band marching past, a revolution coming along the street, up the staircase, smashing in the door)". . . "I'd had the idea of asking for only one thing," he wrote to me. "Right in the very middle of the *Poème électronique*, I thought of having an abrupt and total silence, and white light at the same moment—something to twist the audience's guts inside them. Result: one day as the car was taking us back into Brussels from Eindhoven, Varèse confessed to me: 'My dear Corbu, I haven't been able to fit in that silence of yours; that's exactly the moment in my thing where there's most noise.' My reply: 'Much good may it do you. It doesn't matter! There were supposed to be a few words spoken at that moment in the *Poème électronique,* now they won't be, and perhaps it's just as well for the unity of the work.' Varèse has a rotten character, exactly the same as my own! Moreover, that incident was caught by the film." [5]

This opportunity to create the *Poème électronique* was, if you wish, the miracle that Varése had been awaiting for a very long time. At last he was to have every technical means at his disposal; at last the music would truly be able to move about in space. However, things did not turn out all that easily. Philips continued to try to pressure Le Corbusier into not insisting on having Varèse as his collaborator. They wanted Walton, or Copland, or Landowski. The architect of the pavilion, Xénakis, was entirely behind Le Corbusier in his choice. He wrote to Le Corbusier to let him know of Philips' hostility, and defended Varèse to M. X. . . On January 2, 1957, he wrote to Varèse: "Above all don't let them make you give any ground esthetic-ally. Le Corbusier asked you to create this music. He is obliged to stand up for you. He will defend you *to the end* . . . I think a bang of L.C.'s fist on the table will bring the recalcitrant ones to heel.

Needless to say, I am entirely on your side, because I like your music very much. Le Corbusier will be back soon." [6] At that moment Le Corbusier was away in India. The distance between the three men did not simplify things. Then Le Corbusier returned to Brussels. He immediately reassured Varèse. The latter wrote back: "Thank you. . . Since my last meeting with M. X. . . I have been without any direct news from Philips and have no idea on what conditions they are considering associating me with the project. M. Xénakis tells me that they will certainly write to me directly. I have heard nothing so far, and as far as another trip in April is concerned, that would be financially difficult for me to consider unless I could be sure of recovering the expense. This collaboration with you interests me so much. . . I hope it all comes off!" [7] As this letter indicates, Varèse had already made one journey to Europe—in February, 1957—but at that time he still did not know what the outcome was to be and was unable to begin work. One can imagine what a state of uneasiness he must have been in. But those are things that our great technocrats do not necessarily understand. In a letter written on August 21, 1957, Varèse told me that he was to board the *Westerdam* on Saturday, August 24th, for Rotterdam. He arrived there on September 2nd, went directly to Eindhoven, and settled down immediately to his task. It was to take him seven or eight months, working in a laboratory equipped with the most advanced instruments, assisted by a sound engineer and a group of technicians, to complete his composition. As Le Corbusier wrote to me, he had "480 seconds of music" to create, and moreover "he was in Eindhoven, living in a hotel, not in his own home, and had nothing else to do but keep the Philips technicians at work, and it is high time here to give the latter the praise they deserve." [8]

While Varèse was at Eindhoven, a Varèse exhibition was held in the New York Public Library in November. On November 5th, the composer went to Paris for a few days.

On November 30th, Varèse admitted to Xénakis that his work was progressing at the "slowest possible" rate, but that he soon hoped to have reached the 241st second. Then, on December 21st, again to Xénakis: "There is doubtless going to be something of an explosion. Messers Philips and. . . don't like a fragment of the composition that X. . . played to them. It's true that it was presented to them without much ceremony and with totally inadequate means. Verdict: no melody—no harmony. These gentleman would apparently be happy to be rid of me, but I'm not accustomed to being pushed around . . . The first part has already been recorded on the three tapes. The second is well on in the sketch stage. I have plenty of time, since the sound equipment is far from ready still . . ." Xénakis immediately let Le Corbusier know of the persistent hostility shown by Philips toward Varèse. Whereupon, from Chandigarh, the architect wrote to Philips: "It (the *Poème électronique*) cannot be carried except by Varèse's strange music. . . There cannot for a moment be any question of giving up Varèse. If that should happen, I should withdraw from the affair. . . Varèse is a great name in modern music." But the composer did not allow himself to become demoralized. He wrote to reassure Xénakis on January 2, 1958: "Don't worry—when I have decided something and know that I'm right—and within my right—I don't give way. As for making concessions, that's something that's never happened to me."

Xénakis himself had composed some music on tape for the intermissions, between houses. Varèse, as Xénakis himself told me in a letter, "never took umbrage at this. Quite the contrary, being the truly great man he is, he supported me in all my practical and moral difficulties with Philips, and occasionally with Le Corbusier. And I personally am proud to have succeeded in creating an architecture suitable for his music." [10]

On May 2, 1958, Varèse heard his *Poème électronique* for the first time. He wrote to Xénakis: "Your piece which comes over as sound and spreads admirably—and mine, which comes over well too. Everything will be ready (for the public) next week, and I think we shall have all the sound and fury required." The pavilion had been officially opened on April 17th, then closed again until the reopening on May 2nd. The sound system wasn't ready, which had put Varèse in a rage.

Jean Petit, in his book entitled *Le Poème électronique Le Corbusier* has described the electronic aspect of the tapes as realized by the Philips engineers. "Research was centered, from the very outset, on the principle of three sound images, all different in character, perceived simultaneously, but coming from or moving in different directions. . . The acoustical effects were to be realized by means of a three-track tape, each of its synchronized tracks having its own playback head, a group of amplifiers and loudspeakers, and a multi-track machine with signals to activate the various loudspeaker circuits. . . Varèse's recorded material was extremely disparate. Studio-made recordings were used, machine noises, transposed piano chords and bells, filtered recordings of choruses and soloists. . . oscillators were used to record pure sinusoidal sounds, and literally unheard of sounds were made by mixing and combining all these. Each sound image had its own name, derived from its nature, a process which gave rise to words such as 'peowip,' 'wauwwauw' . . . Some were given the name 'parameter' or 'Parabola,' and these were inspired by the nature of the sound or the movement to be suggested; others were called 'tram,' 'jetplane,' 'cymbals' because of the notions they aroused . . . When these images had at last been recorded and synchronized on the three-track tape—a task which naturally demanded extremely precise cutting—the next step was that of organizing the public performance of the score, which meant spacing it out in all its complexity over the pavilion's surfaces and along the 'sound paths' designed into it. The hundred and fifty (sic) loudspeakers in the pavilion were all divided into 'groups' and 'paths.' The groups were placed above the entrance, above the exit, and at the top of the roofs three concavities; whereas the loudspeakers making up the paths were arranged along the ribs of the roof. A horizontal path had also been installed, and besides this there were also twenty-five large loud-speakers, behind the barrier, right at the bottom, for the reproduction of the deep bass range and special sounds. Since all these loudspeakers were to be switched into circuit at a given moment by the switching system, and since it had been necessary to install them before the composition was completed, they had all been connected by individual cables to the pavilion's control box, where there was a switchboard permitting the necessary choices to be made. The paths and groups of loudspeakers were powered by a series of ten 120-watt ampli-fiers. . . . The distribution of the various sounds on the three-track tapes determined by which group or combination of loudspeakers they would be reproduced. But, since it was also possible, by using special signals, to transpose the entries of the various groups of amplifiers temporarily, this meant that any particular group of loud-speakers could also be employed for the reproduction of any selected sound. For the stereophonic effect, in particular, the two groups of loudspeakers above the exit and entrance were used in conjuction with the horizontal group as one 'channel'—fed by tracks 1 and 2— while the other 'channel' was provided by selected loudspeakers along the paths, so that each listener, in no matter what spot he happened to be, would be able to perceive the reproduced effect in the same way." [11] It is easy to imagine, from this description, what a complex matter the devising of the *Poème électronique* was, and what fascination it must have exerted on Varèse. There were to be, in Le Corbusier's words, "four hundred acoustical mouths completely surrounding the five hundred visitors." [12] This work makes one realize what beauty and power of expression can be attained by such an alliance of creator and technicians. While the music was played, images and colors chosen by Le Corbusier were to be projected on the concrete walls of the building. In the *New York Times*, Howard Taubman described his impressions as follows: "Then pictures begin to appear on the walls. Some are large and some small, and occasionally they join in huge images that seem to cover the assymetric surfaces of the vaulting chamber. They include birds and beasts and fish and reptiles. There are masks, skeletons, idols, girls clad and unclad, cities in normal appearance and then suddenly askew. There are the mushroom explosions so familiar to newspaper readers and moviegoers in an era of atomic bombs." Then, going on to Varèse's music, he commented that "the sounds that accompany these images are as bizarre as the building. One hears rattles, whistles, thunders and murmurs. At one point there is a sound that seems to emerge from a human throat. The score is not compounded of recognizable instruments. It is the work of a man who has been seeking for several decades to return music to a purity of sound that he does not believe possible in conventional music making." [13] The work seems to have been beyond this particular critic. There was no communication between it and him. He himself was careful to avoid the term music. Another critic very aptly remarked that: "Here, one no longer hears the sounds, one finds oneself literally in the heart of the sound source. One does not listen to the sound, one lives it. The unparalleled perfection of the acoustical system and the daring but successful score created by Varèse have brought such perfection to this element of Le Corbusier's *Poème électronique* that the other elements seem to lose all suggestive power. One 'sees' the play of moving and changing colors, but at no point is one 'bathed' in a colored atmosphere. The images are there in front of you, but you never feel yourself inside the image. The father of the *Poème électronique*, M. Le Corbusier, is before all else an architect and a painter, and consequently an artist who sees form rather than movement. He is therefore probably less aware of the extreme possibilities of electronics, certainly less aware, in any case, than M. Varèse and his technical assistant. . . By the use of moving sound they have succeeded in liberating their score from the shackles of reality. The other scores were not conceived in this absolute sense, and that is the cause of a certain imbalance." [14] On November 17, 1958, Le Corbusier wrote to Varèse: ". . .but I declare that you have been the very bones of the *poème* with your magnificent music." Le Corbusier's brother, a musician who was seventy-two years old at the time, confessed to him: "De Brueyn let me hear the music alone between two complete performances and I was filled with joy by that powerful and varied score. I like it much more than when linked with the visual elements, because the two together lessen and dissipate each other. The human voice, at the end, takes on the feeling of a song of liberation, the diagrams for the Radiant City appear as programmatical answers to the images of destruction; the shells, the stone figures as elements of possible perfection. One feels a sense of progress in all this already encountered previously, whereas the music on its own is truly a spontaneous creation endowed with that infinity toward which all music tends. It draws its strength from an originality untouched by a propaganda whose methods have already been encountered elsewhere. I repeat: for the public, for Society, for Philips, it is a success." [15] This letter from Albert Jeanneret is, as it were, a continuation of the *Radio TV* review quoted above. Varèse was to say of the *Poème électronique*: It is an indictment of inquisition in all its forms. When the element of surprise has vanished, the tragic density of the work appears, and its humanity, its singular beauty. That is what two million spectators were able to feel in Brussels. And this great dream was made possible, in its reality, by the determination and the lucidity of Le Corbusier.

During his stay in Brussels, Varèse acted as a member of the jury for an experimental film competition which also included Man Ray, Pierre Prévert, and Norman McLaren. "Particular attention was paid to the remarks of Edgar Varèse, the composer of electronic music, on the relations between sound and light, the eye and the ear." [16]

On July 1, 1958, Varèse left Brussels for Paris, where he took up residence at the Hôtel Madison, Boulevard Saint-Germain. When he wasn't having his tapes played back at the R.T.F. experimental studio (Michaux went to hear them many times), "every day, before an audience of groups of young composers and technicians, Varèse would unfold his graph-paper charts and tirelessly start in yet again on his exegesis of the multi-colored curves and diagrams printed on them. For that is how the score of the *Poème électronique* realized by Philips does in effect appear." [17] Here we have yet one more testimony to Varèse's generosity. He gave his presence. Can there be a greater gift? He gave his time, the rarest, the most precious thing that a creator of seventy-four possesses. But Varèse did not dissociate his life as a man from his life as a creator. He was first of all a living being for whom life itself was the greatest good. And for him, to give himself to the young, to establish contact with others, was to live fully. The affection of the young was without doubt one of the great sources of his inner joy, and perhaps of his strength.

By the time Varèse returned to New York (on the liner *Liberté*) news of his great success in Brussels had already preceded him. As soon as he was back, the newspaper *The Village Voice* and the Record Hunter record store organized a concert at the Village Gate, a small theater in Greenwich Village, Varèse's little homeland. Thus, on November 9, 1958, the first hearing of his *Poème électronique* in the United States took place. But obviously the miracle in Brussels could not be reproduced. Henceforth, all that could be heard of the work was a simple stereophonic version—which is to say, scarcely more than a black and white photograph of some great architectural work. It is this version that has since been included in a Columbia record. Meanwhile, despite Le Corbusier's efforts, the Philips Pavilion in Brussels had unfortunately been demolished. Before this first American hearing of his composition, Varèse gave a lecture on what is usually called electronic music. At the end of it, he announced that the firm of Bogen-Presto, a division of the Siegler Corporation, had offered to put a laboratory at his disposal in order to permit him to go on with his work. But after this one stroke of publicity, Varèse found himself once more without a laboratory. This first hearing was received with such enthusiasm that, as Edward Downes reported, "the work was played a second time." [18] The work was also played on February 20, 1959, at Sarah Lawrence College. *Octandre* was also performed during that particular program.

Another event, towards the end of that memorable year, was the series of performances of *Arcana* conducted by Leonard Bernstein in Carnegie Hall on November 27, 28, 29 and 30, 1958. It was the first time, and in the same auditorium, that the work had been played in the United States since the performance on April 12, 1927. After this concert, Varèse's old friend Slonimsky wrote to him: "Vive *Arcana*. At last we have heard a great work in New York!" [19] At the age of seventy-four, Varèse had at last reached a wide public with his *Poème électronique*. He was beginning to be heard more often in the world. In February, 1957 it was *Ionisation* in London. On October 11, 1957, *Octandre* in Japan. On March 25, 1958, *Arcana* in Cologne, and in the same city, on July 22nd, *Octandre*. During October, 1958, he was played together with Bartók, Schoenberg and Webern at the Karuizama Festival. On October 10th, there were performances of *Densité 21.5* and *Octandre* at the Museum of Modern Art in Stockholm.

At the time of the Karuizama Festival, the Japanese composer Toshiro Mayuzumi wrote in the magazine *Ongaku-Geijutsu:* "At the moment when true music is in its death throes, I know of no music that continues to cry out as agonisingly as that of Varèse, and they are cries of grief for music's death. . . These cries that Varèse has given us are a sort of super-music sprung from the soul of a man who is seeking for the existence of the true music at the time when it is dying." [20] After these various concerts, many young Japanese musicians became passionate admirers of Varèse's work. Another composer, Michiko Toyama, has described her first meeting with Varèse in 1958, after she had followed John Cage's suggestion and gone to knock on his door. "A short while after my visit to Varèse," she wrote me, "I managed to get hold of scores of *Intégrales* and *Octandre*. As soon as I laid eyes on the first page, one thing in particular struck me: 'But it's Gagaku!' I said to myself. The one Gagaku score. . . I had in my possession presented a remarkable resemblance to the Varèse from the point of view of the scoring. Did Varèse know? An opportunity of meeting the Master again presented itself at the house of

Mrs. G., a common friend who had organized a party at which some Gagaku musicians then visiting New York were to play. The concert was about to begin; at my invitation, the Master came over and took a look at my score: 'Your music is very much like Gagaku. . .' Whereupon, beaming with joy, he said: 'You must come and tell my wife that!' He led me over to Madame Varèse so that I could repeat it. 'It happened without my knowing anything about Gagaku,' he added. Several days later, the telephone rang: it was the Master, asking if he could take the score away with him on a trip. Another time, I found him at work in his 'shop'; he was studying the frequency range of the 'Shô,' a sort of mouth organ made up of 17 bamboo tubes which can produce several sounds at the same time, and which was fascinating him at that time. . . Shortly before my departure, he said to me: 'I have just been offered a studio, I don't need to ask for one any more. . .' Varèse, the only composer who really knew how to explore the raw material of sound, had no studio at his disposal where he could be free to work." [21] Varèse was, in effect, fascinated by Gagaku.[22] For him, it was an image of eternity. I still remember the wonder-filled atmosphere when Varèse first introduced me to a Gagaku work. We were in another universe. If one listens attentively to the strings in *Nocturnal,* one can sense in the higher frequencies, certain indescribable sounds in quest of some god far out in the infinite. Gagaku enabled him to conceive, with his use of the strings, another duration, and another meeting of lines in space.

It may be said, if we consider the number of works heard during that year by the new generation, and the number of countries in which Varèse was played, that 1958 was perhaps to remain the most extraordinary year of the composer's life as far as communication was concerned. More than two million people heard the *Poème électronique* alone. Varèse had won a major battle. But there were still many more to be fought. The shock waves from the explosion of *Déserts,* for example, had still not reached the general public. The radiation of that work was still scarcely beginning, and there were plenty of shelters for those who preferred to go to earth. And the same was still true of the majority of his works. The success of the *Poème électronique* was to facilitate the expansion of his work as a whole. But. . . though many people like the *Poème électronique,* they do not for all that look upon it as a *musical* entity: they refuse to talk of it as *music,* but as something else . . . something undefinable. Composers have proved particularly reticent. They are for the most part very ill-prepared in this matter, since they have not had the elementary scientific and technical education that would enable them to undertake such works. Doubtless they find it easier to reject them. And yet there is nothing in the *Poème électronique* that is not sound and expression, nothing that is not music. Perhaps it is always the fate of profoundly new works to produce such paradoxes.

Several months before the first performance of the *Poème électronique,* the Russians launched their first satellite, on October 4, 1957. Humanity was entering a new age. Computers were increasing in numbers and complexity year by year. We had begun to move, not merely toward automation, but toward cybernation. Yet very few people realized what a deep affinity Varèse had with this new age in which nature was being taken more and more out of the hands of men, with this new type of civilization, this complexity of men and things entering into new relationships.

20

Fame, Struggle, and Death

During the year 1959, Varèse continued to be discovered all over the world. On February 2nd, Los Angeles. On June 14th, Pittsburgh. During the summer, at the Donaueschingen Festival, Boulez conducted a performance of *Intégrales*. He wrote to me later: "The best way I had of serving him, both as a friend and as a composer, was precisely that Véga recording." [1] For Boulez did, it is true, make the first recording of several of Varèse's works in France. On July 28th, Varèse sent Pierre Schaeffer a message that the latter had requested as an introduction to a broadcast program of "concrete" music. On September 4th, Varèse gave a lecture at the Princeton Seminar of Advanced Musical Studies. On October 4th, he was invited to appear on the television program *Premier Plan*, broadcast by the French-speaking network of Radio-Canada in Montreal. That same month, the Montreal magazine *Liberté* put out a special number wholly devoted to him, and all the most important Canadian composers took the opportunity of paying tribute to him. Referring to this special issue, the great American critic Alfred Frankenstein remarked: "Perhaps Canadians like Varèse because theirs is a big, spacious country, for no one writes so big and spacious a piece of music as he. He belongs to the heroic generation of Stravinsky, Schoenberg, Webern, Bartók and the other early pioneers of the early century who helped make modern music what it is. Furthermore he is of the same importance as the four composers just mentioned, but recognition of his talents has been long delayed. . . . I suspect that the main reason for the neglect of Varèse is that his work follows no teachable formula. The twelve-tone technique was made to order for academic use, and the school composers use it everywhere; Varèse, however, remains entirely himself, grand master of a style that cannot be reduced to system."[2] Could there be any better reply to the criticisms of R.L. after the Paris performance of *Déserts*?

Meanwhile, Varèse had gone back to work composing. The Koussevitsky Foundation of the Library of Congress, in Washington, had commissioned a work from him. On October 12, 1959, Varèse confided in his old friend Ernst Schoen: "I am working a lot. A choral work on the stocks, with instrumental ensemble: brass, percussion, organ and two ondes Martenot." He added: "I think I'm going to have considerable possiblilities of being performed here in the U.S.A., after all I've waited quite a long while, and am beginning to believe in the proverb: 'everything comes to him who waits.' " On December 31st, he wrote to Michiko Toyama: "I am soon going to start revising the two tapes for *Déserts*. They will be ready in the spring." Nevertheless, Varèse was to have more and more difficulty working. This new (and second) version of the interpolations for *Déserts* was given on August 8, 1960, during the International Conference of Composers held at Stratford in Canada. This was also the first performance of any Varèse work in Canada. Varèse himself arrived in Toronto on August 4th, and in Stratford itself on the 7th. The instrumentalists playing the work under the direction of Frederick Prausnitz visibly neither understood nor felt for the work. During the interpolations, they laughed along with the audience, caught up in the wave of hysterical laughter that shook the latter just as the work reached its tragic climax. In spite of everything, however, there was a great ovation from the fervent admirers and the composers who were present. This performance had been broadcast by both the English and the French-speaking Radio-Canada networks, and was repeated again the following August 15th. After the concert, Varèse said to me: "What do you expect? People laugh because they don't know what to do: it's a defence reaction." One French composer, and a rather well known one moreover, turned to me during the performance and remarked that though he found the instrumental score admirable he could not accept the taped interpolations of organized sounds.

Then, after Stratford, there was the Vienna Festival, the Venice Festival, the Warsaw Festival on September 23rd, not to mention New York, Paris, and Tokyo.

It was also in 1960 that Columbia put out their first recording of Varèse's works conducted by Robert Craft. At last a larger public was able to hear the *Poème électronique,* and others of his works, for the first longplaying record made in 1950 had long been unavailable. The phonograph record is one of the important phenomena of our civilization. Indeed, one might say that its importance is not unlike that of the Gutenberg Bible. How many people would never have heard a work by Varèse were it not for the phonograph! How many orchestras have never dared to perform a work by Varèse—doubtless for fear of offending the ears of their lady patrons, their middle-class subscribers, etc. And for the sake of one lady with a great deal of money, thousands of young people are cheated of a whole universe of sound which they need in order to reach a better understanding of the age they live.

In 1956, the house of G. Ricordi and Co., New York, had undertaken the task of publishing all Varèse's scores. In May, 1960, *Offrandes* was brought out. In 1961 it was to be the turn of *Déserts,* then *Ecuatorial,* etc. Varèse's works had not been republished or published since the twenties.

In September, 1960, there was the memorable meeting with Stravinsky at the Waldorf-Astoria. It was apparently Robert Craft who brought the two men together, for they had never met before. A few photographs were taken, and the two composers parted with a handshake. It was perhaps a sort of tacit reconciliation. We must not forget that Varèse had written once, in 1934, that Stravinsky was finished. Then Stravinsky was to pay tribute to Varèse by calling him the Brancusi of music.

In October, 1960, Varèse began on his third version of the interpolations for *Déserts.* The quality of the sounds still did not satisfy him. This work was both very tiring for him and very time-consuming. The new version he produced was broadcast for the first time, on April 19, 1961, on my program *les Pôles de l'esprit* over Radio-Canada.

On December 22, 1960, a concert was given in Varèse's honor at the Grace Rainey Rogers Auditorium in the Metropolitan Museum of Art. For the first part of the concert, Frederic Waldman had chosen some of Varèse's favorite works: Schütz's *Dialogo per la Pascua,* Monteverdi's *Lamento d'Arianna, Tempro la cetra, Nigra sum* and *Con che soavità,* and Marc-Antoine Charpentier's *Pestis Mediolanis.* The second part was made up of *Ionisation, Offrandes,* and *Intégrales.* All of his friends who were in New York at the time met afterwards at the Jaeger House: Salzedo, Luening and Ussachevsky, Chou Wen Chung, Stefan Wolpe, John Cage, Mayuzumi, and several others. Stravinsky and Craft sent him a telegram from Washington with their good wishes for his birthday. Stuckenshmidt also paid tribute to him, in Germany. That day, Varèse never stopped answering his telephone or going to his front door to accept gifts of flowers or wine. How moved he was. . . What warmth there was, that day, on Sullivan Street. . .

On May 1, 1961, another concert was given in homage to Varèse. This time it was at the New York Town Hall, with Craft conducting *Intégrales, Ecuatorial, (Poème électronique)* , *Offrandes, Nocturnal,* and *Déserts.* Not only was there a performance of the definitive version of *Ecuatorial,* a work that had not been played since its premiere in 1934, but there was also the first performance of Varèse's latest work—*Nocturnal.*

Varèse had "completed" *Nocturnal* two days before the concert. There was only one rehearsal with the entire forces required, on Sunday, April 30th. Carlos Salzedo had himself done the preliminary work with the chorus. This work is composed for soprano voice, men's chorus, piccolo, flute, oboe, two clarinets, bassoon, horn, two trumpets, three trombones, strings, percussion, and two ondes Martenot. The text consists of a few phrases drawn from Anaïs Nin's prose poem *The House of Incest.* A woman dreaming in the darkness shrieks: "I have lost my brother." The chorus answers her: "You belong to the night," etc. The following autumn, Varèse began work on a second version of this composition. For at least four years, while battling ceaselessly against illness, he struggled on with it. On December 10, 1961, he was to write to me: "I am working too, in a bovine fashion, which is to say slowly, but I think I am laying down the right lines for what has to come. One mustn't just sit in the same spot complacently gazing at one's navel."

For the May, 1961, performance of *Ecuatorial* the two ondes Martenot required by the score were replaced by two oscillators "played" by the composer Earl Brown and the engineer Fred Plaut. The Martenot instruments were simply not to be found in New York. The critics of the *New York Times* and the *New York Herald Tribune* were extremely cautious, writing of this and that, but avoiding all judgments. They were unable to conceal their admiration for this "pioneer"; they did not doubt his sincerity, etc.

On August 3, 1961, the *Poème électronique* was played in Montreal as part of the Festival of *"musique actuelle"* in that city. The audience listened to the work in darkness. The only light there was came from the changing colors of two luminous sculptures by the Montreal artist Jean-Paul Mousseau. The Montreal critic Jean Vallerand was to write: "His *Poème électronique* is to my mind an immense masterpiece that accepts the challenge of addressing itself to man in his totality, as he is, unchanged for thousands of years, that accepts the challenge of existing as a venture in which man himself becomes part of the life force, in which, without any involvement of his intellectuality, he can allow himself to be swept up into the maelstrom of telluric energies. . . It is music that one experiences even at the non-conscious level of cellular life. The brightest thing to emerge from this first concert of *'musique actuelle'* will be the immense, the ineluctable invitation to live in the fullness of reality constituted by the music of Edgar Varèse." [3] Next day, in the Redpath Hall of McGill University, a tribute was organized by the composer Pierre Mercure, one of the pillars of the festival, which was attended by composers John Cage, Morton Feldman, Mauricio Kagel, Earl Brown, Serge Garant, and Istvan Anhalt. A letter from Xénakis, sent through me, was read out during the event, as well as a message from the Research Center of the O.R.T.F.

At that time Varèse was still working on his interpolations for *Déserts* at the Columbia-Princeton Electronic Music Center. On August 9, 1961, he informed me that he had just finished his fourth and final version. On February 2nd of the same year, he had written to me to say that the definitive version of *Arcana* was "ready for the table." On March 4th, he spoke to me of the recording of *Arcana* and *Déserts* being prepared by Craft for Columbia. It was with this recording in view that Varèse had completed the interpolations for *Déserts* and the definitive version of *Arcana*. (It is perhaps worthwhile pointing out once again that Varèse himself never employed the terms *"musique concrète"* or *"electronic music"* in reference to his own works. He wrote to me on March 29, 1961: "I don't wish to be associated with *'musique concrète,'* or with any other clique.")

On October 31, 1961, Pierre Mercure and myself organized an "evening of friendship" toward Varèse. The Théâtre Egrégore in Montreal was literally besieged. Varèse had sent us the new recording of *Arcana* for the occasion. Jean Vallerand, in an excellent article, expressed the opinion that "Stravinsky's influence leads to Stravinskyism, which is to say to a style that becomes academic as soon as any composer other than its originator employs it. Schoenberg's influence gives onto a much wider field, but it is a field mined from end to end with compositional technicalities. Varèse's influence, as I see it, provides a three hundred and sixty degree horizon, since it bears, not upon musical language or technique, but upon the very matter of which music is made. Edgard Varèse has rethought all sound in its totality, and his art leads neither to a style nor to a notative discipline, but rather to a new liberalism of musical phenomenology: Varèse's art has redefined the composer's freedom for a half-century to come. . . Varèse's art brings to an end the tyranny of the stave, and that is something even more pregnant with consequences than the escape from the prison of tonality." [4]

After the performance of *Déserts* in England, conducted by Craft, the critic of *The Listener* wrote on November 2nd: " *(Déserts)* is the most satisfying artistic exploration in electronic music I have heard. . . . Have we heard anything of this kind before? Only something in the nature of the Javanese gamelan comes to mind, but an enlarged, fantastic gamelan, somehow rescued from the Orient and enriched by the infinite possibilities of modern music."

During the winter of 1961-62, Varèse suffered a serious bronchial infection, which prevented him from completing *Nocturnal* as he had planned. Louise Varèse wrote to me on April 20th: "He is somewhat better now, it will still take a long while, but the attacks come less and lesss frequently. He has been working despite it all, and seems pleased with the ideas he's had." On November 23, 1962, she mentioned that he was still working on *Nocturnal II*.

The year 1962 was one in which Varèse found himself being loaded with honors. For example, he was elected a member of the Swedish Royal Academy. (A Nobel prize without the money—unfortunately, Saint-John Perse was to comment.) On March 18th, he received the medal of the Brandeis University Creative Arts Awards. Then, the next year, on May 21, 1963 to be exact, he was the hero of a banquet. He became the first recipient of the Koussevitsky International Recording Award, at the age of seventy-nine. The reception took place at the Plaza Hotel in New York. Tribute was paid to Varèse on this occasion by Leonard Bernstein, Aaron Copland, Pierre Boulez, Milton Babbit, Mel Powell, William Schuman, Otto Luening, Mme Serge Koussevitsky, and the great poet Saint-John Perse. Pierre Boulez said: "You are very dear to me because so marginal and solitary. . . You possess the purposefully untamed quality of the hermit, the rarity of a diamond still unset, the stubborn calculation of deep patience." Luening pointed out that Varèse was the first astronaut. And finally, Saint-John Perse paid tribute to the composer in these words: "Varèse, we rise now in your honor, because you are one of those for whom nothing has value, in art, but the truly creative work—by which I mean life itself in its vital impulse and its deep onward flow—you have never yielded to any facility.

"But to that man who, in new forms, deals sincerely in creative art, there comes a day when he becomes a classic figure among the servants of an ancient modernism.

"There is the witness born by an artist's life such as yours, my dear Varèse, a noble lesson of integrity.

"I am one of those who have been able to gauge, on the human level, all that it has meant for you, with your admirable wife and companion at your side, to pursue that long and solitary road while proudly maintaining your own exacting standards.

"Today, as an old friend, I claim my place at your side in order to tell you, quite simply, all the meaning that we—your friends from France, from Europe, and from America—attach to this evening's happy demonstration in your honor."

And Stravinsky had already rendered his tribute, in June of 1962, when he said: "Varèse has been recognized at last, but his is a lonely figure still. That is partly because he, unlike so many composers, preferred composing to the career of 'being a composer.' Instead of lecturing to ladies' clubs, writing articles on the state of music, participating in symposiums, traveling on fellowships, Varèse stayed home and went his own way and alone." [5]

Nevertheless, despite these waves of friendship that were constantly flowing toward him, the winter of 1962-63 was a very hard one for him. It was not until September, 1963, that Louise Varèse was able to write to me: "I am happy to be able to tell you that Varèse feels better. . .and the doctor assures me that according to the X-rays and fluoroscope readings he really is much better. He is beginning to work again. He has had a whole year during which his work has not gone well—a year full of interruptions caused by his bronchial trouble and discouragement. Now he has regained his health, I hope for good, he will be able to finish *Nocturnal II*, which is awaited with impatience." Then Varèse himself wrote to me: "The almost total inability to breathe seems to be willing to go away and my head is beginning to work again. Shall have to make up lost time, and it is unfortunately all taken up."[6] It appears that organically Varèse did not really have anything wrong with his bronchial tubes. Yet he frequently suffered attacks of suffocation during the night. One can only conclude that they were of psychological origin. Perpetually harassed by new ideas, by dreams that would have necessitated a daily rebirth, Varèse was battling wildly against time, against the wearing out of his body, against the weakening of his memory. He felt that he no longer had the time to realize what he was carrying inside him. His strength grew less from day to day, though he tried his best to hide his fatigue from the people who came to see him.

He was struggling with two works in particular: *Nocturnal*, which he wanted to finish, and *Night* (*Nuit*), which was his latest undertaking. This latter work, as I was to learn from a letter written to me by Louise Varèse on March 16, 1963, was also based on words taken from Anaïs Nin's *The House of Incest*. He had conceived it for a soprano soloist and a small orchestra consisting of a flute, an oboe, a clarinet, a horn, one or two trumpets, two trombones, a double-bass, and percussion. He had temporarily laid *Nocturnal* aside, since "he didn't want it played again before he had retouched it." He had also abandoned the project of composing a work based on Henri Michaux's poem *Dans la nuit*. He had been meditating on this text for many years, as though he were unconsciously making an effort to tame the night, the deep darkness that death was for him.

> In the night
> In the night
> I have made myself one with the night
> With the limitless night
> With the night, etc.

Varèse had asked me for a taped transcription of this poem in Morse: he wanted to listen to it through the natural rhythms of a Morse operator.

It is noticeable that *Night* is more austere in its conception than the earlier *Nocturnal*. Varèse had dispensed with the men's chorus and the strings. The title itself reveals the desire for a greater density. As he continued to struggle with these two works, he had a sort of intuition that he would not have the physical strength or the time to complete them as he would have wished. As always, he tried to struggle on, tirelessly; but part of him reacted to these pressures with attacks of suffocation. He felt himself being literally prevented from breathing. He had so any dreams, so many things to create, so little time, that he would have needed to begin his life all over again. And his determination to go on, the tension he was creating inside himself, were perhaps daily diminishing his capacity for work. Hence the attacks of discouragement Louise Varèse mentioned in her letter, the periods of depression. Varèse was quite the opposite of a Taoist, for example. He was the Western man par excellence, full of passion, always preferring struggle to resignation. The whole man, and the whole of his work, lies in that struggle.

On January 23, 24, 25 and 26, 1964, Leonard Bernstein conducted performances of *Déserts* in Philharmonic Hall at Lincoln Center. In a spoken introduction, he compared the work to Picasso's *Guernica*. Varèse wrote to me after these performances: "By far the best. . . the work has had. Magnificent conductor and performers. I have never had such a rendition before: enthusiastic performers, who gave all they had, and a conductor above all praise." [7] Moreover, Salzman remarked in the *New York Herald Tribune*: "The intensity in the air at the Philharmonic last night was palpable. . . . I can recall no piece at the Philharmonic in recent years that has been received with such contrasting boos and bravos." [8] Though there had been a great change in the tone of the critics since that memorable December 2, 1954, the audience was nevertheless still demonstrating its rejection of the work—a work by a composer now eighty years old, but one that still leaves no one indifferent. Is that not the best proof of his personality and his vitality?

At the end of August, 1964, Varèse took part in a composers' conference at Bennington College. *Octandre* was "played marvelously" during the course of it. After his return to New York, he was present, on September 2nd, at a concert in Judson Hall entirely devoted to his works. He himself addressed the audience and was greeted with delirious enthusiasm. On March 31, 1965, he was once more fêted, this time at Carnegie Hall. Most of the important composers in New York were present. On May 12th, he visted Chicago, where his works won him another triumph under the baton of Ralph Shapey (who had also conducted the Carnegie Hall concert on March 31st). Once more, Varèse was greeted by the audience with thunderous applause. This was to be his last contact with the general public, which he had loved all his life, despite all the boos, whistles, and catcalls he had been subjected to at one time or another. On August 21, 1965, he visited the MacDowell Colony to receive that association's medal. On about October 18th, on the occasion of a ceremony in honor of the memory of his friend Le Corbusier, who had just died, Varèse spoke of the man's loyalty and of the insult the Philips Company had inflicted on him by tearing down the pavilion he had built for them.

However, though it was possible to say, in 1965, that the battle for New York had been won, the same was not true of Paris. On March 10, 1964, for example, Boulez conducted the Orchestre National in a performance of *Arcana,* and Antoine Goléa, who had been one of the defenders of *Déserts* in 1954, shied away from his Promethean work. He wrote in his *Seen and Heard* column: "It was certainly not necessary to strain one's ears during the work that brought this varied concert to a close. Boulez conducted Varèse's *Arcana.* It is a thing that makes a great deal of noise; of tiring, boring, ugly, and above all useless noise, it seemed to me. I have a great admiration for certain pages of Varèse, and I know the importance of his work as a precursor (sic). There is no reason why he shouldn't have his off days, like everyone else. But why insist on reminding us of them at all costs?" [9] It is evident that critics tire rather quickly. If a specialist in modern music can react as strangely as the most ill-informed member of the audience, then the path ahead is still a long one. It will take time for the great capitals to fall, one by one.[10] But Paris, the city where Varèse was born and where he suffered, must accept him in the end. And French music must one day look upon him as its own. . . The clarity of Varèse's structures (or rather, of his organisms) is worthy of the French genius, just as their power is worthy of the German genius, or their enthusiasm in harmony with the genius of America. Until now, French musicologists and historians have too often allowed themselves to ignore Varèse because they looked upon him as an American; and certain Americans have neglected him because they said he was French. But the time must come for all to realize that Varèse—who was the embodiment of three cultures—like Monteverdi, like Beethoven, or like Debussy, belongs to the whole world, and to all men. The Japanese, the Swedes, the Canadians have never stopped to wonder what nationality Varèse was before admiring him and recognizing his genius.

On November 6, 1965, I received the following telegram from Louise Varèse: "Varèse died this morning after emergency operation. . . distressed. . . will telephone details." Varèse died at the University Hospital of the New York University Medical Center. He had been admitted as an emergency case on October 27th. A thrombosis had caused an intestinal obstruction that necessitated immediate surgery. He had appeared to be out of danger when he succumbed to an infection. During his last few moments of consciousness, the realization came to him that he was not indestructible, and that death was perhaps almost upon him. He had said to me once: "I loathe death, I hate it." Death, his death, was perhaps the last image of the tyrannical father, the final figure of authority against whom he had to fight, refusing to yield, living his death as he had always lived his life: as a struggle. Had he not himself written: as soon as one ceases

to struggle, one dies. But his body no longer had the powers of re-
sistance necessary for that last struggle with the angel. He lost consciousness. . .

In his will, Varèse had requested that his body be cremated immediately, without any ceremony. He had also requested that his
ashes should not be preserved. So that there no longer exists, anywhere, any sign of the man of flesh and blood who once was. The
news of his death was as abrupt as the collapse of a dam. But I
first became truly conscious of his death on the day when, standing
alone in the room where he had worked, gazing at all those objects
still full of his presence, I suddenly felt the immobility in everything,
the silence in everything. And those gongs that he would never strike
again. . . Then, the flood, after the collapse of the dam, rose like
a swiftly gathering darkness, in an instant. Everything was telling
me that death had truly passed, and that he had become silent
forever, Varèse, that being born for sound.

At the time of his death, preparations were being made, both in
Paris and in New York, to do tribute to him on his eightieth birthday.
The concerts that had been planned for this occasion took place:
on November 24th and December 12th in Paris; on December 15th
at Columbia University in New York. Then, on December 22nd, there
was a ceremony in tribute to him at the Grace Rainey Rogers Auditorium, and another, on December 26th, in the Judson Memorial
Church.

Pierre Boulez wrote after his death: "Your legend is embedded in
our age; from now on, we can rub out that circle of chalk and
water, those magic or ambiguous words: 'experimental,' 'precursor,'
'pioneer.' You have had enough, I think, of being promised the
promised land in perpetuity. Enough of that restricted honor which
has so often been offered you as an embarrassing and embarrassed
gift. . . Farewell, Varèse, farewell! Your time is finished and now it
begins." [11] Xénakis, for his part, wrote: "Away with the scale, away
with themes, away with melody, to the devil with so-called 'musical'
music. . . . His dimension is not in the proportion of combinative
techniques, it is in the parts of music that are not yet expressible. . .
Even while he spent his life fighting for the composers of his time,
conducting the works of Stravinsky, Bartók, Schoenberg, and a hun-

dred others, he never let the goad fall from his hand, he never allowed us to follow our own tails, an insolent prophet, a negator of established values . . . Varèse would not let the directors of Philips doze off. He will forever prevent those for whom music is always a eternal re-beginning from falling asleep. The sound of his music is beginning to awaken us now."[12]

Marc Wilkinson paid tribute to him by broadcasting excerpts from his works over the B.B.C. François Morel and Maryvonne Kendergi devoted programs to him on the French-speaking network of Radio-Canada. Georges Charbonnier did the same in Paris. And now, Luc Ferrari has just given us a film, which he would have liked to make while Varèse was still alive. Yes, Boulez was right in saying that Varèse's time is beginning.

Varèse was a creator of sounds such as the West has very rarely known. He spoke to us of our soul, of our anguish, of our hope, of our faith in man and in the future of humanity. Varèse possessed that very rare power of inflicting wounds that never healed, and of exciting passionate enthusiasm. Few composers have torn at us as cruelly as he did with works like *Densité 21.5,* the *Etude pour Espace,* and *Déserts;* few have so injected us with life as he did with such compositions as *Amériques, Ionsiation,* and *Arcana.* And who has ever spoken to us better of immemorial ages, of age-old origins, or the infinity of the future, than he did in *Ecuatorial* and the *Poème électronique.* Varèse embodied, in exemplary fashion, that quality of man referred to by the analyst Igor A. Caruso: "Man's claim to nobility is his limitless power of development through culture; any 'finished' situation is a bed of Procrustes for him."[13] No one ever understood better this necessity in man to maintain himself in a state of development, no one was ever more man in that sense. He was essentially a being in movement and made for combat. It was only a concatenation of circumstances, casting him into oblivion in Paris, then later in New York, and also the mystery of the creator's tragic destiny itself, that delayed the explosion of Varèse's works in the world's ear, and prevented his expansion.

The man who had been born to transform the universe of music, not to decorate it, fell victim to the time he had defied. Time does not forgive the man who looks upon it as nothing but time. The past tries to rob the present. It attacks that man who will not leave it its illusion of being still present, still living. Yet the Varesian universe has the everlastingness of humanity on its side, the infinite progress of culture and of the spirit of humanity. And the mediocrity of all that stands in Varèse's way is not a force. Varèse "is still going forward." [14]

NOTES AND
BIBLIOGRAPHICAL REFERENCES

Foreword
1. *Le Geste et la parole,* *(technique et langage)* , Albin Michel, Paris, 1964, p. 13.

Chapter 1
1. Colonna di Cesari Rocca, *Armorial corse,* Henri Jouve, Paris, 1892, pp. 21 & 27.
2. Although the Christian name Edgar is spelt without a second *d* in French, a *d* appears in the official certificate confirming the birth of Varèse. So, except during a brief period of his life, Varèse always signed his name with a second *d*.
3. December 22, 1883 is the official date of birth recorded in the register of births at the town hall of the 10th arrondissement.
4. In *l'Essor industriel et l'impérialisme colonial* (1878–1904) , P.U.F., 2nd edition, Paris, 1949, p. 587.
5. Biographical note for Kay Boyle's cook book, sent to Miss Beryl Barr in Paris in July, 1961,
6. *"Pour en finir avec l'aliénation,"* Esprit, No. 12, December, 1965, Paris, p. 1077.
7. This explanation of the central event of Varèse's childhood and adolescence seemed both to Mme Varèse and myself to be essential to an understanding of the many attitudes adopted by him in later life. I think therefore that, as far as I am concerned, it is not worthwhile going over this point again. But these facts should always be kept in mind whenever a criticism of him appears rather unjust.

* According to astrologers, at Varèse's birth the Sun was in Capricorn and Gemini were in the ascendant. The extraordinary versatility of those born under Gemini, together with his comedian's gift (Varèse was a born storyteller), often protected him against *the other*. In this way the tragic character of his underlying Capricorn nature escaped superficial observation. And in the same way his Gemini side would play wicked tricks on interviewers who did not know him. It was necessary to have known him a long time to be able to tell *when* in his replies he was telling the truth. His answers might vary according to his mood, the day or the person interviewing him. It could be said then that Varèse's person is the center of a dialectic between comedy (*homo ludens*) and despair. The astrologer, André Barbault, throws light on the character of those born under Capricorn and Gemini in the following passage: "Two natures co-exist within the person, which, though not necessarily in opposition, remain strangers to one another. One is disciplined, severe, serious, stable, reserved . . . the other all youth, liveliness, versatility, levity . . . united in one person, these two can produce suppleness, ambition, skill, and strength." Cf. *Capricorne*, Seuil, Paris, 1958, p. 50.

Chapter 2
1. In *Littérature et révolution*, Julliard, Paris, 1964, pp. 21 & 30.
2. J. Combarieu, *Histoire de la musique*, vol. III, Armand Colin, Paris, 1947, pp. 532 & 537.
3. In *Visages d'Edgard Varèse*, a collective work, under the direction of Fernand Ouellette, Editions de l'Hexagone, Montreal, 1959, p. 8.
   NOTE: This little book formed the greater part of an issue of the revue *Liberté 59*, September-October, 1959, Montreal. And as the reader may want to refer to it, I shall give the page numbers of the revue in brackets. [p. 276].
4. J. Combarieu, *op. cit.*, p. 473.
5. In *Visages d'Edgard Varèse, op. cit.*, p. 9, [p. 277].
6. Letter to the author, August 9, 1960.
7. In *Visages d'Edgard Varèse, op. cit.*, p. 8, [p. 276].
8. In *la Liberté*, Paris, December 8, 1931.
9. In *Musique nouvelle*, Corréa Buchet-Chastel, Paris, 1956, p. 9, (translation).
10. In *"les Innovations instrumentales d'Edgard Varèse,"* la *Revue musicale*, No. 226, Paris, 1955.
11. How can one not be surprised by the words of the composer Gambara, a character in one of Balzac's works, written in 1837?
"Music seemed to me to be in its infancy. . . All the evidence that remains to us of the world before the seventeenth century proved to me that the ancient composers knew nothing but melody: they were ignorant of harmony and its immense possibilities. Music is both a science and an art. A science

because it has its roots in physics and mathematics, it becomes an art by virtue of the inspiration which, unknown to it, draws on the theorems of science. It is related to physics by the very essence of the substance it uses . . . sound is air modified . . . I believe that the nature of sound is identical to that of light. Sound is light in another form: both the one and the other travel by waves to reach man and are transformed by him in his nerve centers into thought . . . what could we not do if we were to discover the physical laws by which . . . we gather, in a greater or lesser quantity according to certain proportions, that need to be found, an etherial substance, which fills the air and gives us music as well as light . . . These new laws would invest the composer with new powers, by offering him instruments superior to those we know today, and perhaps a harmony, that would be magnificent compared to the harmony governing present-day music. If every modified sound corresponds to a power, that power must be known in order to wed all these forces according to their true laws. Composers are working with substances that are unknown to them . . ." (Then, referring to a work by Gambara, the narrator describes it in the following terms:) "There was no suggestion of any poetic or musical idea in the deafening cacophony that burst upon the ears: the principles of harmony, and even the elementary rules of composition were disregarded in this amorphous creation. Instead of the cunningly linked sequence of notes spoken of by Gambara, his fingers produced a series of fifths, of sevenths, of octaves, of major thirds and of fourths without sixths in the bass, a collection of discordant sounds thrown out at random, which seemed to have combined to torture even the dullest ears. . ." (Finally the narrator tells us more about Gambara himself:) "Then he showed instruments constructed according to his rules, explaining the changes he had introduced into their make-up. Finally he announced, with considearble emphasis, as the crowning touch to that preliminary session, which at most had served to satisfy visual curiosity, that he would let us hear an instrument which could replace a whole orchestra, and which he called a *Panharmonicon* . . . but the imperfect condition of this peculiar machine prevented the composer's expatiating on this theme and thus increased the prestige of his idea. Often perfection in works of art hinders their creator from making them appear yet greater."

We shall see in the course of this work how countless lines of Balzac's are prophetic. It is impossible when one sees the word *Panharmonicon* not to think of the onde Martenot, etc. Of course, with ideas like that, Gambara, in the story, finishes up as a street musician. Now, who has pity on this poor musician (a character out of Balzac, let us not forget) who wanted to hear the angels' concerts? The beautiful Massimilla di Varese. . . I cannot help being perturbed . . . Cf. Balzac, *Gambara, la Comédie humaine,* vol. X, Editions Rencontre, Lausanne, 1963, pp. 503, 504, 505, 519, 521 & 522.

12. *Op. cit.,* note 10.

13. Indeed, the publication in 1597 of the *Sacrae Symphoniae* was really a

great event. For the first time "the instrumentation is clearly indicated." Cf. *Histoire de la musique,* vol. I, Gallimard, Paris, 1960, p. 1330.

14. Claude Samuel, *Panorama de l'art musical contemporain,* Gallimard, Paris, 1962, p. 605.

15. In *Visages d'Edgard Varèse, op. cit.,* pp. 9–10, [pp. 277–278].

16. H. H. Stuckenschmidt, *op. cit.,* note 9, ch. 2.

17. Heinrich Strobel relates that when "Debussy met Satie the latter was setting to music Péladan's *le Fils des étoiles.*" It appears that this meeting took place in 1891. Cf. *Claude Debussy,* Plon, Paris, 1952, p. 79 (translation).

18. I have the photocopy of this letter published under the general title: *Lettres inédites de L. Deubel à Emile Bernard,* IV, p. 227. It is possible that these letters were published in the revue *Franche-Comté et Monts-Jura,* in September, 1930. I have not been able to trace them to their source, though I have asked at several libraries. Varèse, as usual, gave no reference.

19. Cf. *Anecdotiques,* Gallimard, Paris, 1955, p. 126.

20. Letter to Varèse, without doubt of October 2, 1906.

21. In *le Petit Marseillais,* March 13, 1932. (In 1965 the situation is not so very different. If readers are not convinced they should refer to Eric Salzman's article published in *Candide* in December, 1965; or they should ask Pierre Boulez why he left Paris for Germany; or read the following words of Jean-Claude Eloy, when he chose Berkeley: "I set out for California with no regrets. There I shall wait for better days." Cf. *le Nouvel Observateur,* December 15, 1965, pp. 40–41.)

22. J. Combarieu, *op. cit.,* note 2, ch. 2.

Chapter 3

1. *Musique nouvelle, op. cit.,* pp. 66–67.

2. In *les Carnets de Leonard de Vinci,* vol. I. Gallimard, 4th edition, Paris, 1951, p. 67.

3. In "We want Varèse," *Twice a Year,* No. VII, Autumn-Winter, 1941.

4. *Visages d'Edgard Varèse, op. cit.,* p. 10, [p. 278].

5. H. H. Stuckenschmidt, *op. cit.,* p. 160.

6. "Edgard Varèse, musician," *Listen,* 1948.

7. Claude Samuel, *Panorama de l'art musical contemporain, op. cit.,* p. 438.

8. In Varèse's unpublished *Souvenirs* of Busoni. The earlier quotation is taken from Busoni's work translated from the German: *The Essence of Music and other papers,* translated by Rosemond Lay, Philosophical Library, New York, 1957, p. 52.

9. In *FM Listener's Guide,* November, 1962.

10. In *Claude Debussy, op. cit.,* p. 143.

11. *Ibid.,* p. 140.

12. *Ibid.,* p. 35.

13. Cf. *Segalen et Debussy,* Editions du Rocher, Monaco, 1961, p. 107.

14. François Lesure, "Claude Debussy after his Centenary," *The Musical Quarterly,* New York, vol. XLIX, No. 3, July, 1965, pp. 287–288.

15. In *"Souvenirs debussystes,"* *Musica,* Paris, No. 104, November, 1962, p. 4.

16. In a letter of December 22nd to Jean Marnold, Ravel mentions a visit of Varèse. Cf. René Chalupt, *Ravel au miroir de ses lettres,* Laffont, Paris, 1956, pp. 77–78.

17. *Ibid.,* p. 77.

18. Richard Strauss, *Anecdotes et Souvenirs,* Cervin, Lausanne, 1951, p. 47.

19. In *Chère Sofia,* a selection of the letters from Romain Rolland to Sofia Bertolini Guerrieri-Gonzaga, vol. II, Albin Michel, Paris, 1960, pp. 8–9.

20. In *Lettres de Romain Rolland et Richard Strauss,* Albin Michel, Paris, 1951, p. 93.

21. *An Hour with American Music,* J. B. Lippincott, Philadelphia-London, 1929, p. 166.

22. The extracts I quote are from letters translated from the German, with the exception of the two which were written in French.

Chapter 4

1. In a letter to the author, May 30, 1960.

2. *Op. cit.,* p. 107.

3. In *Visages d'Edgard Varèse, op. cit.,* p. 10, [p. 278].

4. Quoted by Michel Philipot, in *Igor Stravinsky,* Seghers, Paris, 1965, p. 54.

5. *Musique nouvelle, op. cit.,* p. 88.

6. *"Verbe"* and *"Que la musique sonne,"* *391,* No. 5, June, 1917, New York, p. 2, or Francis Picabia, *391,* directed by Michel Sanouillet, le Terrain Vague, Paris, 1960, p. 42.

7. Cf. Alan Rich "Varèse Is Waiting For The Audience," *New York Herald Tribune,* (supplement), March 28, 1965, p. 35.

8. *Op. cit.,* p. 126.

9. *Ibid.,* p. 303.

10. *Journal littéraire,* vol III, Mercure de France, Paris, 1956, p. 129.

11. Quoted in *"Edgard Varèse communique avec les lycéens de Fontainebleau,"* Jean Maillard, *le Courrier,* No. 92, Fontainebleau, January 9, 1956.

12. Cf. "Debussy et Edgard Varèse," in *Debussy et l'evolution de la musique du XXᵉ siècle,* Editions du Centre National de la Recherche Scientifique, Paris, 1965, p. 336.

Chapter 5

1. Quoted by Henry Miller in *The Air-Conditioned Nightmare.*

2. In *"Genèse des instruments de musique,"* *Histoire de la musique,* Gallimard, Paris, 1960, pp. 81–82.

3. In *New York Telegraph,* March, 1916.

4. In *Visages d'Edgard Varèse, op. cit.,* p. 8, [p. 276].

5. *Ibid.,* p. 17, [p. 285].

6. In "Some Composers," *Musical America,* New York, June, 1962, p. 11.

7. In *"Innovations instrumentales d'Edgard Varèse,"* Odile Vivier, *op. cit.*
8. "Speaking of Programs," Philharmonic Hall, Lincoln Center, New York, 1963–1964, p. 23.
9. In *Visages d'Edgard Varèse, op. cit.*, p. 11, [p. 279].
10. In *Francis Picabia et 391,* Vol. II, Eric Losfeld, Paris, 1966, p. 73.
11. *391,* No. 5, June, 1917, New York, p. 4; or *op. cit.*, p. 44. Varèse was to write four other poems which he sent to Tristan Tzara. It is probable that these will shortly be published by Michel Sanouillet.
12. Letter from Alexis Léger to Louise Varèse, January 7, 1966.
13. Letter from Carlos Salzedo to the author, August 12, 1960.
14. In *Musique nouvelle, op. cit.*, p. 117.
15. Letter to the author, August 12, 1960.

Chapter 6
1. *My Titles,* unpublished text by Varèse.
2. "Edgard Varèse," *le Cahier,* Paris, No. 8, 1929, pp. 31–32.
3. Note to Odile Vivier.
4. Quoted by Paul Le Flem (from the program of the first performance of the work) who wrongly attributes these words to Lawrence Gilman. Cf. the program for the May, 1929 performance in Paris.
5. *Ibid.*
6. *The Evening Bulletin,* Philadelphia, April 12, 1926.
7. René Bonnot, *"Sociologie de la musique,"* in *Traité de sociologie,* Georges Gurvitch, vol. II, P.U.F., Paris, 2nd edition, 1963, p. 297.
8. In *American Composers on American Music,* Stanford, Stanford University Press, 1933, pp. 43–44.
9. In *Diapason-Microsillon,* Paris, No. 102, December, 1965.
10. In *Visages d'Edgard Varèse, op. cit.*, p. 30, [p. 298].
11. *Ibid.*, p. 20, [p. 288].
12. Cf. *"les Innovations instrumentales d'Edgard Varèse,"* *op. cit.*
13. In "Some Composers," *op. cit.*, note 6, ch. 5.
14. In *Visages d'Edgard Varèse, op. cit.*, p. 32, [p. 300].
15. *Ibid.*, p. 13, [p. 281].
16. *Op. cit.*, note 8.
17. In *Visages d'Edgard Varèse, op. cit.*, p. 19, [p. 287].
18. *Ibid.*, p. 33, [p. 301].
19. In "Edgard Varèse and Alexei Haieff questioned by 8 composers," *Possibilities,* New York, Winter 1947–1948, p. 97.
20. In *op. cit.*, note 8.
21. In *Visages d'Edgard Varèse, op. cit.*, pp. 13–14, [pp. 281–282].
22. Walter Howard and Irmgard Auras, *Musique et sexualité,* P.U.F., Paris, 1957, p. 54.
23. René Bonnot in *"Sociologie de la musique." op. cit.*, p. 297, note 7.
24. *"Vers un nouvel univers sonore,"* *Esprit,* Paris, January, 1960, p. 52, quoted by Umberto Eco, *l'Oeuvre ouverte,* Seuil, Paris, January, 1965, p. 18.

25. Umberto Eco, *op. cit.*, p. 17, note 24.

26. *Ibid.*, p. 17.

Chapter 7

1. Cf. H. H. Stuckenschmidt, *Musique nouvelle, op. cit.*, p. 160.

2. Ray Ellsworth, "The Concert Scene of the Twenties," *Hi Fi Stereo Review*, New York, vol. 15, No. 4, October, 1965, p. 56.

3. This letter of Varèse's was at first sent to the newspapers.

4. Ivo Supicic, *"Problèmes de la sociologie musicale,"* *Cashiers internationaux de sociologie*, Paris, P.U.F., vol. XXXVII, July-December, 1964, p. 127.

5. Cf. Michel Sanouillet, *Dada à Paris*, Jean-Jacques Pauvert, Paris, 1965, pp. 235, 286, 620 and 623.*

 * This work was finished when I met M. Michel Sanouillett. The publication of his next work: *Dada à New York*, will most certainly throw a very interesting light on Varèse in his relations with Duchamp, Picabia, Gleizes, Stieglitz, Juliette Roche, W. C. Arensberg and Gabrielle Buffet during the years 1916-1920. In this book, which I have not had the good fortune to read, M. Sanouillet devotes a whole chapter to Varèse.

6. In *les Lettres françaises*, Paris, November 11, 1965, p. 11.

7. Quoted by Chou Wen-Chung in "Varèse: a Sketch of the Man and his Music," *The Musical Quarterly*, vol. LII, No. 2, April, 1966, New York, p. 156.

8. Cf. *Le Style et le cri*, Seuil, Paris, 1965.

9. Pierre Schaeffer, in *le Nouvel Observateur*, Paris, November 17, 1965.

Chapter 8

1.   *SONG OF THE HEIGHTS*

The Seine sleeps in the shadow of her bridges.
I see the earth turning,
And follow the flight of your perfume,
Sound my horn to every sea.
All the words and bees are gone
Oh! Queen of the Polar dawn,
Compass rose whom autumn fades,
In her head a bird sings all year long.

THE SOUTHERN CROSS

Women with the gestures of the madrepore
Have hair and lips in orchid red.
The monkeys from the pole are albinos
Amber and snow they leap
                    clothed in Aurora Borealis.

In the sky there is a poster
For margarine.
Here is the quinine tree,
And the virgin of sorrows.
The Zodiac turns in the night of the yellow fever,
While rain encloses the tropics in a crystal cage.
And now it is time to stride through the twilight
Like a zebra to that ancient isle,
Where slaughtered women awake.

(Translated by Anthony Pagden)

2. *The Evening World,* April 19, 1928.
3. Cf. "Edgard Varèse," *le Cahier, op. cit.,* p. 33, note 2, ch. 6.
4. In "Some Composers," *Musical America, op. cit.,* note 6, ch. 5.
5. April 29, 1922.
6. Letter to the author, August 12, 1960.
7. April 29, 1922.
6. Letter to the author, August 12, 1960.
7. April 29, 1922.
8. July 8, 1922.
9. *Le Don Juan de Mozart,* Plon, Paris, 3rd edition, 1948, p. 15.
10. In *Esthétique et Création musicale,* P.U.F., Paris, 1947, p. 31.
11. Record sleeve, Vega C30 A 271.
12. Gisèle Brelet, *op. cit.,* p. 92, note 16.
13. In "Edgard Varèse," *le Cahier, op. cit.,* p. 34. Cf. note 2, ch. 6.
14. Record sleeve, Columbia ML-5478.
15. *"Artistes d'avant-garde en Amérique,"* le *Figaro littéraire,* July 25, 1928.
16. March 5, 1923.
17. *Twice a Year,* New York, No. 7, Autumn-Winter, 1941.
18. *The Dial,* February, 1925, pp. 172–173.
19. December 17, 1924.
20. *The Daily News,* July 31, 1924.
21. *The Evening News,* July 31, 1924.
22. *The Evening Standard,* July 31, 1924.
23. "The Music of Tomorrow," *The Evening News,* June 14, 1924.
24. Boris de Schloezer et Marina Scriabine, *Problèmes de la musique moderne,* Editions de Minuit, Paris, 1959, p. 79.
25. In "Edgard Varèse," *le Cahier, op. cit.,* p. 34, note 2, ch. 6.
26. In *"les Innovations instrumentales d'Edgard Varese,"* la *Revue musicale, op. cit.*
27. *The Christian Science Monitor,* Boston, January 14, 1924.
28. January 14, 1924.
29. An English translation from the Spanish appears in the revue *Eolus,* January, 1927.

Chapter 9
1. "An Introduction to the Music of Edgard Varèse," *The Score and I.M.A. Magazine,* London, No. 19, March, 1957, pp. 7-8.
2. Record sleeve, Vega C 30 A 271.
3. In order not to overload the body of the book with quotations, I have preferred to quote here Marc Wilkinson's analysis of *Intégrales.*

> "*Intégrales,* written in 1926, embodies with unusual clarity all the aspects of Varese's style and technique, and can therefore well be used as an illustration. . . The work is in one movement, divided into three almost equal sections. The first (a), subdivided symmetrically, serves the introductory purpose of presenting the material in two different but similar forms, and on two levels of transposition . . . Harmonic movement (taken in the sense of changing vertical structure) occurs only at the cadential points, that is, very briefly between the two parts of the section, and quite extensively at the end. The second section (b), built of two highly contrasting patterns, each derived from the original material, is subdivided asymmetrically, and the interchanging patterns again are harmonically static, though on separate levels. In this case, however, the main harmonic development is found in the central cadence, which takes on the proportions of a small coda, and the cadence which closes the section is no more than a desinance. The final section (c), a continuous free development, maintains a constant if limited harmonic fluctuation, and all but the last of the several cadential points are secondary. This last cadence is a development of the coda in the second section; it is longer and more involved than any other in the work, and closes on a chord of nerve-rending finality."

4. In the *Poème électronique Le Corbusier,* Paris, Editions de Minuit, 1959, p. 192.
5. In "Varèse envisions 'Space' Symphonies," *New York Times,* December 6, 1936.
6. In "Edgar Varèse 'Great Sound Builder' is Here," *The Santa Fe New Mexican,* June 15, 1936.
7. March 2, 1925.
8. March 2, 1925.
9. March 2, 1925.
10. *The Dial,* May, 1925.
11. March 2, 1925.
12. In "Edgard Varèse," *le Cahier, op. cit.,* p. 34, note 2, ch. 6.
13. On the advice of Louise Varèse, I have adopted for the titles of the scores the spelling used by Varèse himself when he wrote them, though he may sometimes have talked of *Arcanes* with a French-speaking friend.

Chapter 10
1. April 10, 1926.
2. *The Sun,* April 14, 1926.

3. *The Christian Science Monitor,* April 15, 1926.

4. *New York Herald Tribune,* April 14, 1926.

5. In *An Hour with American Music,* J. B. Lippincott, Philadelphia-London, 1929, pp. 168–169.

6. In *"les Instruments de musique et la machine électronique," l'Age nouveau,* Paris, No. 92, May, 1955, pp. 28–29.

7. In *"Artistes d'avant-garde en Amérique," op. cit.,* p. 9, note 15, ch. 8.

8. Quoted by Marius Richard, *"Une partition moderne sous le signe de l'alchimie," la Liberté,* February 24, 1932.

9. In *"les Innovations instrumentales d'Edgard Varèse," op. cit.*

10. *The Dial,* June, 1927.

11. In "Edgard Varèse," *le Cahier, op. cit.,* pp. 34–35.

12. April 13, 1927.

13. April 13, 1927.

14. April 13, 1927.

15. *The Evening World,* April 13, 1927.

16. *The Dial,* June, 1927.

17. *New York Herald Tribune,* April 13, 1927.

18. *Twice a Year,* No. 7, Autumn-Winter, 1941.

19. The reader may be interested to know what the English composer and critic Ernest Newman thought of Varèse, when, in 1927, he published an article on the music of "today." Of course there is no doubt that he based his criticism on the published scores. He may possibly have heard *Hyperprism.*

"Edgard Varèse's experiments are curiously interesting. One does not know how far he is serious and to what extent he is merely pulling our leg; but things like the *Hyperprism* are decidedly interesting, though Varèse makes the same mistake here that Honegger does—he mixes music, and inferior music at that, along with his noises. His scores are largely unreadable because we cannot imagine how most of his noises will sound, but in performance it becomes evident that Varèse himself is not merely splashing nonsense at random on the paper: he has an excellent idea of what he wants and how to get it. I should very much like to hear a performance of his latest work, *Amériques,* that has been published by *Messrs. Curwen and Co.* at five guineas. The score is about 22 inches long by 16 broad, and is surely the most astonishing effort in the way of 'freak' music that the freak mind has ever put forth. . . It would take perhaps a year's hard study of the mammoth score to get any accurate idea of what it all sounds like, and life, I am afraid, is too short for that; and as no orchestra in this country is likely to attempt a performance of the work, we shall probably go down to our graves in ignorance of most of what Varèse has been driving at. If the composers of noise-music want to lay the foundations for a new art, they should be more modest in their demands upon orchestras and conductors and students. But that some sort of new art along these lines is possible I am convinced."

(Ernest Newman, *The Glasgow Herald*, January 13, 1927.) *Amériques* has had no concert performance since 1929. It was recorded, however, by Maurice Abravanel in 1965, and the record appeared on the market in 1966.

Chapter 11

1. In J. H. Klaren, *Edgar Varèse*, C. C. Birchard & Co., Boston, 1928.
2. *The Christian Science Monitor*, Boston.
3. *"Artistes d'avant-garde en Amérique, op. cit.,* p. 9, note 15, ch. 8.
4. Antoine Goléa, *20 ans de Musique contemporaine*, vol. 1, Seghers, Paris, 1962, p. 29.
5. In *Comoedia*, Paris, April 20, 1929.
6. *La Liberté*, April 27, 1929.
7. No. 4, April 30, 1929, signed D. M.
8. *The Christian Science Monitor*, Boston, June 5, 1929.
9. June 7, 1929.
10. *Le Monde musical*, No. 6, June 30, 1929.
11. *Le Merle*, Paris, June 21, 1929.
12. Letter of May 1, 1960.
13. In "Edgard Varèse," *le Cahier, op. cit.,* p. 35, note 2, ch. 6.
14. In *Arts et Spectacles*, November 8–14, 1954.
15. Marius Richard, February 24, 1932.
16. This can be found in Georges Charbonnier, *Essai sur Antonin Artaud*, Seghers, Paris, 1959.

Chapter 12

1. In *l'Echo de Paris*, March 3, 1930.
2. In *"la Mécanisation de la musique,"* *Bifur*, Paris, No. 5, April, 1930, pp. 124–127.
3. Cf. Jean-Jacques Matras, *le Son*, P.U.F., Paris, 1957, p. 41.
4. In J. Vidal, *"le Film sonore engendrera-t-il de nouvelles tendances musicales,"* *Pour Vous*, January 30, 1930.
5. June 15, 1931.
6. *Arts*, Brussels, June 26, 1931.
7. Paris, October 9, 1931.
8. *Comoedia*, June 15, 1931.
9. In *Olivier Messiaen*, Seghers, Paris, 1965, p. 41.
10. Record sleeve, Time 58000.
11. Odile Vivier has well described the instruments used by Varèse in this work. Cf. *"les Innovations instrumentales d'Edgard Varèse,"* note 10, ch. 2.
12. Record sleeve, Columbia ML-5478.
13. In *le Cahier*, March, 1932, p. 74.
14. In "Some Composers," *Musical America, op. cit.,* note 6, ch. 5.
15. "Arcana," *la Revue musicale*, Paris, No. 124, March, 1932, p. 217.
16. *le Feuilleton du Temps*, Paris, November 26, 1932.
17. *le Cahier, op. cit.,* pp. 74–75, note 13 above.

18. *Comoedia,* February 29, 1932.
19. March 8, 1932.
20. March 7, 1932.
21. March 7, 1932.
22. In *Hi Fi Stereo Review,* New York, vol. XIV, No. 4, April, 1965, p. 57.
23. In *Aspects du Drame contemporain,* Georg et Cie, Geneva-Paris, 1948, p. 158.

Chapter 13
1. February 14, 1933.
2. In *Letters of Composers, an Anthology (1603–1945),* compiled by Gertrude Norman and Miriam Lubelle Shrifte, Alfred A. Knopf, New York, 1946.
3. March 18, 1933.
4. Gallimard, Paris, 1961, pp. 91–110.
5. Cited by Guy Dumur, in *le Nouvel Observateur,* Paris, January 19, 1966, p. 22.
6. *"Edgard Varèse ou la musique sidérale,"* Arts et Spectacles, Paris, December 8–14, 1954.
7. "Varèse and Monteverdi," *The New Republic,* April 26, 1933.
8. March 16, 1933.
9. March 7, 1933.
10. July 22, 1933.
11. July 22, 1933.
12. In *El Imparcial,* March 31, 1932.
13. "Hail ye builders, ye molders! You see. You hear. Oh ye gods, do not abandon us, do not forsake us! In the sky, on the earth, Spirit of Heaven. Spirit of Earth. Grant us offspring, grant us posterity, as long as there shall be dawns. Let germination thrive! May they be numerous the green paths, the green ways that you give us. May the tribes live in peace, in deep peace. May the tribes be perfect, wholly perfect. May the life, the existence that you grant us be perfect. Oh Giant, oh Master, oh Lightning Trail, oh Lightning Flash, Trail of the Most Wise, Flash of the Most Wise, Wind-hover, master-magi, dominions, powers of Heaven, procreators, engenderers, Ancient Secret, Ancient Mistress of Secrets, Ancestor of the Day, Ancestor of the Dawn! . . . Let germination thrive, let dawn arise!

"Hail Beauties of the Day, Giant-Masters, Spirits of Heaven and Earth, Givers of Yellow and Green! Givers of Daughters and Sons! Return to us, spill out the yellow, the green, give life, life to my children, to my offspring. May they be engendered, may they be born those who support and those who feed you, invoking you in the paths, in the lanes, by river sides, in ravines, under the trees, under the creepers! Give them daughters, give them sons! Protect them from sorrow and misfortune! May lies not enter their lives, neither before nor behind them! Let them fall, let them not be hurt, let them not be torn. Let them not be burnt! Let them not fall neither on the hills nor in the valleys of their journey! Let there be neither danger nor hindrance to them, neither before nor behind! Give them green ways, green paths! May your power and your magic not bring on them either sorrow or misfortune. May the life of your supporters, of your nurturers, be blessed, before your mouths and before your faces, oh Spirits of Heaven, oh Spirits of Earth, oh Enveloped Strength, oh Rain-bringer! Oh Volcano! In the sky, in the earth, at the four corners, at the four ends, as long as dawn shall last, as long as the tribe shall endure, oh ye gods." (Translated by Jane Brooks.)

For his work, Varèse omitted some passages from this text.

14. In *"les Innovations instrumentales d'Edgard Varèse,"* *la Revue musicale,* No. 226, Paris, 1955.
15. May-June, 1934, p. 146.
16. *The Christian Science Monitor,* April 19, 1934.
17. *New York Times,* April 16, 1934.
18. April 16, 1934.
19. April 25, 1934.
20. In "Varèse and Contemporary Music," *Trend,* May-June, 1934, pp. 124–128.

Chapter 14
1. Cf. *la Faillite de la paix,* Vol. II, P.U.F., Paris, 1961, p. 536.
2. *Ibid,* p. 537.
3. *Ibid,* pp. 538–539.
4. Letter of May 5, 1941.
5. This letter and others by Varèse that I cite here were written in English.
6. Edgar Varèse, *"Ionisation—Espace,"* *Twice a Year,* No. 7, Autumn-Winter, 1941.
7. In *"les Innovations instrumentales d'Edgard Varèse,"* *la Revue musicale,* Paris, cf. note 14, ch. 13.
8. Cf. *New York Times,* February 17, 1936; *New York Herald Tribune,* February 17, 1936; *New York World Telegram,* February 17, 1936.
9. "An Introduction to the Music of Edgard Varèse," *The Score and I.M.A. Magazine, op. cit.,* pp. 15–18, cf. note 1, ch. 9.

Chapter 15
1. *The Santa Fe New Mexican,* July 13, 1937.
2. *Ibid,* September 1, 1937.
3. *Ibid,* September 9, 1937.
4. Cf. Igor Stravinsky, "Some Composers," *Musical America,* note 6, ch. 5.
5. *The Santa Fe New Mexican,* September 22, 1937.
6. *Ibid,* September 30, 1937.
7. December 2, 1937.
8. January 10, 1938.

9. Cf. *Problèmes de la Musique moderne, op. cit.,* pp. 167–168, note 24, ch. 8.

10. Cited by Claude Samuel, in *Panorama de l'Art musical contemporain, op. cit.,* pp. 646–647, note 14, ch. 2.

11. December 13, 1940.

12. In *op. cit.,* pp. 760–761, note 10.

13. In *Cahiers du Cinéma,* Paris, No. 152, February, 1964, p. 27.

Chapter 16

1. Letter of May 5, 1941.

2. Letter to the author, February 18, 1960.

3. Corréa Buchet-Chastel, Paris, 1960, p. 298.

4. Claudel had met Varèse in November, 1927, while he was Ambassador in Washington. Cf. Paul Claudel, *Cahiers,* No. 3, *Correspondance Paul Claudel-Darius Milhaud,* Gallimard, Paris, 1964, p. 84.

5. March-April, 1946.

6. March 31, 1947.

7. Cf. *New York Times,* July 25, 1948.

8. Letter to the author, June 25, 1960.

9. Letter to the author, August 15, 1960.

10. In "Edgard Varèse: an Appreciation," *The Juilliard Review,* New York, vol. 1, No. 3, Autumn 1954, p. 3.

11. In *New York Herald Tribune,* January 24, 1949.

12. In *9 Artes,* No. 3, June, 1948.

13. Edgard Varèse, *"Musik auf Neuen Wegen,"* Stimmen, No. 15, Berlin, pp. 400–404.

14. Winter, 1947–1948.

Chapter 17

1. Letter from Xénakis to the author, April 1, 1960.

2. Cf. Antoine Goléa, *Rencontres avec Pierre Boulez,* Julliard, Paris, 1958.

3. Letter to the author, June 25, 1960.

4. Letter to Varèse, April 19, 1951.

5. Letter to Varèse, October 12, 1952.

6. Quoted by F. Waldman, "Edgard Varèse: an Appreciation," *op. cit.,* note 10, ch. 16.

7. New York, W. W. Norton, 1953, pp. 363–364.

8. Paris, Nos. 4 and 5, August-November, 1951.

9. *A la recherche d'un musique concrète,* Seuil, Paris, 1952, p. 180.

10. In *Vues,* la Table Ronde, Paris, 1948, p. 41.

11. Letter of September 29, 1953.

Chapter 18

1. *New York Herald Tribune,* January 24, 1954.

2. Gallimard, Paris, 1961, p. 305.

3. Paris, December 11, 1954.
4. Paris, December 4, 1954.
5. In *Derrière le miroir*, Paris, ed. A. Maeght, No. 73, February-March, 1955.
6. Paris, December 7, 1954.
7. R. L. in *l'Express*, December 11, 1954.
8. December 11, 1954.
9. In *Carrefour*, Deccember 8, 1954.
10. *Op. cit.*, note 5.
11. In *la Gazette littéraire*, No. 299, December 18–19, 1954.
12. Letter to the author, June 25, 1960.
13. In "Some Composers," *Musical America, op. cit.*, note 6, ch. 5.
14. Letter to the author, April 1, 1960.
15. Cable published in the *Musical Courrier*, January 15, 1955, p. 36.
16. March 18, 1955.
17. March 11, 1955.
18. No. 780, p. 14.
19. Paris, No. 92, May, 1955, p. 28.
20. *Ibid.*, p. 28.
21. *Ibid.*, p. 30. (In connection with this question of number, I offer the reader a fascinating idea put forward by a specialist from the Cameroons:

"Thus European music obeys a numerical rhythm. Without doubt we cannot deny that theirs are creative works of a rational nature; but this kind of creation is a slave to number; it is a regulated determinism: it is logical.

"In contrast, African rhythm is dialectical. It is the expression of the primordial struggle of life with death. It rises up and rebels against all enslavement to numbers. It is spoken of as being multiple, syncopated and disconcerting. In fact, it is like a diagram of a life of agitation, and of the creative outbursts of its triumphant liberty." Cf. P. Englebert Mveng, *"L'Art africain, II-le rythme"*, *Présence africaine*, Paris, No. 52, 4th quarter, 1964, p. 105.
22. May 20, 1955.
23. In *The Musical Quarterly*, New York, vol. XLI, No. 3, July, 1955, pp. 372–373.
24. Edward Tatnall Canby, "Epoch at Bennington," *Harper's Magazine*, New York, July, 1955.
25. December 1, 1955.
26. "Noisy Week," December 10, 1955.

Chapter 19
1. Text quoted again in *Disques*, December, 1956.
2. Letter to the author, June 4, 1960.
3. *Ibid.*
4. *Ibid.*
5. *Ibid.*
6. Letter from Xénakis to the author, April 1, 1960.

7. Letter to Le Corbusier, February 24, 1957.

8. Letter to the author, June 4, 1960.

9. Letter from Le Corbusier, December 24, 1957.

10. Letter from Xénakis to the author, April 1, 1960.

11. Editions de Minuit, Paris, 1958, pp. 201–203.

12. *Ibid.*, p. 25.

13. July 8, 1958.

14. J. O., *"le Poème électronique,"* *Radio et T.V.*, No. 5, May, 1958, pp. 349–355.

15. Letter from Albert Jeanneret to his brother Le Corbusier, October 14, 1958. Readers will doubtless remember that following Jacques-Dalcroze's example Albert Jeanneret had founded a School of Rhythm and Physical Education in Paris in the 1920's.

16. In *le Soir*, Brussels, April 30, 1958.

17. Michel Pobers, in *Arts et Spectacles*, Paris, July 30, 1958.

18. In *New York Times*, November 10, 1958.

19. Quoted by Mary Kersey-Harvey, in "Edgard Varèse: 'Stratospheric Colossus of Sound,' " *The Diplomat*, May 1959, p. 40.

20. August, 1958. Text translated from the Japanese.

21. Letter to the author, August 31, 1960.

22. *"Gagaku,* apparently of Indian origin, was the court music of the ancient T'ang dynasty in China (618-907). It has disappeared in that country now, but is fortunately preserved in Japan. A dozen different instruments are used for its performance (transverse flutes, *hichiriki,* mouth-organs giving the chords, *biwa, koto,* small metallic gongs and drums of three different sizes). In Japan this music should not be listened to in a concert hall, but in the open air, during a Shinto ceremony. Then the effect of its different timbres is wonderful and this music of past centuries takes on a great sweetness and harmonizes with those light rustlings that are part of nature's calm. . . Records can give no idea of this; or at any rate not unless the gramaphone can be turned to pianissimo."*

    *Armand Hauchecorne, *"La Musique japonaise"* in *Histoire de musique,* vol. I, Encyclopédie de la Pléiade, Gallimard, Paris, 1960, p. 314.

Chapter 20

1. Letter to the author, September 2, 1960.

2. In "The 'Big and Spacious Music' of Edgard Varèse," *High Fidelity,* New York, No. 10, October, 1960, p. 69.

3. *Le Devoir*, Montreal, August 5, 1961.

4. In *le Nouveau Journal*, Montreal, November 28, 1961.

5. In "Some Composers," *Musical America, op. cit.*, p. 11, note 6, ch. 5.

6. Letter to the author, September 1, 1963.

7. Letter to the author, February 3, 1964.

8. January 24, 1964.

9. *Musica-disques,* Paris, No. 122, May, 1964, pp. 16–17.

10. A few days after the death of Varèse, November 24th, Maderna conducted a Varèse concert in the Domaine musical. In the *Nouvel Observateur* for December 1st, it was said of *Déserts* that this work "seems like an ill-controlled improvisation, the work of a none too gifted amateur. . . It is his masterpiece, *Arcana,*" the writer added, "that should have been performed to honor the memory of Varèse." Let the reader look back at what Goléa wrote about *Arcana*. Decidedly laymen who have only their ears, their imagination and their heart are quite right to smile at the "pearls" that specialists of journalistic criticism have for centuries been amassing. It is about time that these gentlemen learned to restrict themselves to reviewing; it is difficult enough to be an objective witness. Thinking of certain critics, Varèse told me one day that he felt tempted to have them examined before a tribunal to obtain their "experts'" diploma. "They have the right," he said, "to say that they *do not like* my works, but they are not competent to assert that they are *bad.*"

11. In *le Nouvel Observateur,* Paris, November 17, 1965, p. 39.

12. *Ibid.*

13. In *"Psychanalyse et souveraineté de l'homme,"* *Esprit,* Paris, No. 1, January, 1966, p. 3.

14. I began this book in 1960 and finished it in April, 1965, having been unfortunately delayed for various different reasons. I sent my work to Varèse immediately. His wife, Louise, read him the whole book, except for the quotations. As I was certain of Varèse's support, I sent my manuscript to a publisher, in June, 1965. In the interval Varèse had died. After Louise Varèse had re-read my manuscript, and we had had many conversations together, I felt compelled to rewrite the book in its entirety, taking into account the new information that had been given me. Varèse had asked me to set all this down, and I think I have kept my word. I shall therefore take the liberty of quoting here the telegram that he and his wife sent me on April 27, 1965: "Manuscript arrived. What a wonderful job. Glanced through only. Will write after reading." Failing health prevented Varèse from writing to me. But I am convinced that he would have done so, as Mme Varèse in confidence assured me. Without the certainty of having his agreement I should never have offered my manuscript to a publisher.

Works of Varèse

WORKS*

1905   *Trois pièces,* for orchestra.
(the end of)
         La Chanson des jeunes hommes.
         Souvenir.
         Le Prélude à la fin d'un jour, for large orchestra.
1906   *Rhapsodie romane.*
1908   *Bourgogne,* for large orchestra.
         Berlin, December 15, 1910.
1909   *Gargantua,* for orchestra. Unfinished.
1912   *Les Cycles du Nord,* opera.
1908–14   *Öedipus und die Sphynx,* opera. Libretto by Hugo von Hofmannsthal.
1920–21   *Amériques,* for large orchestra.
         Philadelphia, April 9–10, 1926.
         New York, April 13, 1926.
         Paris, May 30, 1929. (Revised version.)
1921   *Offrandes,* for soprano and chamber orchestra.
         New York, April 23, 1922.
         Berlin, November 1, 1922.
         Paris, March 14, 1930.

---

* (Works written before 1915 were either destroyed by Varèse or lost in a fire in Berlin. Concerning these works, I have mentioned only those whose existence is confirmed by precise evidence. Following the title of each work, I have indicated the place and date of its first execution in a number of major cities.)

1922–23   *Hyperprism,* for small orchestra and percussion.
New York, March 4, 1923.
London, July, 1924.

1923   *Octandre,* for flute, clarinet, oboe, bassoon, horn, trumpet, trombone and string bass.
New York, January 13, 1924.
Mexico, December 18, 1925.
Paris, June 2, 1927.

1923–25   *Intégrales,* for small orchestra and percussion.
New York, March 1, 1925.
Paris, April 23, 1929.

1926–27   *Arcana,* for large orchestra.
Philadelphia, April 8–9, 1927.
New York, April 12, 1927.
Paris, February 25, 1932.
Berlin, March 5, 1932.

1931   *Ionisation,* for 13 percussionists.
New York, March 6, 1933.
Havana, April, 1933.

1934   *Ecuatorial,* for choir, trumpets, trombones, piano, organ, 2 ondes Martinot and percussion.
New York, April 15, 1934.
New York, May 1, 1961. (Revised version.)

1936   *Densité 21.5,* for solo flute.
New York, February 16, 1936.

1947   *Etude* for *Espace,* for choir, 2 pianos and percussion.
New York, February 23, 1947.

1950–54   *Déserts,* for orchestra and two tracks of "organized sounds" on magnetic tape. (As Varèse indicated on the score, the orchestra part can be played without the interpolation of the taped sounds.)
Paris, December 2, 1954.
Hamburg, December 8, 1954.
Stockholm, December 18, 1954.
Bennington, Vermont, May 17, 1955.
New York, November 30, 1955.

1955   *La Procession de Vergès,* organized sounds on tape, for a sequence of the film, *Around and About Joan Miro,* by Thomas Bouchard.

1958   *Le Poème électronique,* for tracks of organized sounds on magnetic tape.
Brussels, May-October, 1958. Le Corbusier's Pavillon Philips, International and Universal Exposition.
New York, November 9, 1958. (Concert version for two or three tapes.)
Montreal, August 3, 1961.

| 1961 | *Nocturnal,* for soprano, choir and orchestra. New York, May 1, 1961. |
| 1965 | *Nuit (Night)*, for soprano, flute, oboe, clarinet, 2 trombones, 1 or 2 trumpets, horn, string bass and percussion. Unfinished. |

SCORES

1. The scores of the works of Varèse are published by G. Ricordi & Co., New York, except for *Arcana,* which was published by Franco Colombo, Inc., New York, 1964 (N.Y. 2274).
2. Publications prior to 1950:
   Amériques, J. Curwen & Sons, Ltd., No. 90781, London, L925, 168 pp.
   Offrandes, C.C. Birchard & Co., No. 1237–39, Boston, 1927.
   Hyperprism, J. Curwen & Sons, Ltd., No. 90747, London, 1924. 17 pp.
   Octandre, Id., No. 93023, 1924. 23 pp.
   Intégrales, Id., No. 90794, 1926. 47 pp.
   Arcana, Max Eschig, Paris, No. Me 3316, 1931. 110 pp.
   Ionisation, New Music Orchestra Series, San Francisco, 1934, No. 11. 23 pp.
   Densité 21.5, New Music American Music Center, New York, 1946, No. XIX 4b.

DISCOGRAPHY

Amériques
   Utah Symphony (Maurice Abravanel, cond.), Vanguard (7) 1156.
Offrandes
   Columbia Symphony (Robert Craft, cond.), Columbia ML5762, MS6362*.
Hyperprism
   Columbia Ensemble (Robert Craft, cond.), Columbia ML5478, MS6146*.
Octandre
   Columbia Ensemble (Robert Craft, cond.), Columbia ML5478, MS6146*.
   New York Wind Ensemble (Frederic Waldman, cond.), EMS401.
Intégrales
   Columbia Ensemble (Robert Craft, cond.), Columbia ML5478, MS6146*.
   Julliard Percussion Orchestra (Frederic Waldman, cond.) EMS401.
Arcana
   Columbia Symphony (Robert Craft, cond.), Columbia ML5762, MS6362*.
   Chicago Symphony (Jean Martinon, cond.), Victor LM2914, LSC2914*.
Ionisation
   Columbia Ensemble (Robert Craft, cond.), Columbia ML5478, MS6146*.
   American Percussion Society (Price, cond.), Urania (5)106.

Julliard Percussion Orchestra (Frederic Waldman, cond.), EMS401.
Densité 21.5
   Columbia Ensemble (Robert Craft, cond.), ML5478, MS6146*.
   René LeRoy, EMS401.
Déserts
   Columbia Symphony (Robert Craft, cond.), Columbia ML5762, MS6362*.
Le Poème électronique
   Direct magnetic tape creation, Columbia Ensemble (Robert Craft, cond.),
   Columbia ML5478, MS6146*.

ARTICLES BY VARÈSE AND EXTRACTS FROM PUBLISHED INTERVIEWS

1916   *The Morning Telegraph* (or *The New York Telegraph*), New York,
        March.
1917   *391*, No. 5, New York, June. ("Oblation," a poem, and a manifesto.)
1919   *The New York Times,* March 20. ("A League of Art.")
1920   *391*, November. ("Aphorism.")
1921   A Manifesto for the International Composers' Guild, New York.
        Dada soulève tout, Paris, January 12.
        391, Paris, July 10. ("Le Pilhaou-Thibaou.")
1922   *The Christian Science Monitor,* July 8.
        The New York Herald, November 12.
        Musical America, December 23.
1923   *The New York Review,* December 22.
        The Sackbut, London, December.
1924   *Eolian Review,* February.
        The Evening News, London, June 14.
        The Musical News and Herald, London, June 21.
        The Musical Standard, July 12.
1925   *Musical America,* October 10.
1926   *The Evening Bulletin,* Philadelphia, April 12.
        The Public Ledger, Philadelphia, April 12.
1928   *Le Figaro hebdomadaire,* Paris, July 25.
1930   *Pour Vous,* Paris, January 30.
        Bifur, Paris, April.
1931   *La Liberté,* Paris, December 8.
1932   *The New York Herald,* January 11.
        La Liberté, Paris, February 24.
        Le Petit Marseillais, March 13.
        Eolus, April.

---

* Stereo.

1933   "Letter to Jose Rodriguez," Paris, March 1. (Published in *Letters of Composers*, an anthology edited by Gertrude Norman and Miriam Lubell Shrifte, Alfred A. Knopf, New York, 1946.)
La Liberté, Paris, February 14.
Musical Courier, New York, March 18.

1934   *Trend*, New York, May-June. (Michael Sperling, "Varèse and Contemporary Music.")

1936   *The Santa Fe New Mexican*, August 21.
The New York Times, December 6.

1937   *The New York Times*, March 4.
The Santa Fe New Mexican, August 25.
The Santa Fe New Mexican, September 1.
The New Mexico Sentinel, September 21.
The Santa Fe New Mexican, September 22.

1938   *The San Francisco News*, January 10.

1940   *The Commonweal*, New York, December 13.

1941   *Twice a Year*, New York, Autumn-Winter.

1945   *La Voix de France*, New York, February.
Newsweek, June 11.

1946   *Listen*, June.
The Musical Digest, New York, March-April.

1948   Paul Rosenfeld, *Voyager in the Arts*, Creative Age Press, New York, p. 237.
Possibilities, Winter 1947–48.
The New York Times, July 25.

1949   David Ewen, *American Composers Today*, The H.W. Wilson Co., New York, p. 250.
Stimmen, Berlin, No. 15.
Musical Quarterly, October.

1955   G. Apollinaire, *Anecdotiques*, Gallimard, Paris, p. 126.
L'Age Nouveau, Paris, May.

1958   *Le Poème électronique Le Corbusier*, Editions de Minuit, Paris, pp. 188–93.

1959   *Liberté 59*, Montreal, September-October. Or *Visages d'Edgard Varèse*, Edit. de l'Hexagone, Montreal, pp. 8–15.
Buenos Aires Musical, December.

1960   *Châtelaine*, Montreal, November.
Exposition Cadoret, notes, Galerie Norval, New York, November.

1961   G. Bernard, *L'art de la musique*, Seghers, Paris, pp. 480, 528.

1962   *FM Listener's Guide*, New York, November.

1965   *Candide*, Paris, November 15–21.

Bibliography[*]

BOOKS

APOLLINAIRE, GUILLAUME   *Anecdotiques,* Gallimard, Paris, 1955, pp. 126, 203.

ARTAUD, ANTONIN   *Oeuvres complètes,* tome 2, Gallimard, Paris, 1961, p. 91.

ASTURIAS, MIGUEL ANGEL   *Leyendas de Guatemala,* Madrid, 1930.

AUSTIN, WILLIAM   *Music in the Twentieth Century,* W.W. Norton Co., New York, 1966.

BARZUN, JACQUES   *Music in American Life,* Doubleday, New York, 1956.

BERNARD, GUY   *l'Art de la musique,* Seghers, coll. Melior, Paris, 1961, pp. 480, 528.

BOULEZ, PIERRE   *Relevés d'apprenti,* Seuil, coll. Tel Quel, Paris, 1966, pp. 224–225.

BUSONI, FERRUCIO   *The Essence of Music and other Papers,* Translated from the German by Rosamond Lay, Philosophical Library, New York, 1957, p. 52.

CESARI-ROCCA, COLLONA DE   *Armorial corse,* Henri Jouve éditeur, Paris, 1892, pp. 21, 27.

CHALUPT, RENÉ   *Ravel au miroir de ses lettres,* Laffont, Paris, 1956, pp. 77–78.

CHARPENTREAU, SIMONNE ET JACQUES   *Panorama de la Musique Contemporaine,* Editions Ouvrières, Paris, 1960, p. 193.

---

[*] This does not pretend to be a complete bibliography in all languages. However, I have left out nothing which came to my attention in either English or French.

CHASE, GILBERT   *America's Music,* McGraw-Hill, New York, 1955, p. 585.

CLAUDEL-MILHAUD   *Correspondance Claudel-Milhaud,* Gallimard, coll. Cahiers, Paul Claudel, No. 3, Paris, 1964, p. 84.

COHN, ARTHUR   *20th-Century Music in the Western Hemisphere,* Keystone Books, J.B. Lippincot, New York, 1961, p. 213.

COWELL, HENRY   *American Composers on American Music,* Stanford University Press, Stanford, 1933, pp. 43–48.

DEMARQUEZ, SUZANNE   *André Jolivet,* Ventadour, Paris, 1958, pp. 8–9.

DUMESNIL, RENÉ   *la Musique Contemporaine en France,* tome 2, Colin, Paris, p. 27.

EWEN, DAVID   *Composers of Today,* The H.W. Wilson Co., New York, 1934, p. 284.
American Composers Today, The H.W. Wilson Co., New York, 1949, pp. 249–251.
The Book of Modern Composers, Alfred A. Knopf, New York, 1950, pp. 17–18.

GOLEA, ANTOINE   *Esthétique de la Musique contemporaine,* P.U.F., Paris, 1954, pp. 152–153, 174, 192.
Dictionnaire des biographies, tome 2, P.U.F., Paris, 1958.
Rencontres avec Pierre Boulez, Julliard, Paris, 1958, pp. 33, 82.
20 Ans de Musique contemporaine, Seghers, Paris, 1962.

GRAF, MAX   *Modern Music,* Philosophical Library, New York, 1946, p. 203.
The Harmonica of Aristoxenus, Oxford Press, Clarendon Press, Oxford, 1902.

HODEIR, ANDRÉ   *la Musique étrangère contemporaine,* P.U.F., coll. Que Sais-je?, Paris, 1954, p. 113.

HOWARD, JOHN TASKER   *Our Contemporary Composers,* Thomas Y. Crowell, New York, 1941, pp. 254–256.

KOSICE, CYULA   *Géoculture d'Europe d'aujourd'hui,* Editions Losange, Buenos Aires, 1959, pp. 254–256.

MACHLIS, JOSEPH   *Introduction to Contemporary Music,* W.W. Norton Co., Inc., New York, 1961, pp. 624–630.

MANUEL, ROLAND   *Histoire de la Musique,* tome 2, Gallimard, coll. Encyclopédie de la Pléiade, Paris, 1963, pp. 1152–1153, 1193, 1401.

MARI, PIERETTE   *Olivier Messiaen,* Seghers, coll. Musiciens de tous les temps, Paris, 1965, p. 41.

MARTIN-BARZUN, HENRI   *Orpheus, Modern Culture and the 1913 Renaissance,* New York, 1960, pp. 32, 39, 40, 71, 89, 93, and 98.

MILLER, HENRY   *The Air-Conditioned Nightmare,* New Directions, New York, 1945.

MOOSER, R.-ALOYS   *Visage de la Musique contemporaine,* (1957–1961), Julliard, Paris, 1962, pp. 105–108.
Neue Musik in der Bundesrepublik, Deutschland, (Documentation) 1963–1965, pp. 77, 106, 166, 169, 172, 173, 260.

OUELLETTE, FERNAND   *Visages d'Edgar Varèse,* Editions de l'Hexagone, Montreal, 1959, 56 pp.

PAZ, JUAN CARLOS   *Introduccion a la musica de nuestro tiempo,* Editorial Nueva Vision, Buenos Aires, 1955, pp. 187, 327, 328, 330, 385, 387, 447.

PITTION, PAUL   *la Musique et son histoire,* tome 2, Editions Ouvrières, Paris, 1961, p. 540.

ROLLAND, ROMAIN   *Lettres de Romain Rolland et Richard Strauss,* Albin Michel, coll. Cahiers Romain Rolland, No. 3 Paris, 1951, p. 93.
Chère Sofia, tome 2, Albin Michel, coll. Cahiers Romain Rolland, Paris, 1960, p. 8.

ROSENFELD, PAUL   *An Hour with American Music,* J.B. Lippincott Co., One Hour Series, Philadelphia, London, 1929, pp. 160–179.

ROY, JEAN   *Musique française,* Nouvelles Editions Debresse, Paris, 1962, pp. 123–143.

SACHS, CURT   *Rhythm and Tempo,* W.W. Norton Co., New York, 1953, pp. 363–364.

SAMUEL, CLAUDE   *Panorama de l'Art musical contemporaine,* Gallimard, coll. le Point du jour, Paris, 1962, pp. 569, 570.

SANOUILLET, MICHEL   *Dada à Paris,* Pauvert, Paris, 1965.

SCHAEFFER, PIERRE   *A la recherche d'une Musique concrète,* Seuil, Paris, 1952, p. 180.
Situation de la recherche, Cahiers d'études de radio-television, No. 27–28. Flammarion, September-October, Paris, 1960, pp. 58, 65, 66, 71, 83, 87, 90, 94, 101–102.

SCHLOEZER, BORIS DE, AND SCRIABINE, MARINA   *Problèmes de la Musique moderne,* Editions de Minuet, Paris, 1959, p. 177.

SLONIMSKY, NICOLAS   *Music since 1900,* W.W. Norton Co., 2nd Edition, New York, 1938, pp. 95, 215, 233, 273, 278, 295, 336, 340.

STRAUSS, RICHARD   *Correspondance de Richard Strauss et de Hugo von Hofmannsthal,* (In German), Atlantis Verlag, Zurich, 1952, pp. 63, 66, 67.

STRAVINSKY, IGOR   *Memories and Commentaries,* Doubleday, Garden City, 1960.
Dialogues and a Diary, Doubleday, Garden City, 1963.

STUCKENSCHMIDT, H. H.   *Musique nouvelle,* Corrêa, Paris, 1956, pp. 80, 107, 155, 160, 252, 254.

THOMSON, VIRGIL   *Music Right and Left,* Henry Holt & Co., New York, 1951.

URBAIN, G.   le Tombeau d'Aristoxène (Essays on Music), Gaston Doin, éditeurs, Paris, 1924.

WOLFF, PIERRE   *la Musique contemporaine,* Nathan, Paris, 1954, p. 172.

PERIODICALS

(Since this is the first biography of Varèse, it seemed to me necessary to compile the most complete periodical bibliography possible. However, so that the reader might not be overwhelmed, I have marked with an asterisk those articles which I believe to be the most important. I did not feel it indispensable to put in this section those articles cited in other parts of the bibliography. Furthermore, I felt it unnecessary to repeat each time that *Musical America,* for example, is published in New York.)

1914
Prager Tageblatt, Prague, January 6.
Prazske Noviny, Prague, January 6.
Samostatnost, Prague, January 7.
Union Prague, January 7.
Narodni Listy, Prague, January 9.
Narodni Politika, Prague, January 9.

1915
l'Intransigeant, Paris, April 18.

1917
The Evening Mail, New York, April 2.
The Globe and Commercial Advertiser, New York, April 2.
The New York Herald, April 2.
The New York Evening Sun, April 2.
The Sun, New York, April 2.
*The Seven Arts Chronical, New York, June. (P. Rosenfeld.)

1918
The Cincinnati Commercial Tribune, March 18.
The Cincinnati Times Star, March 18.
The Cincinnati Post, March 18.

1919
The New York Times, April 12.
The Globe and Commercial Advertiser, New York, October 10.

1921
Musical America, New York, July 23.
The Morning Telegraph, New York, July 25.

1922
Musical America, February 11.
The Greenwich Villager, New York, February 11.
The World, New York, February 20.
The New York Tribune, February 20.

The Greenwich Villager, February 25.
The Christian Science Monitor, Boston, March 11.
Musical America, April 29. (*Offrandes*.)
The Christian Science Monitor, April 29. (*Offrandes*.)
The Greenwich Villager, April 29.
Heraldo de Cuba, May 5. (José Juan Tablada.)
Revista-de-Revista, New York, May 21. (Tablada, "La Musica Moderna.")
The Christian Science Monitor, July 8.
Musical America, November 11.
The Christian Science Monitor, November 18.
The New York Times, November 26.
The New York Telegraph, December 3.
Musical America, December 9.

    1923

The New York Herald, January 14
The New York Evening Post, February 17.
The Evening Sun, March 5.
The New York Tribune, March 5.
The Globe and Commercial Advertiser, March 5.
The New York Times, March 5.
The World, March 5.
The Christian Science Monitor, March 5. (*Hyperprism*.)
The Sun, March 5.
The New York Evening Post, March 5.
Musical Courier, New York, March 8.
Eolian Review, New York, Vol. 2, No. 2, March. (Carlos Salzedo, "Music of
   the Young America.")
The Christian Science Monitor, March 10. (D. Rudhyar, "Future Music of
   America and Varèse as its Pioneer.")
The New York Herald, March 11. (W.J. Henderson.)
The Brooklyn Standard Union, March 11.
The New Pearsons, April. (D. Rudhyar, "The Music of Fire.")
Musical Courier, April 1.
The New York Tribune, April 15.
Musical Courier, April 26.
The Christian Science Monitor, July 7. (W.P. Tryon, "Edgar Varèse's New
   Orchestral Work, *Amériques*.")
Musical America, September 29. (Jerome Hart, "Plea for Tolerance on Part
   of Creators of 'New' and Lovers of 'Old' Music.") Cf Varèse's answer in
   Eolian Review, February 24, 1924.
The New York Tribune, October 28.

    1924

The Christian Science Monitor, January 12. (*Octandre*.)
The Morning Telegraph, January 14.
The Evening Mail, January 14.

*_The Evening Telegram,_ January 14.
The New York Herald, January 14.
The Evening World, January 14.
The New York Times, January 14.
The New York Evening Post, January 14.
The Brooklyn Eagle, January 14.
The Brooklyn Standard Union, January 14.
*_The Christian Science Monitor,_ January 14.
The Sun and the Globe, January 14.
Musical Courier, January 17.
Musical America, January 19.
Musical Advance, New York, January 19.
The New York Review, January 19.
The Brooklyn Eagle, January 20.
The Brooklyn Standard Union, January 20.
The New York Tribune, February 10.
*_The Dial,_ March. (Paul Rosenfeld on _Octandre._)
The Musical News and Herald, London, March 1.
The New York Tribune, March 5.
The New York Evening Post, May 21.
The Daily Express, London, June 12.
The Evening Standard, London, June 12.
The Evening News, London, June 12.
The Evening News, London, June 14.
The Morning Post, June 18.
The Belfast Evening Bulletin, June 19.
The Nottingham Journal & Express, June 20.
*_The Bristol Evening News,_ June 20.
*_The Daily Express,_ London, June 26. (Eugene Goosens, "England in Need of Bells.")
The Northern Daily Telegraph, July 12.
The Musical Standard, July 12.
Radio-Time, July 25.
The Morning Post, July 26.
The Observer, July 29.
The Star, July 29.
The Liverpool Evening Express, July 29.
The Daily News, London, July 30.
The Manchester Guardian, July 31.
The Daily News, July 31.
The Star, July 31.
The Evening News, July 31.
The Evening Standard, July 31.
The Sheffield Mail, July 31.
*_Jewish Guardian,_ August 8. (Eugene Goosens, "Notes on the Newest Music.")

The Chicago Tribune (Sunday Magazine) , August 31.
Musical Advance, September.
The Musical Quarterly, New York, Vol. X, No. 4, October.
**El Universal,* October 19. (J.J. Tablada.)
The Christian Science Monitor, November 8.
The Christian Science Monitor, December 6.
**Musical America,* December 13.
**The New York Herald Tribune,* December 17. (Lawrence Gilman.)
**The New York Times,* December 17. (Olin Downes on *Hyperprism.*)
The New York Telegraph and Evening Mail, December 17.
The Evening World, December 17.
**The New York Evening Post,* December 17. (Ernest Newman.)
The Sun, December 17.
The World, December 17.
The Evening Telegram and Mail, December 17.
The Sun, December 20.
The Musical Digest, December 23.

1925

**The Glasgow Herald,* January 7. (Ernest Newman, "Music of the Day.")
The Christian Science Monitor, January 9.
**The New York Herald Tribune,* January 11. (Lawrence Gilman.)
The Globe, January 14.
**The Sackbut,* London, February. (Kenneth Curwen, "Edgar Varèse.")
**The Dial,* February. (Paul Rosenfeld on *Hyperprism.*)
The New York Times, February 15. (Olin Downes.)
The Sackbut, March. (Ursula Greville, "An American Jaunt.")
**The New York Herald Tribune,* March 2. (Lawrence Gilman on *Intégrales.*)
The Brooklyn Eagle, March 2.
**The Sun,* March 2. (W.J. Henderson.)
The World, March 2.
**The Evening Post,* March 2.
The New York Times, March 2. (Olin Downes.)
**The New York Evening Journal,* March 2.
**Musical Courier,* March 5.
Musical America, March 7.
The Brooklyn Eagle, March 25.
The Brooklyn Eagle, March 29.
The Christian Science Monitor, March 25.
The Christian Science Monitor, March 29.
**The Dial,* May. (Paul Rosenfeld, on *Intégrales.*)
Music and Musicians, August.
**Musical Digest,* September 22. (Arthur Bliss, "In America Lives the Future of Music.")

The Herald, Los Angeles, October 23.

Musical America, October 24. (Oscar Thompson, "An Outline of History.")

Los Angeles Times, October 24.

Los Angeles Record, October 25.

Los Angeles Express, October 25.

Los Angeles Examiner, October 26.

The Evening Standard, London, October 27.

Chronache d'Art, December. (Massimo Zanotti-Bianco, *"Un compositore americano d'avanguardia, Edgard Varèse."*)

1926

The Christian Science Monitor, January 9.

Musical America, January 26.

The Evening Bulletin, Philadelphia, April 10.

The Philadelphia Inquirer, April 10. (*Amériques.*)

*The Philadelphia Evening Public Ledger, April 10.

The Philadelphia Record, April 10.

The Philadelphia Evening Public Ledger, April 12.

*The New York Herald Tribune, April 14. (Lawrence Gilman on *Amériques.*)

The New York Times, April 14.

The New York Evening Journal, April 14.

The New York Evening Post, April 14.

*The New York Sun, April 14.

The New York Telegram, April 14. (P. Sanborn.)

*The Evening World, April 14. (P. Morris.)

The Daily Express, London, April 14.

*The Christian Science Monitor, April 15. (W.P. Tryon.)

The Christian Science Monitor, April 17.

Musical Courier, April 22.

Musical America, April 24.

Le Cri de Paris, May 9.

Musical News and Herald, May 29.

*The Dial, June. (Paul Rosenfeld.)

The Christian Science Monitor, August 28.

Musical News and Herald, October 2.

1927

*Eolus, New York, January 4. (Carlos Chavez, "Antecedents and Consequences.")

*Modern Music, New York, February. (Pitts Sanborn, "A Glance Towards the Left.")

Musical Courier, February 3.

*Musical Courier, February 17. (Carlos Salzedo.)

*The Glasgow Herald, January 13. (Ernest Newman, "Music of the Day.")

*The Philadelphia Evening Public Ledger, April 9. (Arcana.)
The Philadelphia Inquirer, April 9.
*The Evening World, April 13 . (R. Stokes on Arcana.)
The New York Sun, April 13.
The New York Evening Post, April 13.
*The New York Herald Tribune, April 13. (Lawrence Gilman on Arcana.)
The New York Times, April 13. (Olin Downes.)
*The New York Telegram, April 13. (Pitts Sanborn, "From Varèse to Bach.")
The Brooklyn Daily Times, April 13.
The Brooklyn Eagle, April 13.
Musical America, April 16.
*The Christian Science Monitor, April 21.
Musical America, April 23.
Town and Country, May.
*The Dial, June. (Paul Rosenfeld on Arcana.)
Comoedia, Paris, June 13. (Paul Le Flem on Octandre.)
*Comoedia, September 19. (Pierre Mandru, "Les Principaux Compositeurs actuels en Amérique du Nord.")
The San Francisco News, September 26.
The San Francisco Chronicle, October 26.
The Argonaut, San Francisco, November 5.
*Radio Times, March 16. (Dion Gow, "How Music Defies Analysis.")

  1928

*Modern Music, New York, January-February. (Henry Cowell, "The Music of Edgar Varèse.")
The Evening World, March 19.
The Christian Science Monitor, June 10.
The Christian Science Monitor, July 7.
*Le Figaro Hebdomadaire, Paris, July 25. (Ruth Phelps and Henri Morane, "Artistes d'avant-garde en Amérique.")
*The Christian Science Monitor, October 4. (W.P. Tryon.)

  1929

The Chicago Tribune, Paris, January 2.
The New York Herald, Paris, January 4.
The Christian Science Monitor, January 19.
The New York Herald, Paris, April 25.
*La Liberté, Paris, April 27. (Pierre Wolff on Intégrales.)
*Comoedia, Paris, April 29. (Paul le Flem on Intégrales.)
*Le Monde Musical, Paris, April 30.
l'Ami du Peuple, Paris, May 5.
The New York Herald, Paris, May 31.
The Chicago Tribune, Paris, May 31.
Le Courrier musical, Paris, June 1.
The Chicago Tribune, June 1.

le Petit Parisien, June 3.

le Journal des Débats, June 3.

*Comoedia, Paris, June 3. (Paul Le Flem on *Amériques.*)

l'Intransigeant, June 4.

*le Ménestrel, Paris, June 7. (J. Barusi on *Amériques.*)

le Progrès de Lyon, June 8.

la Griffe, June 13.

le Courrier musical, June 15.

*The Christian Science Monitor, June 15. (W.P. Tryon, "A Musical Siege of Paris.")

*la Revue Internationale de Musique et de Danse. Paris, June 15. (Carol Bérard on *Amériques.*)

la Presse, June 17.

*le Merle, Paris, June 21. (Robert Desnos, *"Varèse musicien."*)

*le Monde musical, Paris, June 30. (Adolphe Piriou.)

*la Revue musicale, Paris, July. (J. Baruzi.)

The Boulevardier, July.

Midi, Brussels, July 9.

*le Cahier, Paris, August. (Alejo Carpentier, "Edgar Varèse.")

Lumière et Radio, Paris, September 10.

la Revue musicale, Paris, September-October. (Raymond Petit.)

Cahier de Belgique, October.

la Revue musicale, Paris, December. (Arthur Hoérée.)

1930

*la Revue de France, Paris, January. (Florent Schmitt on *Amériques.*)

*le Cahier, Paris, January. (Louis Mouilleseaux.)

*Comoedia, Paris, March 3. (Paul Le Flem on *Offrandes.*)

L'Echo de Paris, March 3. (Adolphe Boschot.)

le Courrier musical, March 15.

le Ménestrel, Paris, March 21. (J. Baruzi.)

les Nouvelles littéraires, Paris, March 22.

*le Monde musical, Paris, April. (F. Goldbeck.)

*Comoedia, April 6. (Paul Le Flem on *Octandre.*)

*La Nacion, Buenos Aires, April 20. (José André, "Edgar Varèse y la musica de Vanguardia.")

la Revue musicale, June.

The New York Herald Tribune, June 1. (Lawrence Gilman.)

1931

*The New York Herald, Paris, January 11.

Musical America, January 25.

Musical Advance, May.

*Scribner's Magazine, New York, June. (Paul Rosenfeld, "The New American Music.")

*Excelsior, Paris, June 15. (Emile Vuillermoz on Intégrales.)
*Comoedia, June 15. (Paul Le Flem on Intégrales.)
*le Candide, June 18. (Emile Vuillermoz.)
le Ménestrel, June 19.
A Paris, June 26.
The New York Times, July 12. (Henri Prunières.)
*Schweizerische Musikzertung Und Sëngerblatt, Zurich, September 9. (Arthur Hoérée.)
la Revue Musicale, Paris, October.
*Kinéo, Paris, October 9. (Alexis Remizov, "la Géométrie sonore.")
*Musical Courier, New York, October 31. (Irving R. Sussman, "We May Dislike It, but It is Here.")
*la Liberté, Paris, December 8. (Marius Richard.)

1932

*la Liberté, Paris, February 24. (Marius Richard.)
The Daily Mail, London, February 27.
le Petit Journal, February 29.
*Comoedia, Paris, February 29. (Paul Le Flem on Arcana.)
*la Revue musicale, Paris, March. (F. Goldbeck on Arcana.)
*le Cahier, March. (René Julliard on Arcana.)
*le Ménestrel, March 4. (Marcel Belvianes.)
B.Z. am Mittag, Berlin, March 5.
Vossische Zeitung, Berlin, March 6.
*Vossische Zeitung, March 7.
*Berliner Tageblatt, March 7.
*Berliner-Zeitung, March 7.
Cottbuser Anzeiger, Cottbus, March 8.
Musical Courier, March 19.
*Musical America, March 25. (Gilbert Chase on Arcana.)
El Nacional, March 26.
*le Temps, Paris, March 26. (Florent Schmitt on Arcana.)
*El Imparcial, Guatemala, March 31. (Miguel Angel Asturias on Arcana.)
*Eolus, New York, April. (Carlos Salzedo, "The American Left Wing.")
*The Christian Science Monitor, April 23. (R. Kustner.)
*Zig-Zag, July 14. ("Edgar Varèse, un gran valor de la musica contemporanea.")
The New York Herald Tribune, October 30.

1933

*The New York Herald Tribune, March 7. (On Ionisation.)
The New York Times, March 7.
Musical Courier, March 18. (On Ionisation.)
Musical America, March 25.
*La Voz, Havana, April 25. (F.V. Portela.)

*The New Republic, April 26. (Paul Rosenfeld.)
The Havana Evening Telegram, April 27.
La Voz, Havana, May 2.
The Havana Post, May 2.
*La Presse Universelle, June 2. (Paul Rosenfeld.)
*The San Francisco Examiner, July. (Redfern Mason.)
The Los Angeles Record, July 17. (On Ionisation.)
*The Los Angeles Times, July 22. (On Ionisation.)
The Christian Science Monitor, October 16.

1934

*The New Republic, January 24. (Paul Rosenfeld, "The Assault on the Battery.")
The Boston Sunday Advertiser, February 25.
The Christian Science Monitor, March 31.
The New York World Telegram, April 16. (On Ecuatorial.)
*The New York Herald Tribune, April 16. (On Ecuatorial.)
*The New York Times, April 16. (On Ecuatorial.)
*The Christian Science Monitor, April 19. (On Ecuatorial.)
*Musical Courier, April 21.
The New York Times, April 23.
*Trend, May-June. (Michael Sperling, "Varèse and Contemporary Music.")
*Musical America, April 23. (On Ecuatorial.)
*Trend, May-June. (Harrison Kerr on Ecuatorial.)
*Musical Digest, December 23.

1935

*Trend, January-February.
The San Francisco Chronicle, January 27.
Jewish Advocate, March 5.

1936

*The New York Times, February 17. (On Densité 21.5.)
The New York Herald Tribune, February 17.
The New York World Telegram, February 17.
The New York World Telegram, February 18.
*The Santa Fe New Mexican, June 15.
*The Santa Fe New Mexican, August 24. (Aphorisms.)
The New York Sun, December 5.
*The New York Times, December 6. (Espace.)

1937

*The New York Times, March 4.
*The Santa Fe New Mexican, July 13. (On the Spanish Civil War.)
*Ibid, August 7.

*Ibid, August 25.
*Ibid, September 9.
Ibid, September 22.
Ibid, September 30.
The Albuquerque Journal, November 8.
*The San Francisco Chronicle, November 28. (Alfred Frankenstein.)
*le Courrier du Pacifique, San Francisco, December 2. (Jehanne Bietry-Salinger.)

1938
*le Courrier du Pacifique, February. (Jehanne Bietry-Salinger.)
The San Francisco News, February 14.
*The San Francisco Chronicle, February 16. (Alfred Frankenstein.)
The San Francisco Examiner, February 16.
The San Francisco News, February 16.

1941
*Twice a Year, No. VII, Autumn-Winter. (Paul Rosenfeld, "We Want Varèse.")
Panta, Santiago, Chile, October. (E. Maturana.)
The New York Post, May 31.

1942
Noyoye Russkoye Slovo, New York, October 11.
Pour la Victoire, New York, November 28.

1943
Amerikai Magyar Nepszaya, New York, February 14.
*The New York Times, April 25.
The New York World Telegram, April 26.
*Musical Courier, May 5.
*The Daily Worker, May 6.

1945
*Pour la Victoire, New York, February. (Lucie de Vienne.)
*The New York Times, June 3.
*View 5, No. 4, November. (Lou Harrison, "Ruggles, Ives, Varèse.")
*Contrepoints, No. 1, Paris, December. (Jolivet.)

1946
*Musical Digest, March-April.

1947
*Possibilities, Winter.
*The New York Herald Tribune, March 31.
*The New York Times, March 31.
Le Figaro Littéraire, July 26. (F. Goldbeck.)

1948
Listen, (?). (Kurt List, "Edgar Varèse, musician.")
9 artes, Buenos Aires, June. (Juan Carlos Paz.)
The New York Times, July 25.
Radio Electronics, October.

1949
The New York Herald Tribune, January 24. (Virgil Thomson on
  Hyperprism.)
The New York Times, May 14. (Olin Downes.)
Revival, June.
Expressen, Lördagen, July 9. (Olaf Starkenberg.)
Colorado Springs Gazette Telegraph, August 21.
Mus Q 41, October.

1950
Mademoiselle, New York, November.
Vogue, November 15. (Peggy Glanville-Hicks, "Musical Explorers.")

1951
The Chicago Daily Tribune, April 9.
The New York Herald Tribune, April 15. (Virgil Thomson.)
l'Age du cinéma, Paris, August-November.

1952
La Revue musicale, Paris, No. 216.
La Revue internationale de musique, Paris, No. 13, Summer. (A. Goléa.)

1953
Mus. 8, London, December 9.

1954
The New York Herald Tribune, January 24. (Abraham Skulsky.)
La Tribune de Genève, August 13. (Elisabeth Bourquin.)
Hi Fi 4, September. (Fred Grunfeld.)
The Julliard, Review, New York, Autumn. (Frederic Waldman.)
Le Monde, December 4.
Arts-Spectacles, Paris, December 8–14. (Brassai.)
Carrefour, Paris, December 8. (Claude Rostand.)
l'Express, Paris, December 11. (A.G. for and R.L. against *Déserts.*)
Le Journal du dimanche, December 12.
The New Yorker, December 18.
La Gazette de Lausanne, December 18–19. (G. Ribemont-Dessaignes.)

1955
La Parisienne, Paris, January.
le Revue Musicale, Paris, No. 226. (Odile Vivier.)
Musical Courier, New York, January 15. (Yves Tinayre.)

*Derrière le miroir, Paris, February-March. (Jean Roy on Déserts.)
*El Nacional, Havana, February 13. (Alejo Carpentier on Déserts.)
*Combat, Paris, March 11. (Robert Thill.)
*Le Monde, March 18.
*L'Age nouveau, Paris, May. (Jean Roy.)
The New York Herald Tribune, May 20. (On Déserts.)
Buenos Aires Musical, June. (J.C. Paz.)
*The Musical Quarterly, New York, July. (Henry Cowell on Déserts.)
*Harper's Magazine, New York, July (Edward Tatnall Canby on Déserts.)
Musical Quarterly, October.
Musical Courier, November 30.
*The New York Herald Tribune, December 1.
The New York Times, December 1.
*The New Yorker, December 10. (On Déserts.)
Time, New York, December 12.
Musical America, December 15.
Musical Courier, December 15.
*Der Tagesspiegel, Berlin, December 21. (H.H. Stuckenschmidt.)
*l'Education musicale, Paris, No. 23, December. (J. Maillard.)

1956
*le Courrier, Seine-et-Marne, January 9. (J. Maillard.)
*l'Education musicale, Paris, No. 24, January. (J. Maillard.)
*Hi Fi Music at Home, New York, January-February. (Henry Cowell.)
Metronome, February.
Etude, March 22. (On Déserts.)
Musical Courier, May.
*Disques, Paris, Christmas issue. (Jean Roy.)

1957
*The Score and I.M.A. Magazine, London, March. (Marc Wilkinson.)
Arts-Lettres-Spectacles, Paris, April 3–9.
The World of Music, October.
Koerier, Eindhoven, October 26.
le Soir, Brussels, November 3.

1958
*Hi Fi Music at Home, March. (John Edmunds, "Edgard Varèse, engineer-composer.")
L'Espresso, March 2.
L'Espresso, March 20.
le Soir, Brussels, April 30.
*Radio-T.V. Revue, No. 5, May. (On le Poème électronique.)
*The New York Times, July 8.
*Arts-Lettres-Spectacles, Paris, July 30.

La Nacion, Buenos Aires, August 10. (Cyula Kosice.)
*Ongaku-Geijutu Magazine, August. (Toshiro Mayusumi.)
La Musique dans le monde, October.
*The New York Times, November 16. (Edward Downes.)
*The Village Voice, December 31. (H.B. Lutz.)

1959
*la Revue musicale, Paris, No. 244. (Yannis Xénakis, "Une geste électronique.")
*John Edmunds and Gordon Boelzner, "Some Twentieth Century American Composers," a selective bibliography, with introductory essay by Peter Yales, New York Public Library.
*Antares, Hamburg, January.
*Ord och Bild, Stockholm, (?). (A.V. Bengt Hembraeus.)
*Darmestädter Beiträge zur Neuen Musik. (Heins-Klauss Metzger.)
*Nutida Musik, January. (John Cage.)
Harper's Magazine, April.
*The Diplomat, May. (Mary Kersey Harvey.)
Arts and Architecture, August.
Frankfurter Allgemeine Zeitung, August 29.
*le Devoir, Montreal, September 19. (Jean Vallerand.)
The Times Literary Supplement, London, November 6.
*The New York Times, November 10. (Edward Downes on *le Poème électronique.*)
Mademoiselle, New York, November.
The San Francisco Chronicle, December 4.

1960
*Esprit, Paris, January.
Indice, Madrid, January. (R. Garcia.)
*Jeunesses musicales françaises, February. (Jean Roy.)
Combat, Paris, February 1.
Arts, Paris, February 3.
La Revue des disques, Brussels, May.
*Liberté, Montreal, June-July. (F. Morel.)
The Telegram, Toronto, August 9.
The Stratford Beacon-Herald, August 9.
The Kitchener-Waterloo Record, August 9.
*The Toronto Daily Star, August 9. (Alfred Frankenstein.)
The Globe and Mail, Toronto, August 10.
Lunes de Revolucion, Havana, September 12. (Edmundo Desnoes.)
*High Fidelity, New York, October. (Alfred Frankenstein.)
Hi Fi Stereo Review, New York, October.
Harper's Magazine, New York, October.
*The New York Times, October 30. (Eric Salzman.)
*Châtelaine, Montreal, November. (M. Lasnier.)

The New York Times, December 23. (Harold Schonberg.)
The New York Herald Tribune, December 23.
The Saturday Review, New York, December 31. (Mel Powell.)

1961

High Fidelity, January.
The Canadian Music Journal, Toronto, Winter. (Istvan Anhalt.)
The New York Post, February 9.
The New York Times, May 2.
The New York Telegram, May 2.
The New York Herald Tribune, May 2 or 3. (Paul Henry Lang.)
Time, New York, May 12.
Newsweek, New York, May 15.
The Miami Herald, June 18.
Musical America, June.
La Presse, Montreal, August 4.
The Gazette, Montreal, August 4.
Le Devoir, Montreal, August 5. (Jean Vallerand.)
The Times, London, October 27.
Le Nouveau Journal, Montreal, October 28. (Jean Vallerand.)
Musical America, November.
Le Nouveau Journal, November 1.
The Listener, London, November 2. (E. Lockspeiser.)
Musica, Paris, December. (Paul Le Flem.)

1962

The Musical Quarterly, New York, January.
Le Nouveau Journal, January 24.
Le Devoir, March 12.
The Boston Globe, April 19.
The Christian Science Monitor, April 20.
Musical America, June. (Igor Stravinsky, "Some Composers.")
Musical America, October.
Musica, Paris, November. (Paul Le Flem.)
High Fidelity, November.
Musica d'Oggi, Milan, November-December. (Pablo Castaldi.)

1963

Musical America, January.
The New York Times, May 22.
Musical America, May.
*The Musical Quarterly, July. (François Lesure.)
Les Nouvelles Littéraires, Paris, September 26.

1964

The New York Herald Tribune, January 24. (Eric Salzman on *Déserts.*)

Musical America, February.
*Musica, Paris, May. (A. Goléa.)
*Philharmonic Hall Program, 1963–64. (Irving Kolodin.)
*Philharmonic Hall Program, 1963–64. (Edward Downes on *Déserts.*)

1965

*François Lesure, *"Debussy et Edgard Varèse,"* in *Debussy et la Musique au XXᵉ siecle,* Edition du Centre National de la Recherche Scientifique, Paris, 1965.
*The New York Times, February 21. (Theodore Strongin.)
The Alliance Bulletin, March.
The San Francisco Chronicle, March 1.
The San Francisco Examiner, March 2.
The New York Herald Tribune, March 28.
The New York Herald Tribune, April 1. (Alan Rich.)
The New York Times, April 1. (T. Strongin.)
The Evening Bulletin, Philadelphia, April 3.
Tempo, April 7.
The Chicago Sun Times, April 17.
*The Chicago's American, May 12.
The Chicago Sun-Times, May 12.
The Chicago Daily News, May 12.
The Chicago Tribune, May 12.
l'Express, Paris, May 10–16.
*Perspectives of New Music, Spring-Summer. (Gunther Schiller, "Conversation with Varèse.")
The New York Times, July 4.
The New York Times, July 25.
The Rotunda, October 18.
Hi Fi Stereo Review, October.
*The New York Times, November 7. ("Edgard Varèse, 81, Composer, is Dead.")
The New York Herald Tribune, November 7.
Le Monde, Paris, November 9.
Les Lettres françaises, Paris, November 11. (Aragon.)
The New York Times, November 12.
*La Presse, Montreal, November 13.
*The New York Times, November 14. (Harold Schonberg.)
The Boston Sunday Globe, November 14.
The Christian Science Monitor, November 14.
*Le Nouvel Observateur, Paris, November 17.
*Le Figaro Littéraire, November 18. (Claude Rostand.)
*Les Nouvelles littéraires, Paris, November 18. (Marc Pincherle.)
*Arts, Paris, November 17–23. (Jacques Bourgeois.)
Les Lettres françaises, November 18. (L. Ferrari.)
Newsweek, New York, November 22.

Contemporanne, November 26. (George Batan.)

*The New York Times, November 28. (Igor Stravinsky on the *Times* and Edgard Varèse.)

*The Los Angeles Times, November 28.

The San Francisco Chronicle, November 28.

The Nation, November 29.

*Le Quartier latin, Montreal, December 2. ("Hommage a Edgard Varèse," under the direction of Daniel Saint-Aubin.)

*Les Lettres françaises, December 2. (Martine Cadieu.)

Contemporanne, December 3.

The Christian Science Monitor, December 8.

Les Lettres françaises, December 16.

The New York Times, December 27.

Diapason-Microsillon, Paris, December. (André Jolivet.)

1966

La Presse, February 2.

Le Devoir, February 3. (Gilles Potvin.)

*The Musical Quarterly, New York, April. (Chou Wen-Chung.)

Les Lettres françaises, June 16. (Pierre Schasffer on *Déserts*.)

SPECIAL ISSUES

1928

J.H. Klaren, "Edgard Varèse, Pioneer of New Music in America," C.G. Birchard & Co., Boston, 24 pages.

1959

Liberté 59, Montreal, No. 5, September-October. Special issues under the direction of Fernand Ouellette.

Index

This Book was set on the linotype in Baskerville,
a type designed by John Baskerville, (1706–1775),
which is a transitional face between the classic
and the modern. The display type is Bulmer,
designed by John Martin in 1795.
Composed, printed and bound at Kingsport Press,
Kingsport, Tennessee.
Designed by Jacqueline Schuman.